IMAGES
of America

WALDEN AND MAYBROOK

To our Walden and Maybrook friends
and especially to Patsy and Geri Iorlano
for their special gift of friendship.

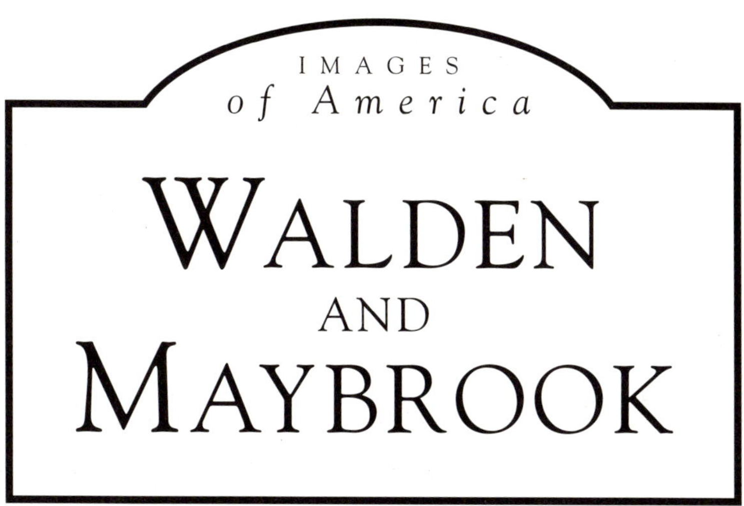

Marc Newman

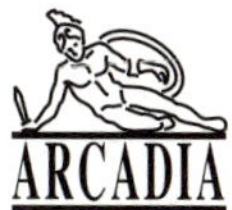

ISBN 0-7385-0956-6

First printed in 2001.

Published by Arcadia Publishing,
an imprint of Tempus Publishing, Inc.
2A Cumberland Street
Charleston, SC 29401

Printed in Great Britain.

Library of Congress Catalog Card Number: 2001093038

For all general information contact Arcadia Publishing at:
Telephone 843-853-2070
Fax 843-853-0044
E-Mail sales@arcadiapublishing.com

For customer service and orders:
Toll-Free 1-888-313-2665

Visit us on the internet at http://www.arcadiapublishing.com

Contents

ACKNOWLEDGMENTS

Many people have been instrumental in making this project a reality. Dozens of residents and community friends have given their time and donated photographic material to help present a meaningful history of their communities Walden and Maybrook. It is hoped that this history will be used for posterity, as well as educationally, and will enhance the understanding of the contributions of both communities to the growth of Orange County, New York State, and the United States.

From Walden, with appreciation, I want to thank Robert Kidd for many of the postcards that have been used in the text. Marcus "Mickey" Millspaugh has been of great help, supplying information about the community and the use of photographic material from his own collection, as well as those of the Walden Historical Society. I am grateful for the support, information, and photographic materials given by friends and community leaders, including Ella Orndorff, Walden's historian; Sam Phelps Jr., the "American Farmer"; Jeff Sohns; Dave Lustig; Joseph Fowler; Walter Roosa; and especially from the "Senior Community Father" John Clarke; and Nancy Mitchell of the Village of Walden Municipal Office.

From Maybrook, I want to express my deep appreciation by thanking especially those men of the Maybrook Railroad Museum, who dedicated their lives to the rail line that served the continental United States: Albert Alexander, Sam Christian, and Tony Marano. These men extended a great deal of time and photographic materials that were necessary to tell the story of Maybrook, the "Gateway to the East." With sincere appreciation for the support, information, and photographic materials, I dedicate a portion of this book to my close friends at CB: Pat and Geri Iorlano, Manny and Danny Green, Cindy and Doug Badendyck, Caren and Mike Aiello, Kathy and Norm McVey, Bonnie and Neil Van Wagenen, and Carole and Ivan Jennings. Special appreciation goes to Jennie Gesso, Robert Brown Jr., and Aunt Doris Christian. Additional photographs were supplied by June Johnston Hess, Dan Saracino, and Eric Kruger regarding life in Maybrook, as well as the rail industry. I want to especially thank Tom Kirby of Yellow Freight Transit Company for the history lesson. Special mention goes to Eugene Bastianio, who gave me information and stories about life in Maybrook during the 1940s and 1950s. Roberta "Roby" Petzold, Maybrook historian, provided resources and time that made the story of Maybrook, the community, come to life. I want to thank two members of the Harness Racing Museum & Hall of Fame in Goshen, Gail Cunnard, director, and Marcia Faber, library technician, for material relating to Dexter. Finally, thanks to Pat Iorlano, who spent many years telling me wonderful stories about growing up in a small village (Maybrook) in which friendship, honesty, and sincerity were the rules of daily living. If any person, group, or organization has been omitted, please accept my apology.

Introduction

Walden and Maybrook were once centers of mass production and mass transportation in the heart of the Mid-Hudson Valley. These two villages (two of the township's three municipalities, Montgomery being the third) are located in northern Orange County, which borders Ulster, Sullivan, and Rockland Counties. Each of the two villages is distinctive and has its own identity; yet, each is dependent on the other, both politically and economically. Maybrook, the "Gateway to the East," was a rural area that became a major rail center and later a trucking center, having Interstate 84 within its borders. Walden, initially a rural community with woolen and cotton cloth mills, eventually became the cutlery capital of not only New York but also the country, known as the "Sheffield of America."

The village of Walden is located at the junctions of state Routes 208 and 52. A mill town during the first industrial revolution, it used the power of the Wallkill River, flowing north and northeast. Walden and her neighboring communities were able to harness the strong and swift current of the "kill" for both waterpower and steam power. By the 1830s, Jacob T. Walden's mill was creating woolen cloth for New York consumers through the power of the "mighty Wallkill."

By the 1850s, many of the local businesses, including mills, were going bankrupt or beginning to lay off many of their employees, the result of the depression of the period. Employing various economic incentives to keep profits high and production costs, some of the "village fathers" encouraged businesses in other counties, such as Dutchess, to move to Walden. In 1856, the New York Knife Company left Mattewean and came to Walden. This company became the first of three major companies to locate its factories along the banks of the Wallkill. In the decades that followed, the two other companies, Walden Knife Company and Schrade Cutlery Company, established their cutlery businesses and made use of steam power and, later, electrical power for the mass production of pocketknives, penknives, and the like. One of the means of transportation for workers to travel to Walden from Maybrook and from Maybrook to Walden, was the Wallkill bus, which traveled along Route 208, connecting Walden to Maybrook.

Along Route 208, a meetinghouse was constructed at the present site of the Goodwill Church. As a result of an extended road from Shawangunk to Goshen, a settlement grew and prospered. Maybrook was settled by the John Blake family, who prior to the Revolutionary War received a land grant for a large tract. During the Federalist era, the 1790s, other settlers, including Col. John Nicholson, journeyed south from Walden into Maybrook and erected homes and farms. During the early years, most of the development of the area consisted of agriculture and horse farms.

By the 1880s, rail lines were surveyed throughout the area. In 1887, as food, clothing, and cutlery production increased in the region, a bridge was built across the Hudson River, connecting Newburgh to Poughkeepsie, in Dutchess County. This enabled goods to be shipped from the West (Pennsylvania) to the East (New England).

The railroad system was established in 1889, and the Orange County Rail Junction was later renamed Maybrook. By the 1920s, the railroad industry had expanded and, in 1925, Maybrook was incorporated as a village.

The railroad merger of the Central New England Railroad and the New York, New Haven, and Hartford Railroad helped to expedite employment and housing within the newly created village. By the early 20th century, the village of Maybrook was the largest railroad terminal in the East, while Walden was the largest knife manufacturer in the United States. By the 1970s, trucking slowly began to replace rail freight. Yellow Freight was one of several trucking firms in Orange County, located in Maybrook. As the rail industry suffered layoffs and cutbacks in the early 1970s, the trucking industry gradually replaced rail service. Part of this was the result of the construction of Interstate 84, which serviced truck freighting thru Pennsylvania and New York to Connecticut.

During the same time period, the doors of the last knife company, Schrade, closed. Schrade was purchased by the Imperial Knife Company and relocated to Ellenville. During the latter part of the 19th century, Walden had become the very symbol of mass production during the height of the second Industrial Revolution, while its sister village, Maybrook, was the symbol of mass transportation. Immigrant workers flocked to both villages, seeking employment in either the railroad yards as construction workers (for example, the Italian Americans) or on the assembly lines at factories in Walden (for example, the German Americans and Scotch-Irish Americans). Today, both villages have been "suburbanized" through the construction of planned communities and developments. In the 21st century, Orange County has become the largest growing county in New York State. The town of Montgomery has become the fastest growing town in the state, and its villages of Maybrook, Montgomery, and Walden, the fastest growing municipalities. Although the rail industry of Maybrook and the knife industry of Walden have waned with the passage of time, the villages are now home to small companies and businesses with descendants from the early founding families who gave life and economic growth to the mid-Hudson Valley.

One
Early History

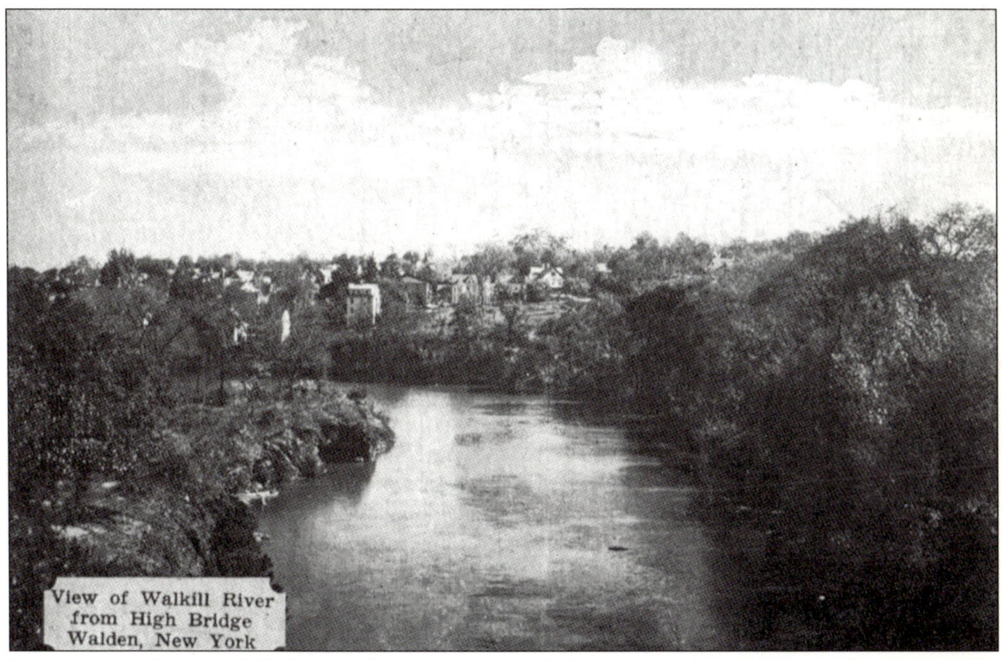

Located on the Wallkill River, Walden was settled prior to the American Revolution by Scotch-Irish, English, and German immigrants. This view of the river and the village was taken *c.* the 1920s. (Courtesy of Robert Kidd.)

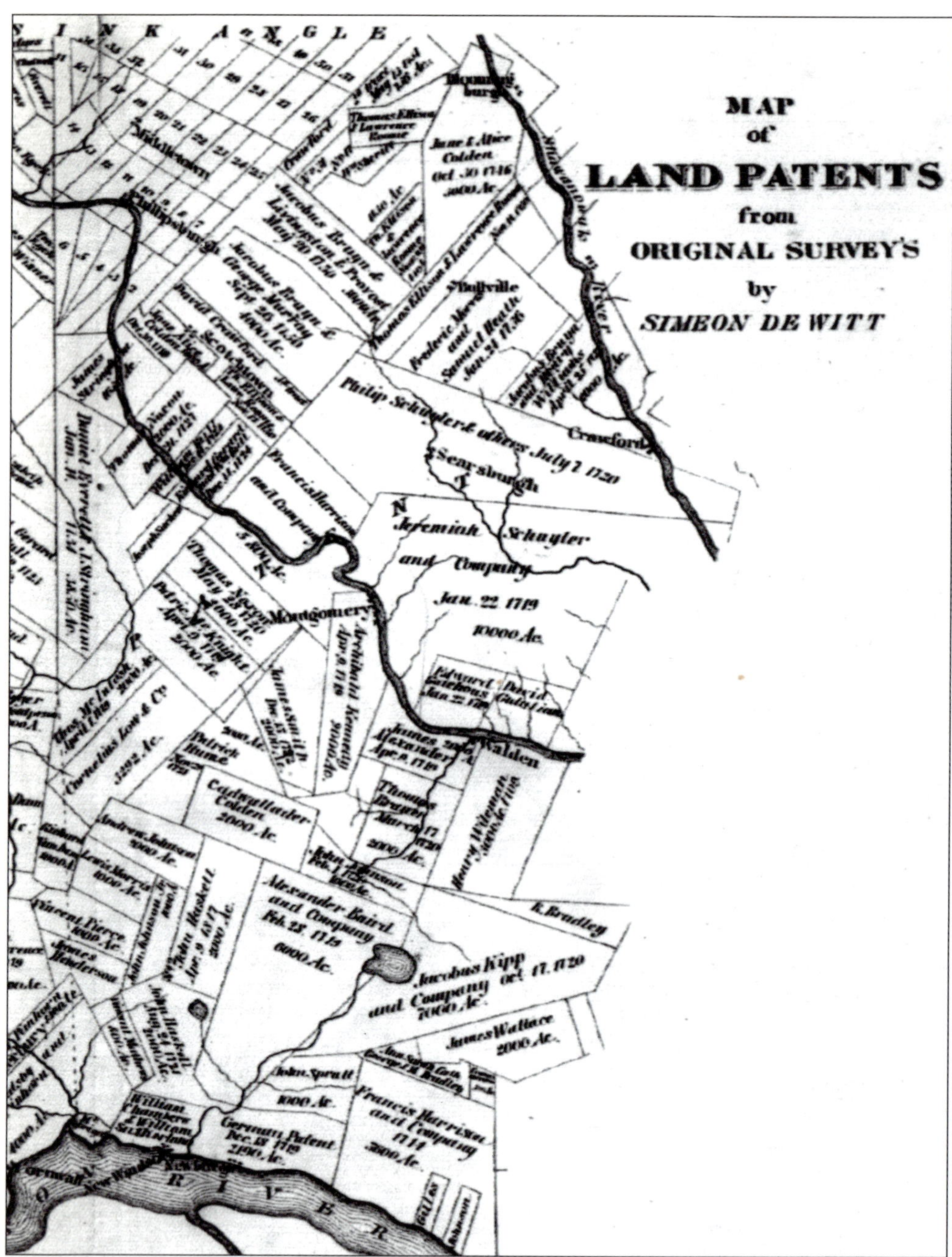

Several farms were built within the area by English and German families. One of the businesses was the breeding of livestock, especially sheep, by the Clineman family. In 1736, Alexander Kidd, a Scotch-Irishman, purchased a large tract of land in the area and created several farms that were divided among his three sons. Many of the early residents in the vicinity were Native Americans, who resented the expansion of these early settlements along the banks of the Wallkill River and on the west side of the Hudson River. This map shows the land patents in Orange County and the Walden area *c.* the 18th century. (Ruttenber & Clark, *History of Orange County New York*, page 17–18.)

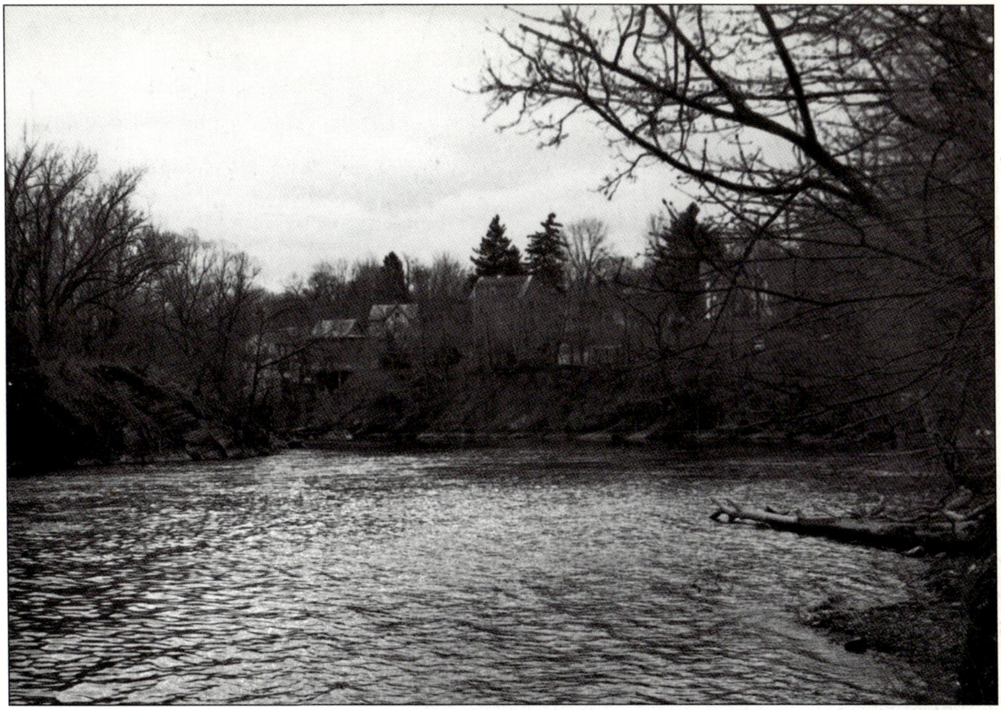

On the east bank of the Wallkill, the first settlement was established in and around Walden. Henry Wileman received a grant of about 3,000 acres of land. Wileman Town was built in 1713. This *c.* 1910 photograph shows the river's east bank. (Courtesy of Marcus Millspaugh.)

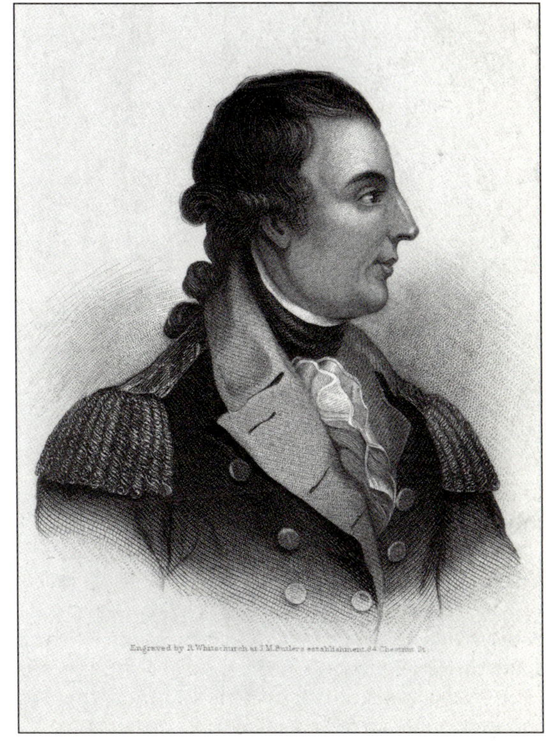

Neighboring Indian settlements throughout the county, mostly Lenape members of the Delaware family of Algonquin Indians, were considered a threat to the new white settlers. Farmers and tradesmen who lived in the surrounding Orange and Ulster Counties formed their own militia company. Several hundred volunteers were later used to support the colonists and the British in the French and Indian War. During the American Revolution, the Continental Congress passed a law in 1775 that led to the creation of regimental districts. Volunteers came from Walden and neighboring communities to become part of the 2nd Regiment New York Militia. These regiments served under Brig. Gen. Richard Montgomery *c.* 1775, during the Champlain-Canadian campaign. (Courtesy of Marc Newman.)

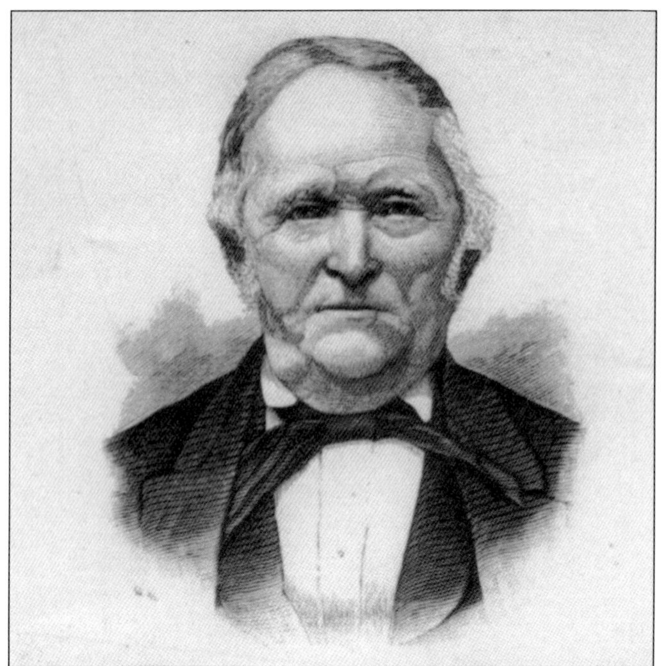

John Kidd, pictured *c.* the 1840s, built a gristmill on the banks of the Great Falls of the Wallkill prior to the Revolutionary War. He built it on the tract of land that was sold to Alexander Kidd. (Ruttenber & Clark, *History of Orange County New York*, page 411.)

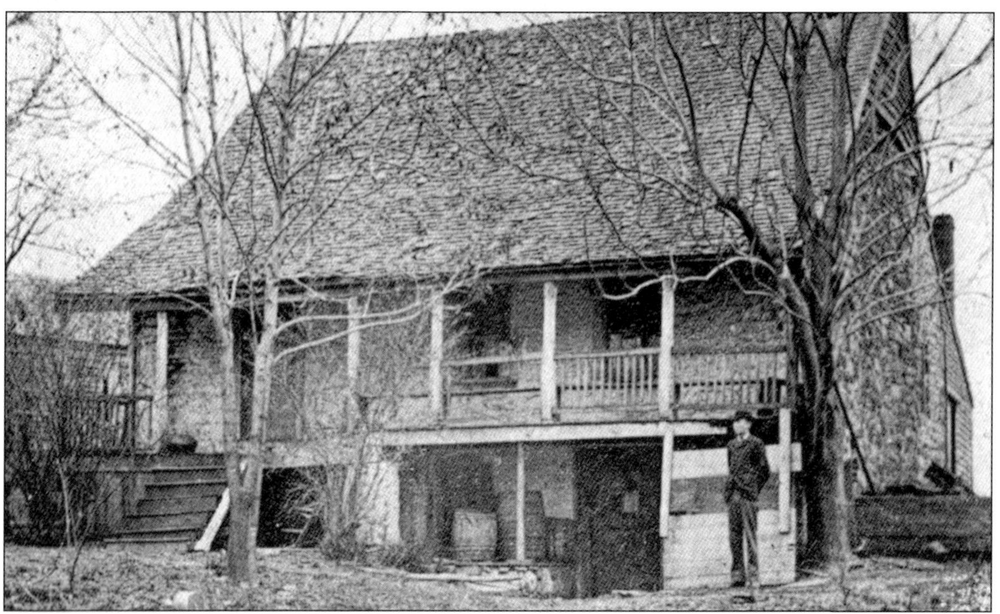

James Kidd built this old stone house sometime before 1775. The Kidd family made a great deal of money from the Kidd Mill, which converted wheat to flour for neighboring communities and settlers. By 1768, the mill was sold to Johannes Decker and later, in 1789, to Cadwallader Colden Jr. The Colden family was well known within the towns of Montgomery and Newburgh. Cadwallader Colden Sr. was the last royal lieutenant governor of the colony of New York. He owned what was called Colden's Hamlet, a large tract of land that bordered Kidd Town. His daughter was Jane Colden, the first woman botanist in the American colonies and a close associate and friend of famed botanist Carl Linnaeus. Cadwallader Colden Jr. was the grandson of Colden Sr. and the nephew of Jane Colden. (*Walden and Its Environs*, page 40.)

Two

INDUSTRIALIZATION AND MASS PRODUCTION

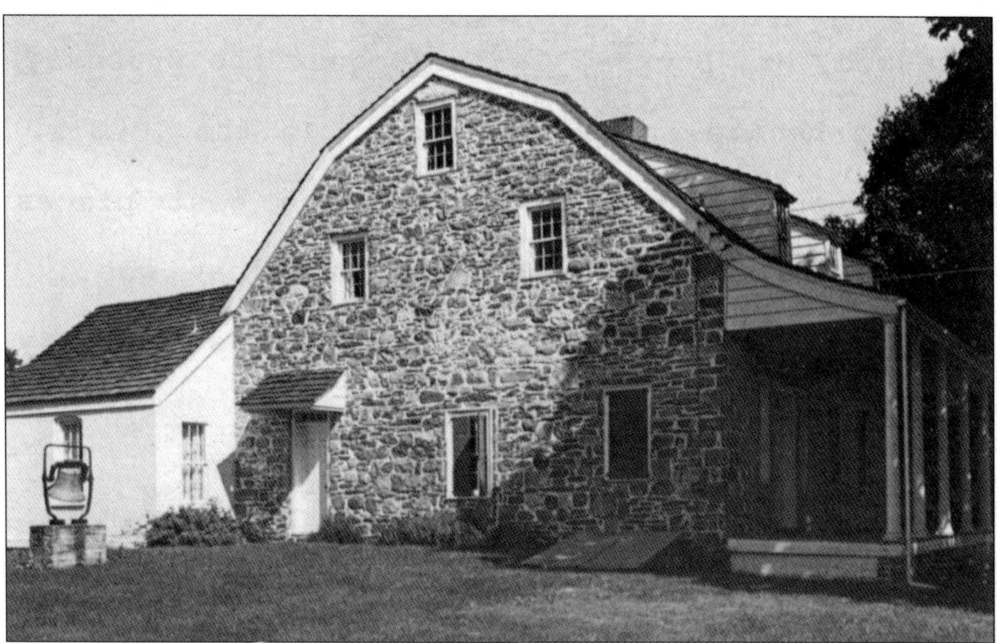

When Samuel Slater created the first textile mill in Pawtucket, Rhode Island, using steam and water power to harness the spinning and weaving looms, the North began to convert slowly from an agricultural to an industrial economy. By the early 1800s, New England was the leader in textile production, later reaching its pinnacle of success with the Lowell system, which developed in Massachusetts. The cotton gin of the 1790s further enhanced the development of textile production with the use of both woolen and cotton clothing. New York joined this first industrial revolution and, a century later, became the garment center of the United States. Kidd Town contributed to the textile industry through the auspices and business investments of Jacob T. Walden, whose house is pictured here *c.* the 1820s. (Courtesy of Walden Historical Society.)

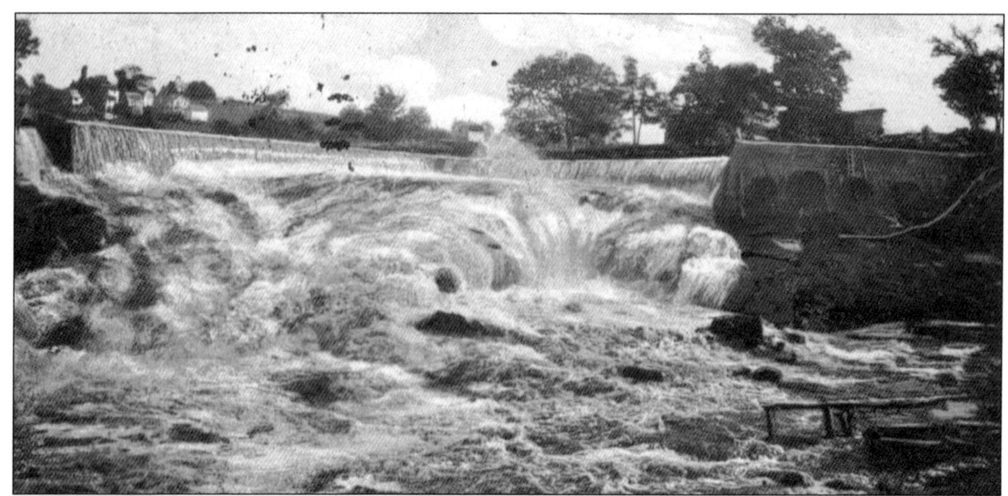

Jacob T. Walden purchased land in Kidd Town during the 1820s by the "Great Falls of the Wallkill River," pictured above *c.* 1908. Walden and his family were wealthy and successful shipping merchants in New York City. During a summer in the highlands of the Hudson Valley, the Waldens purchased a large tract of land, a land patent originally owned by George Gatehouse. Walden was able to convince New York City businessmen Jesse Scofield and Seth C. Capron to create a woolen mill using the Wallkill River as the source of power. The business investors formed the Franklin Company in 1822 for the production and processing of woolen goods. A number of years later, Jacob T. Walden established a cotton factory below the Great Falls. The woolen factory was considered to be the most extensive manufacturer of flannel woolen goods in the state. By the 1830s, several textile companies were producing woolen and cotton cloth. Shown below, *c.* the 1840s, are ruins of the Old Mills of Scofield, Capron & Company. The Wallkill River was able to provide both water and steam power for the gristmills, sawmills, and textile factory houses of Walden. The area had expanded, with businesses on the Great Falls and the lower river and falls. By the 1840s, Orange County had more than a dozen woolen mills. Walden and Montgomery were considered the center of woolen production within the county. Approximately one third of woolen production within the county was produced in Walden. (Above, courtesy of Robert Kidd; below, *Walden and Its Environs*, page 38.)

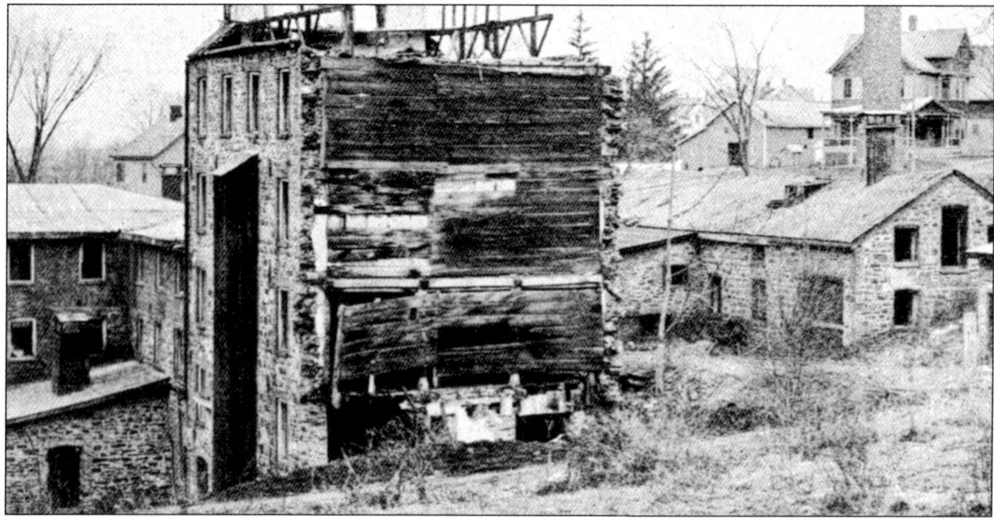

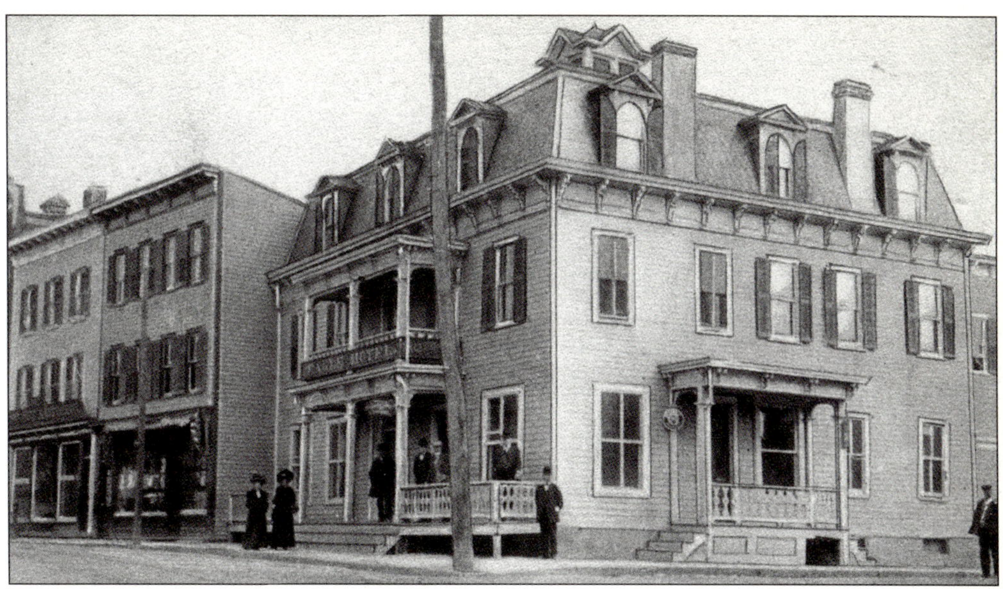

On the outskirts of Kidd Town was the Albany Post Road. This major highway intersected the Boston Post Road in and around present-day Yonkers. Both roads were used for freight and passenger service and especially for the delivery of the U.S. mail. In 1823, New York City businessman Jesse Scofield built the Eagle Hotel on Main Street in Kidd Town, a few miles away from the Albany Post Road. The hotel, shown *c.* the 1850s, became a popular stop for travelers in the region prior to the Civil War. (Courtesy of Robert Kidd.)

OFFICIALS

OF THE

VILLAGE OF WALDEN

Village Office

8 Scofield Street
Walden, New York 12586
Telephone: 914/778-2177

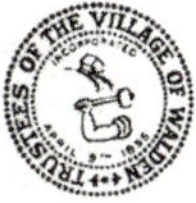

1982

MARCY L. SPERRY — **Mayor**
ANTHONY GARCIA — **Trustee**
BARBARA C. MILLSPAUGH — **Trustee**
KEVIN J. MULQUEEN — **Trustee**
J. BRUCE SEGUIN — **Trustee**
LINDA SEISS — **Trustee**
PETER WOLVEN — **Trustee**

DAVID R. HEACOCK
Village Manager

NANCY MITCHELL
Village Clerk

GERALD N. JACOBOWITZ, ESQ.
Village Attorney

During the decade of the 1850s, a fire company was established, as well as a municipal band. In 1855, the village of Walden was incorporated and named after its chief resident who brought business and growth to Kidd Town, Jacob T. Walden. Shown on this 20th-century listing of village officials is the seal of the village of Walden, incorporated in 1855. (Courtesy of the Village of Walden.)

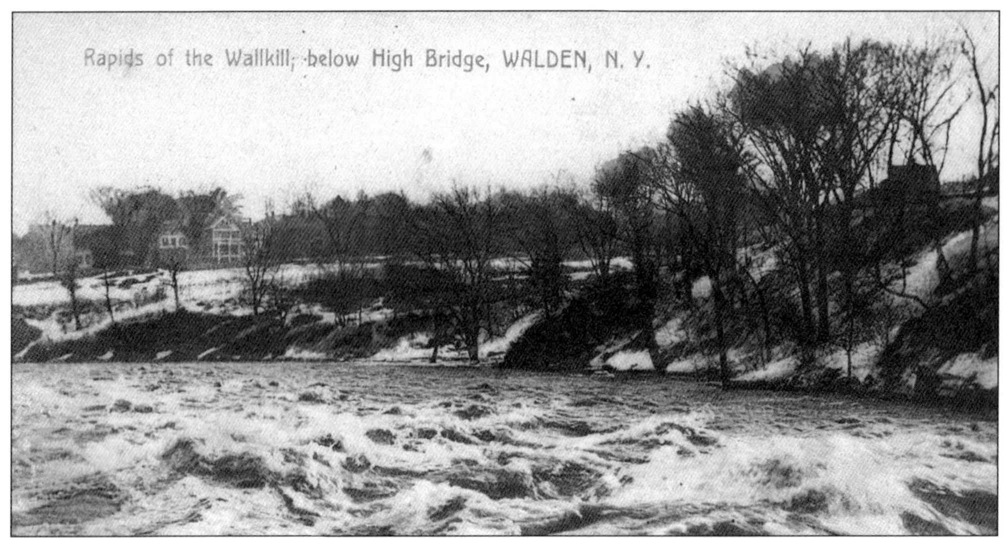

During the 1850s, the United States experienced an economic depression that affected major cities in New York State and small municipalities, such as the village of Walden in 1855 and 1856. Many businesses went bankrupt or were forced to cut jobs severely. Woolen factories and cotton factories began to close as early as the 1840s as a result of the panic of 1837. By the early 1850s, businesses had experienced a recession and, by 1857, a depression. This is a view of the rapids of the Wallkill below the High Bridge. (Courtesy of Jeff Sohns.)

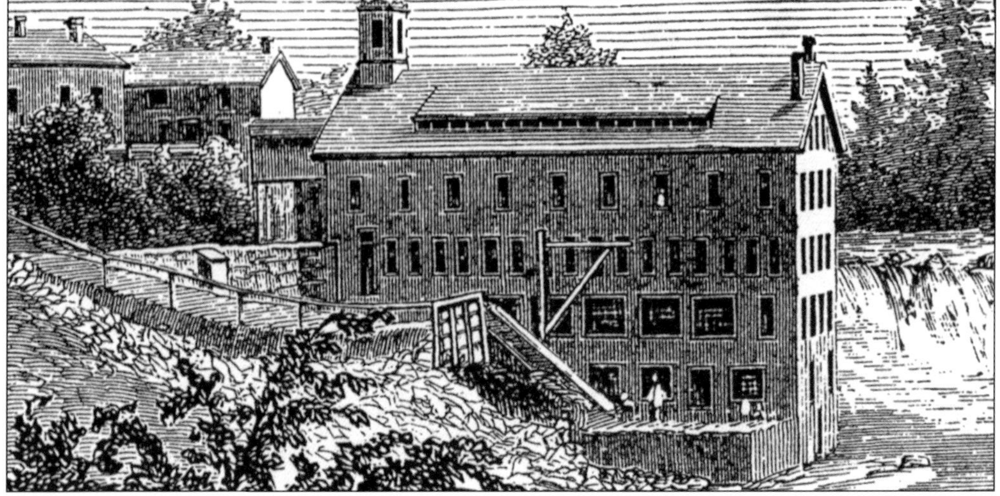

Towns and villages in Orange and Ulster Counties offered incentives to attract companies from Dutchess and other neighboring counties across the Hudson River. One incentive was good access to the Hudson River for shipping goods south to New York City and to the Albany Post Road for freight deliveries. Another incentive was the use of vacant buildings and warehouses, former factories and storage houses for the woolen and cotton businesses. In 1856, the village of Walden offered the New York Knife Company of Mattewean, a town in Dutchess County, the use of several buildings. Dozens of townspeople from Walden agreed to assist with the transporting of machines and materials. The newly relocated company meant the salvation of jobs for area residents. Pictured is the Wallkill River Knife Works *c.* 1860. The company was established at the High Falls, as had been many previous businesses. The president and manager of the company was Thomas J. Bradley. (Courtesy of Marc Newman.)

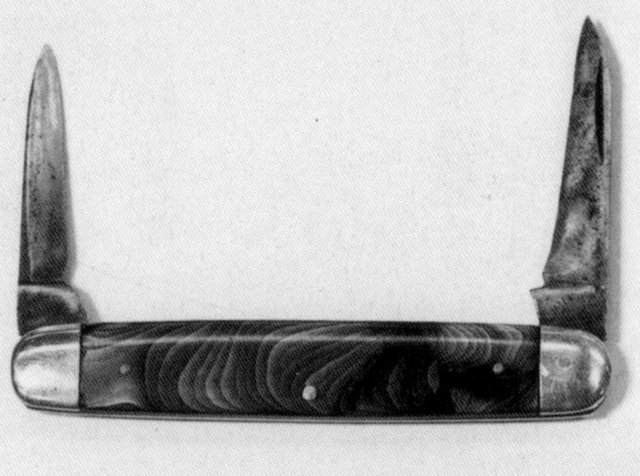

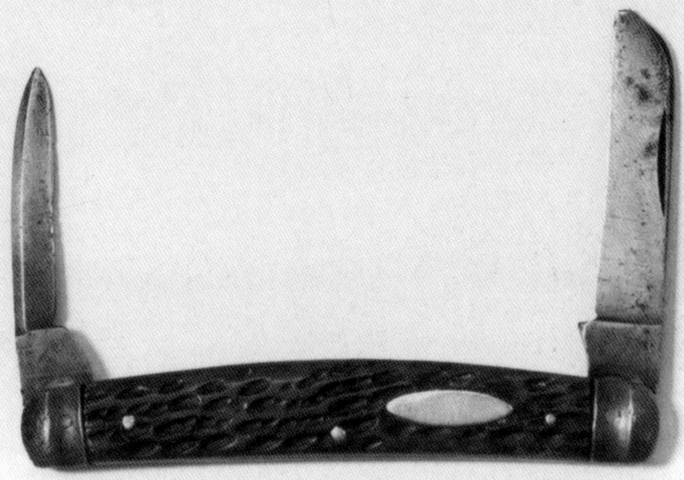

Thomas J. Bradley brought many of the Mattewean employees and residents with him. Among them were

Joseph Rowland Sr.	Isaac Newton	Alfred Donnelly
James Ward	George Barker	James Roberts
Alfred Simpson	George Mathews	George Kilner
Thomas Waley	George Robinson Sr.	Dennis Handy
Martin Marshall	Alfred Lockwood	Lewis Lockwood
Joseph Kilner	Joseph Brown	Edward Lawton
Robert Sutcliff	Jacob Bradwell	Samuel Trickett
Harvey Trickett	John Lindley	

Many of these men were stockholders in the company, which produced pocketknives, penknives, and tableware. Shown in the photograph are two 1860s penknives manufactured by the Wallkill River Knife Works; the lower one is a Congress penknife. (Photograph by Liz Bassett, courtesy of Marc Newman.)

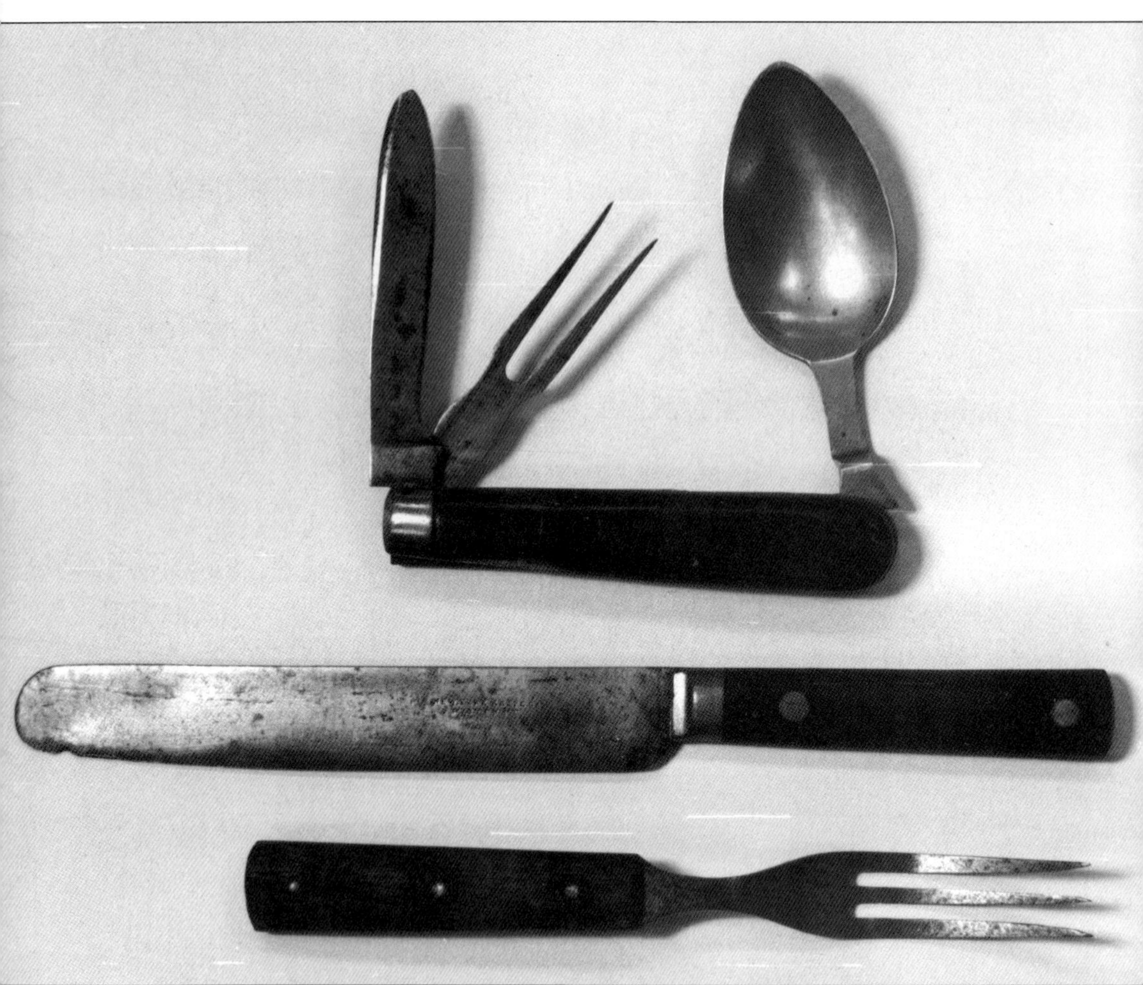

By the 1860s, the company had changed its name back to the New York Knife Company. During the Civil War, the company produced a variety of knives that were used by both civilians and the Union army. Mess tableware was produced for soldiers in camp; the knife and fork were usually sold in sets. Shown at the top is a combination pocketknife that had the knife, spoon, and fork easily accessible for the soldier in camp. In the center is a mess knife. Below is a mess fork. During the 1860s, most employees of the company were immigrants or first-generation Americans from either Sheffield, England, or Solingen, Germany. As production levels increased, more area residents and family members were hired. (Photograph by Liz Bassett, courtesy of Marc Newman.)

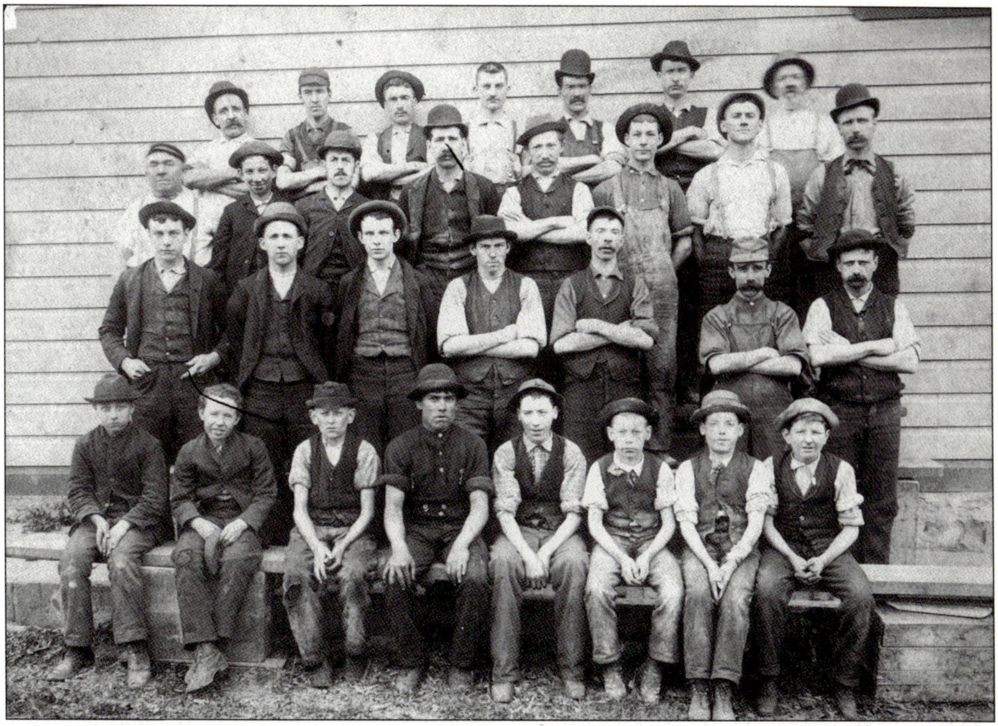

These were the blade finishers of the New York Knife Company *c.* 1889. (Courtesy of the Walden Historical Society.)

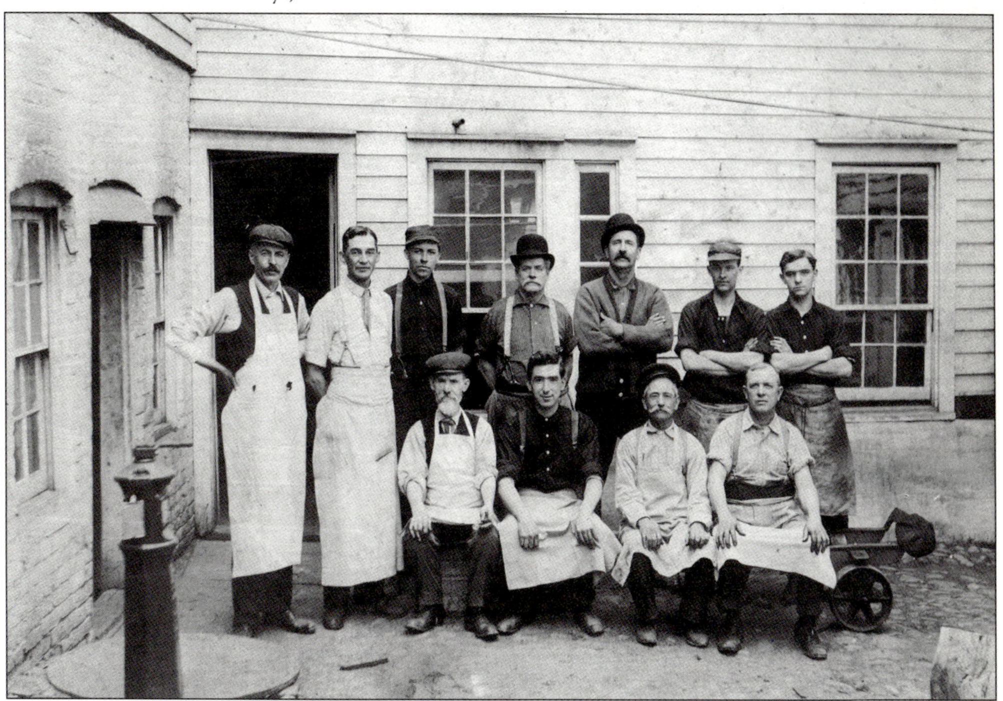

These were the grinders of the New York Knife Company *c.* 1900. (Courtesy of the Walden Historical Society.)

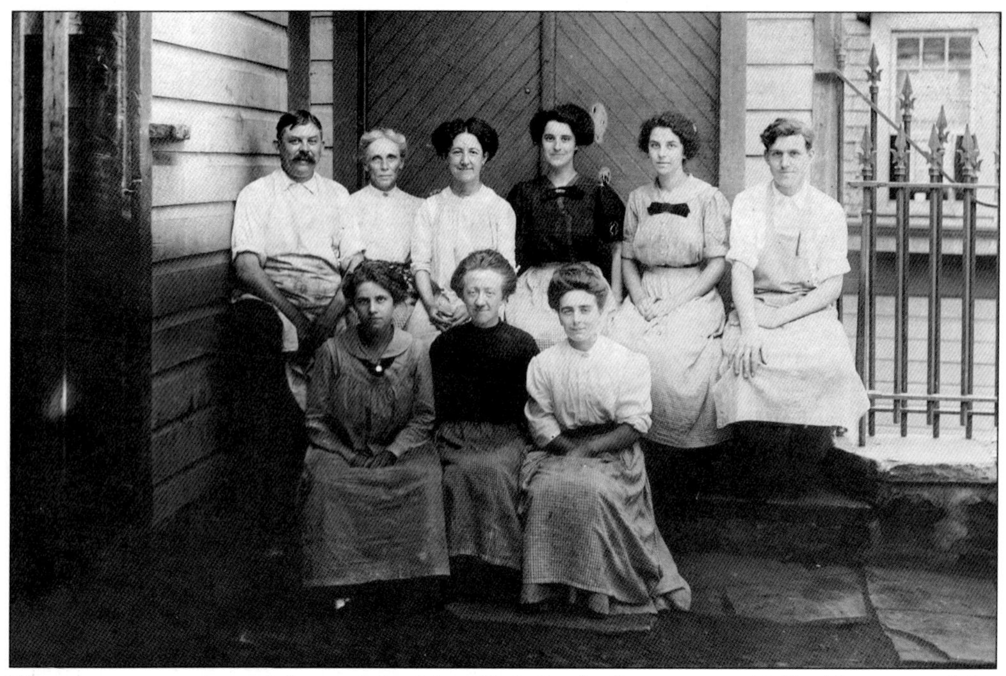

These men were the polishers of the New York Knife Company *c.* 1900. (Courtesy of the Walden Historical Society.)

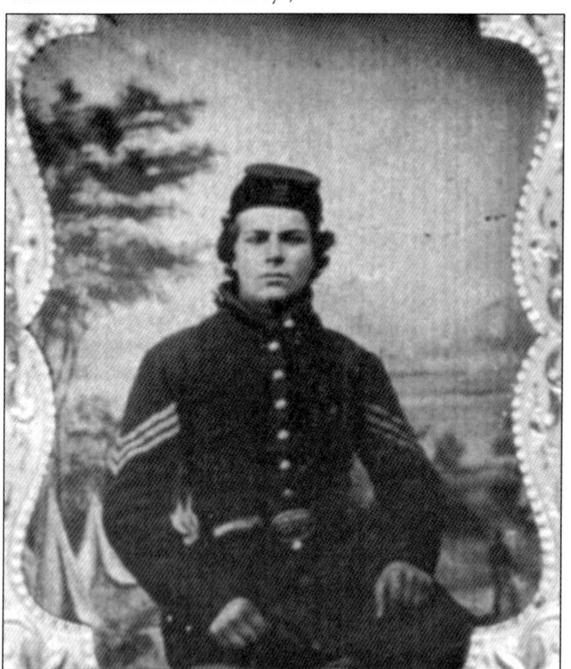

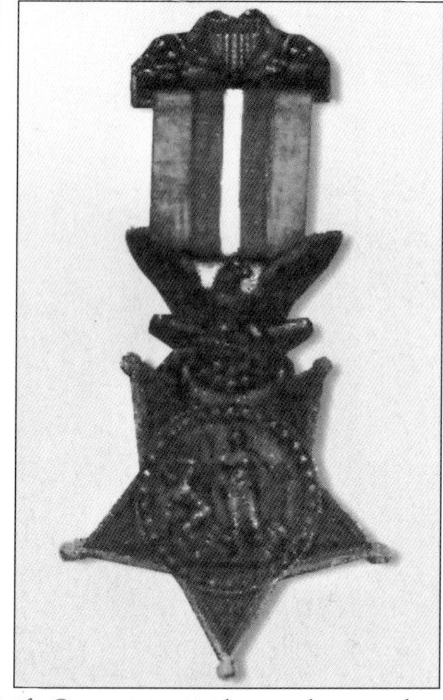

Thomas W. Bradley (left), the son of the New York Knife Company president, volunteered in the Civil War. At age 18 he joined as a private in the 124th Company H, which was commissioned in 1862. Four men of the 124th received a Congressional Medal of Honor (right). Among them were Sgt. Thomas W. Bradley and Pvt. Archibald Freeman of Walden. (Left, courtesy of Marcus Millspaugh; right, courtesy of the Walden Historical Society.)

Sgt. Thomas W. Bradley had "volunteered in response to a call and alone, in the face of a heavy fire of musketry and canister, went and procured ammunition for the use of his comrades."—from Sharp & Dunnigan, *The Congressional Medal of Honor*, page 726.

By 1865, Bradley was promoted from sergeant to major. He was wounded several times during the Civil War, including the Gettysburg campaign and the Battle of the Wilderness. When the war ended, he resumed his job of employee under his father, Thomas J. Bradley, at the New York Knife Company. The company flourished at its factory in the old cotton mill building, manufacturing thousands of knives with the hammer brand logo; the one shown here dates from c. 1910. (Courtesy of the Walden Chamber of Commerce.)

Wallkill River Works - Incorporated 1852

New York Knife Co.

Walden, New York

Works
Walden, N. Y.

Office
225 5th Avenue
New York

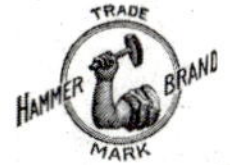

Hammer Brand Pocket Knives

Table Knives and Forks

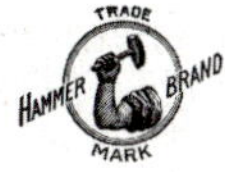

J. E. Fuller, President
Walter Geer, Vice Pres.
C. B. Fuller, Treasurer

G. B. Townsend, Secretary
F. R. Benedict, Manager
Thomas Brookfield, Superintendent

New York Knife Co.'s Factory, Walden, N.Y.

After the death of his father in 1880, Thomas W. Bradley took over the management of the knife company. (Courtesy of Marc Newman.)

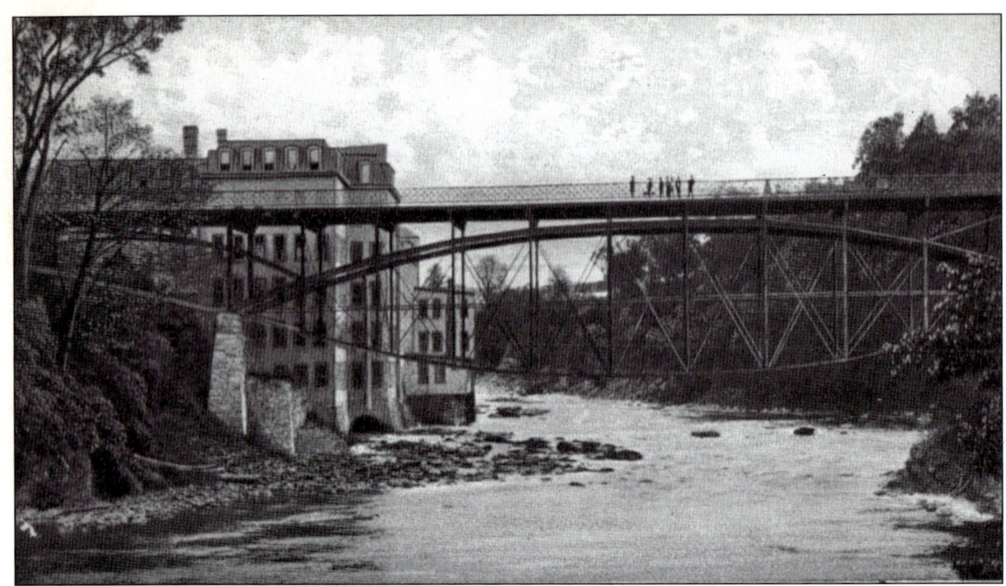

Near the Great Falls, the New York Knife Company constructed a new seven-story building, shown *c*. 1910. A suspension bridge, called the High Bridge, created a walkway across the Wallkill for residents to use. Workers gained access to the large building through the top floor. (Courtesy of Marc Newman.)

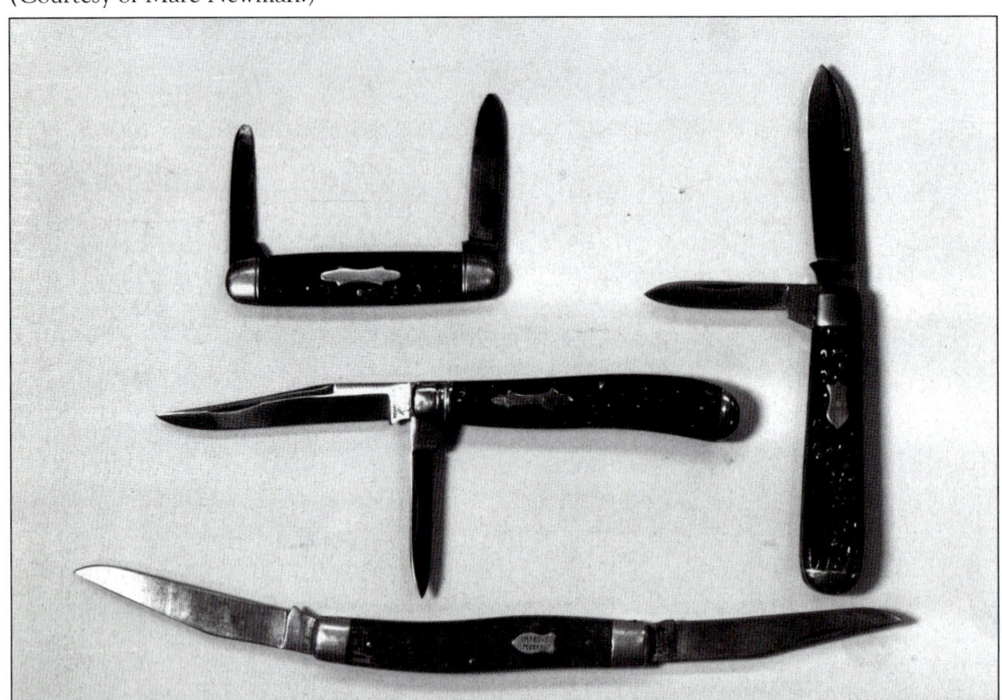

The company produced hundreds of different styles of pocketknives, penknives, and tableware. By the 1880s, the New York Knife Company had mass-produced hundreds of thousands of knives per year and sold them both nationally and internationally. The pocketknife usually had two to four blades and was used as a utility tool. The four shown date from 1870 to 1920. (Photograph by Liz Bassett, courtesy of Marc Newman.)

The penknife was smaller and thinner than the pocketknife and generally contained only two blades. It was used for mundane practices such as opening letters. The bolsters were made of steel and the frames of brass. Stag and antler were the most common materials used for the scales, or handles, of the knives. Exotic woods such as walnut were also used. The four penknives on the right date from *c.* 1870 to 1920. Other penknives, such as the two below from *c.* the 1920s, were 14-carat gold-filled and were carried either inside a man's vest pocket or suspended on a long chain like a watch fob. Some of these knives were mother-of-pearl and often bore a plate or escutcheon at the center of the knife handle. Often owners had their initials engraved on the handle to personalize these works of art. (Photograph by Liz Bassett, courtesy of Marc Newman.)

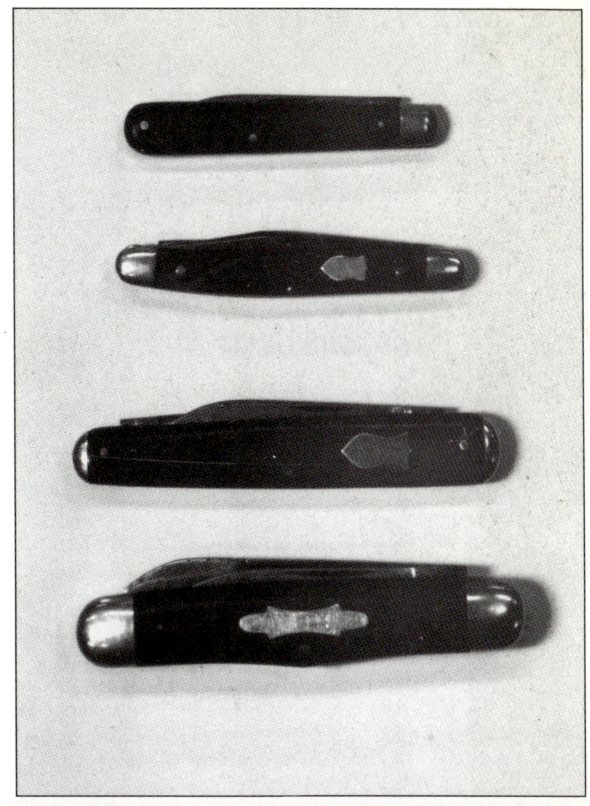

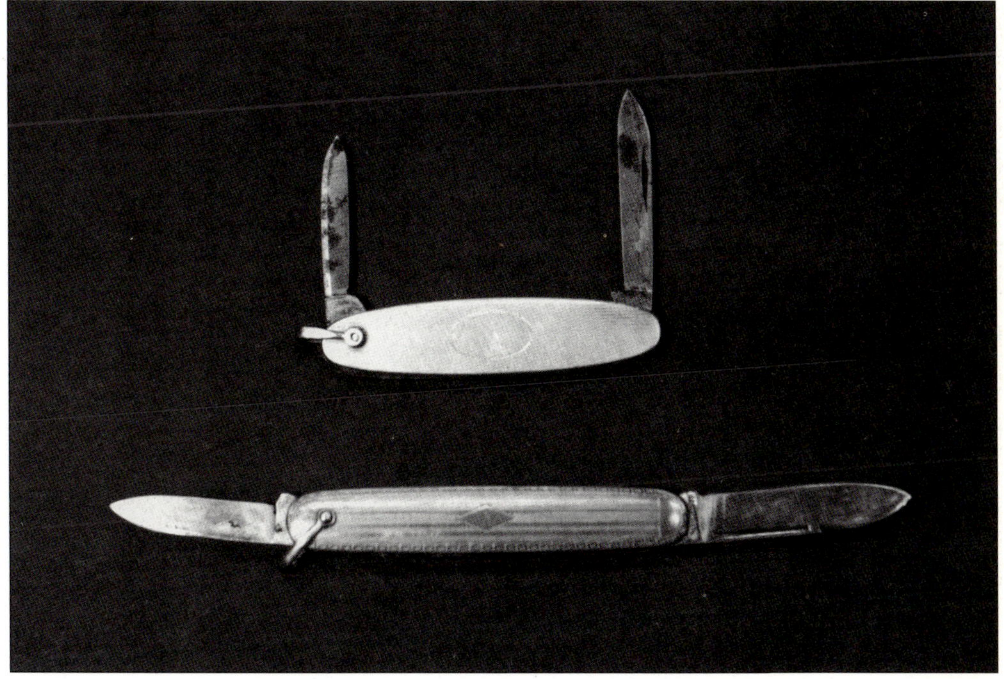

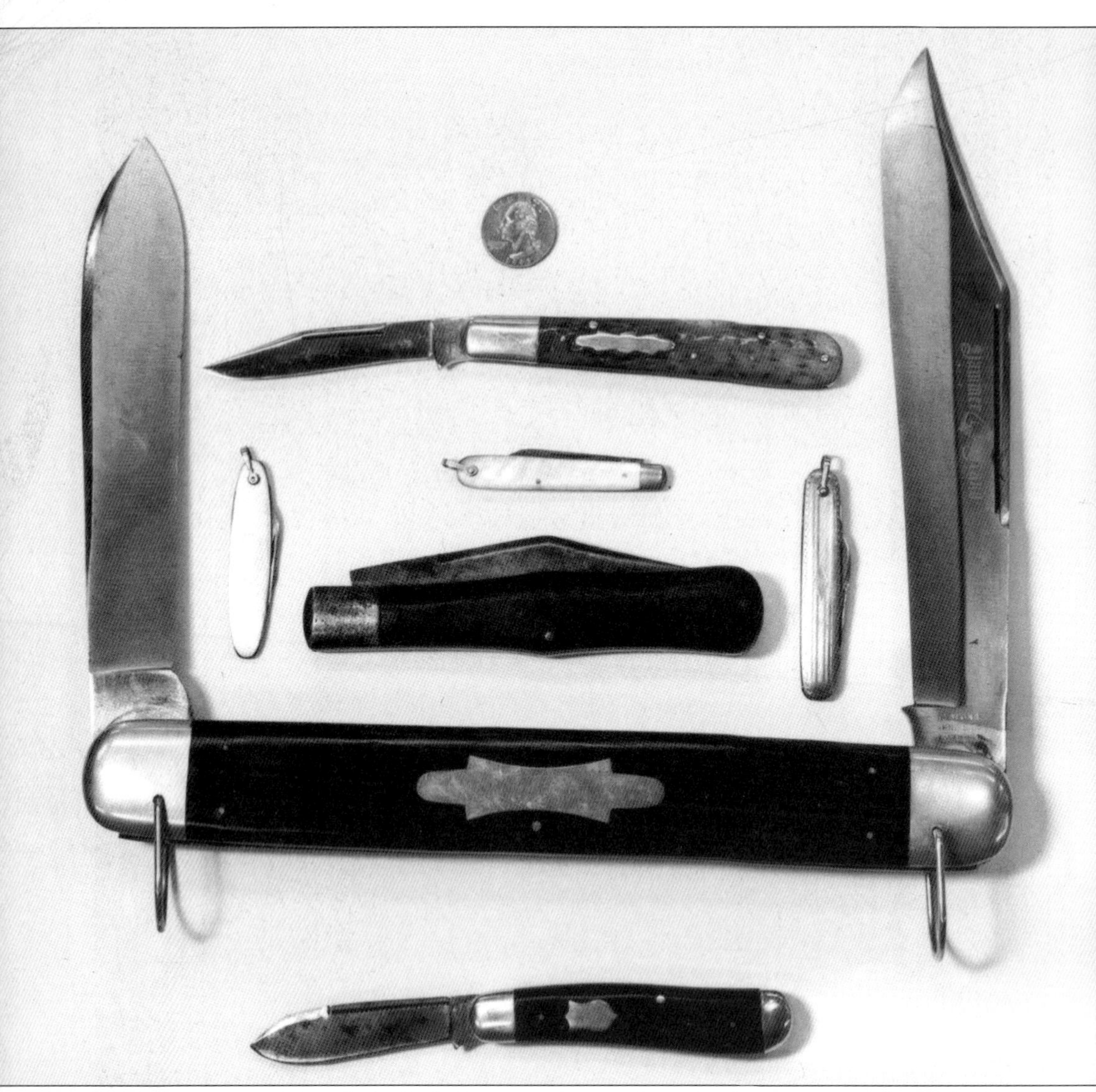

This assortment of New York Knife Company knives from the first quarter of the 20th century includes, from top to bottom, a lock-blade knife, penknives in gold plate and mother of pearl, a hunting knife, a promotional pocketknife, and a regular pocketknife. (Photograph by Liz Bassett, courtesy of Marc Newman.)

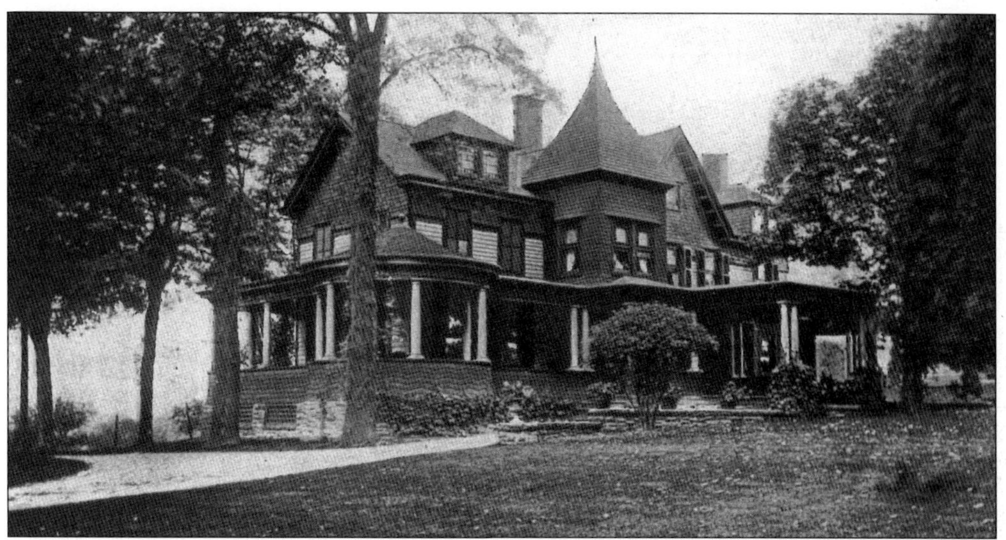

By the late 1880s, the New York Knife Company had expanded its operation. As president, Thomas W. Bradley had assets in excess of $250,000 in 1890. Employment was high, and housing and real estate expanded in and around the village of Walden. This *c.* 1880 photograph shows the Bradley home. (Courtesy of Marcus Millspaugh.)

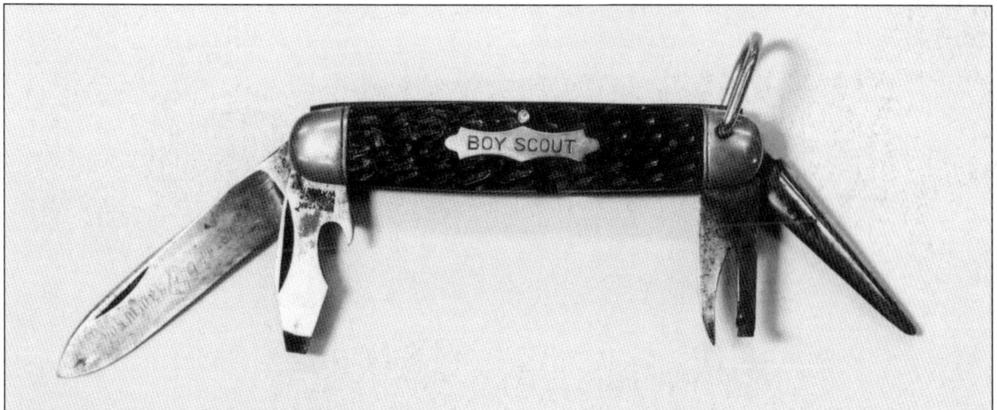

In the late 1880s, Congress and Pres. Grover Cleveland decided to lower the tariff on foreign exports, specifically steel products from Europe. This "reform tariff" lowered the tax rate on imports. German cutlery companies, especially from Solingen, Germany, took advantage of the lower rates and flooded the American market with less expensive knives. This threatened to force the New York Knife Company to lower prices and profits during a period of recession. Congressman William McKinley sponsored a tariff in 1890 (the McKinley Tariff), during the administration of Pres. Benjamin Harrison. That tariff raised the tax on foreign goods. By 1893, the United States was in the worst depression in the history of the nation up to that time. The downturn led to serious cutbacks and layoffs in major industries including rail service. By 1894, the economy had not rebounded under Cleveland. The Pullman Strike of 1894 led to armed conflict between the U.S. Army and the American Railway Union, resulting in casualties on both sides. Foreign steel products were coming into the United States, threatening to force the New York Knife Company to lay off many of its workers. The company continued to produce knives, such as this *c.* 1920 Boy Scout knife, but under a shortened four-day workweek, with production maintained for each day. Excess knives were stored in warehouses and barns in Walden and throughout Orange County. (Courtesy of Michael Newman.)

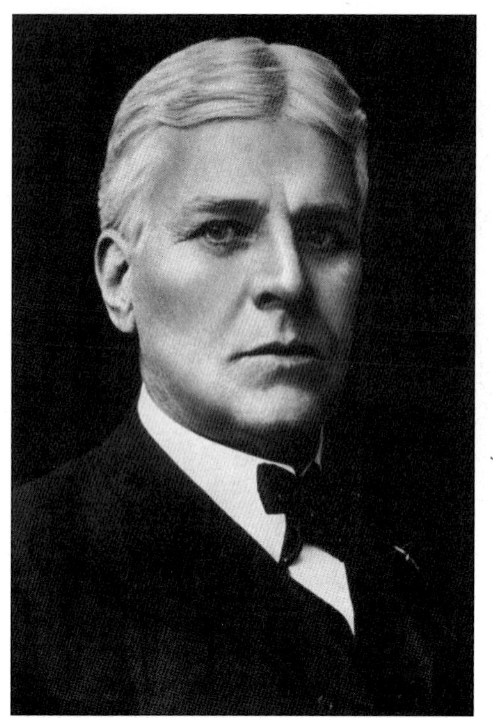

Having lost $250,000 of his assets, Thomas W. Bradley, New York Knife Company president, borrowed $100,000. Bradley's friend and comrade in arms from the Civil War became Pres. William McKinley, who convinced Congress to pass the Dingley Tariff. By 1897, that tariff had raised duties to the highest level in the history of the United States, especially on steel products made in Europe. Bradley earned back the $350,000 originally lost and borrowed, plus another $200,000 to $250,000. In 1903, he decided to sell his company to the Fuller brothers of New York City and to begin his 10-year career as a U.S. congressman, as pictured here *c.* 1910. When he died in the 1920s, money was left in his will for the establishment of a statue, in gratitude, to honor Pres. William McKinley. The Fuller brothers continued the production level of the New York Knife Company until the company went out of business in 1931. By the advent of World War II, the buildings had been torn down and destroyed. (Courtesy of the Walden Historical Society.)

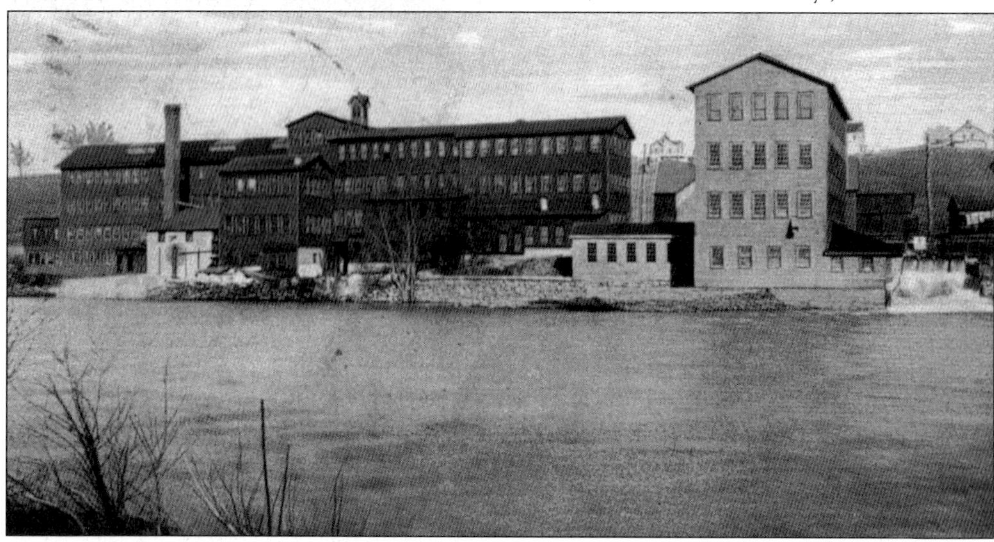

A baseball game led to the creation of the second cutlery company within the village of Walden. During lunch hour, some of the male employees of the New York Knife Company spent their time playing a baseball game on the company field. There were several teams, and female employees looked on and cheered their team and fellow workers. Apparently, there was a bad call regarding whether the baseball player was safe or out. As the men started to argue, several of the women found Thomas J. Bradley and asked him to stop the game. The company president told the men to stop the game and prohibited them from playing baseball on their lunch hours. The workers refused and, after losing their jobs, decided to form their own company in rented several rented rooms in the Rider Engine company plant. Shown *c.* 1900 is the Walden Knife Company. (Courtesy of Marc Newman.)

W.E. Gowdy was named president of the new Walden Cooperative Knife Company. In 1874, the name was changed to the Walden Knife Company. The company made pocketknives and penknives (shown, c. the 1880s to the 1930s) similar in design to those of the New York Knife Company. The original building of the knife company was four stories and was approximately 128 feet long and 20 feet wide. Water and steam power were used as the principal source of power and energy for some of the machines. There were 225 employees in the company. Many of the knives produced were purchased by hardware tycoon E.C. Simmons of St. Louis, Missouri. (Photograph by Liz Bassett, courtesy of Marc Newman.)

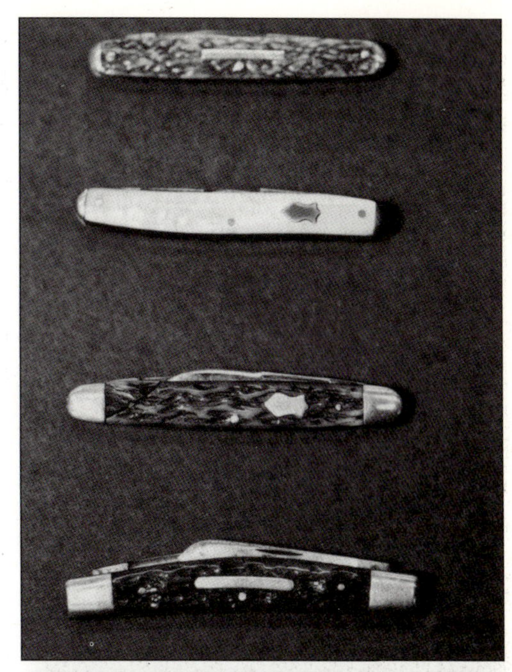

Walden Knife Company

INCORPORATED 1852

Walden - New York

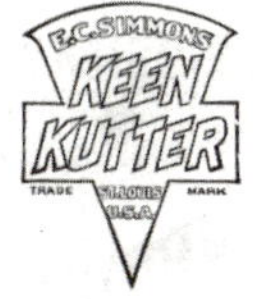

Manufacturers of

Keen Kutter Pocket Knives

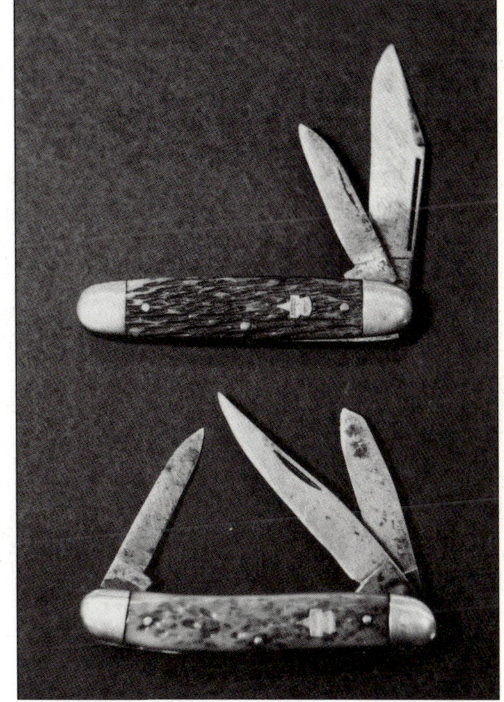

Walden pocketknives (right, c. the 1920s) were one of the main utility tools stocked by E.C. Simmons hardware stores. When principal stockholder George Weller sold his majority shares in the Walden Knife Company, they were purchased by Simmons. The company's logo (left) was Keen Kutter, symbolizing the fine cutting edge and durability of its knives. (Left, courtesy of the Walden Chamber of Commerce; right, photograph by Liz Bassett, courtesy of Marc Newman.)

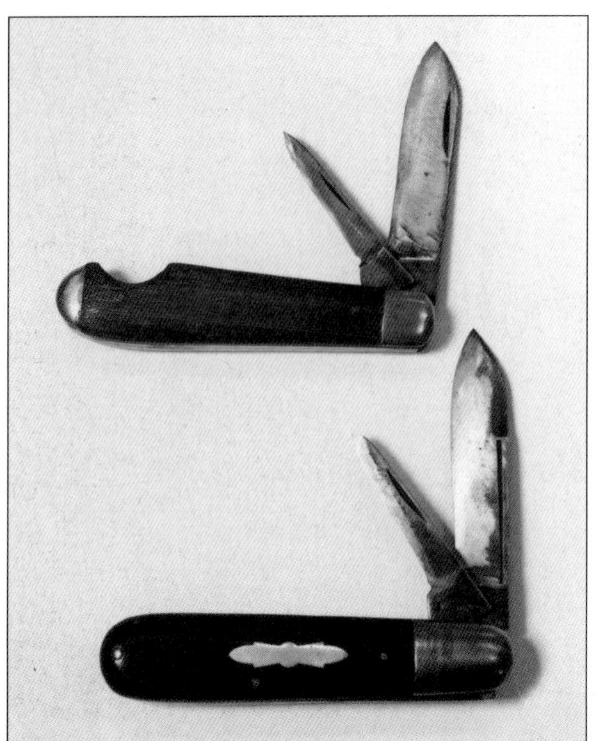

These jackknives were manufactured by the Walden Knife Company *c.* the 1930s. (Courtesy of Marc Newman.)

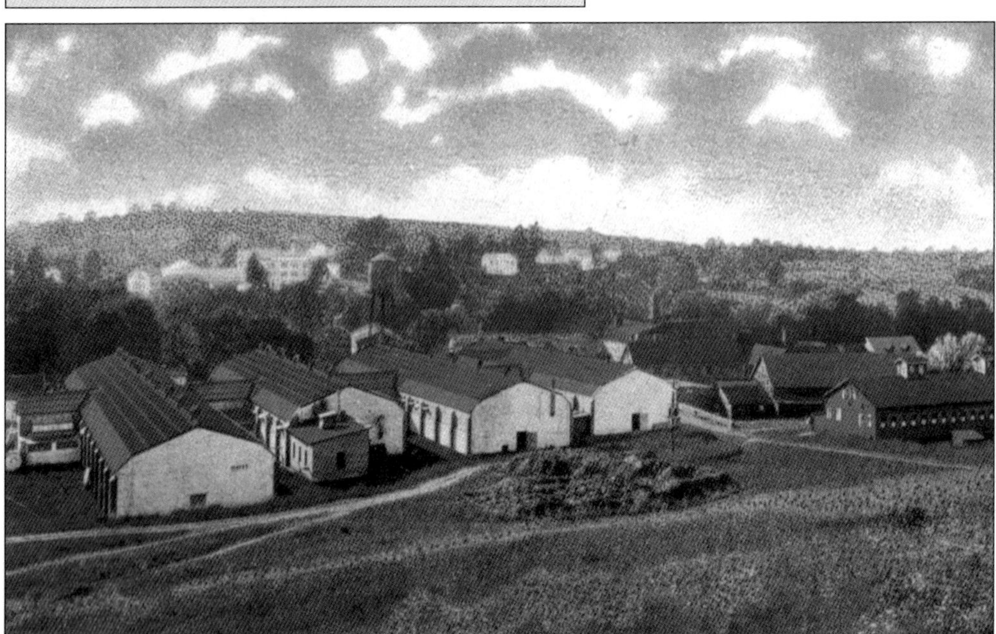

The Walden Knife Company was known as the "Lower Shop" because it was located at the Lower Falls of the Wallkill River. The "Upper Shop," the New York Knife Company, was located at the Upper Falls of the Wallkill River. Many of the workers from the Lower Shop had been former employees of the New York Knife Company and were highly skilled in the various phases of the cutlery process. Shown are extension buildings *c.* the 1920s. (Courtesy of Robert Kidd.)

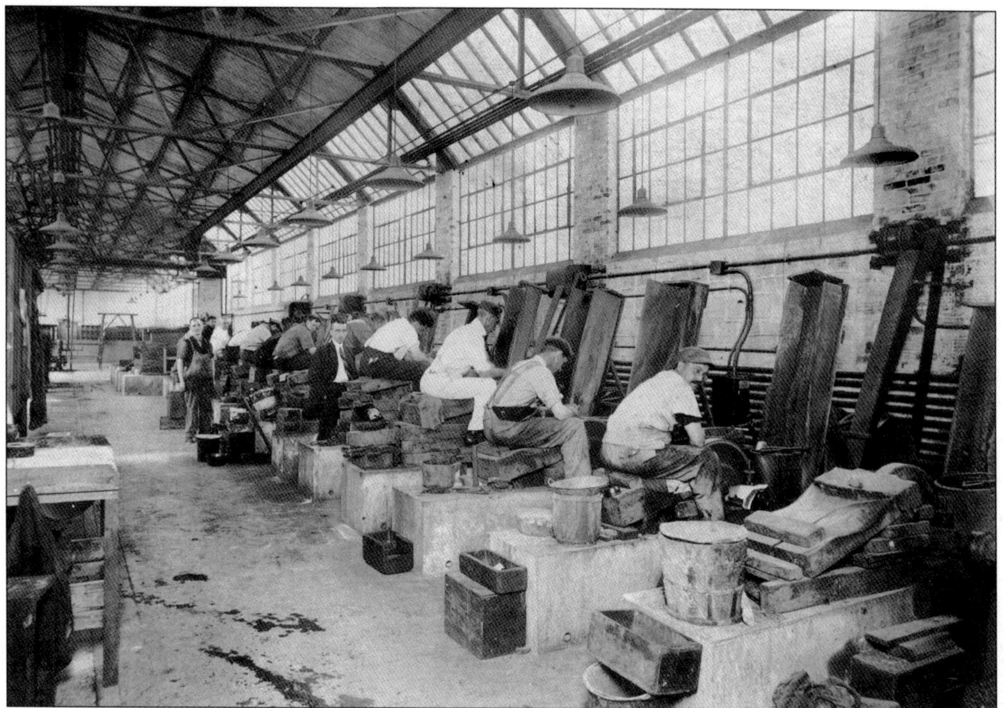

Shown *c.* 1910 are the grinders (above), who shaped the blades of the knives, and the hefters (below), who were responsible for shaping and creating the frames that held the blade, bolsters, pins, and scales of the knife. (Courtesy of the Walden Historical Society.)

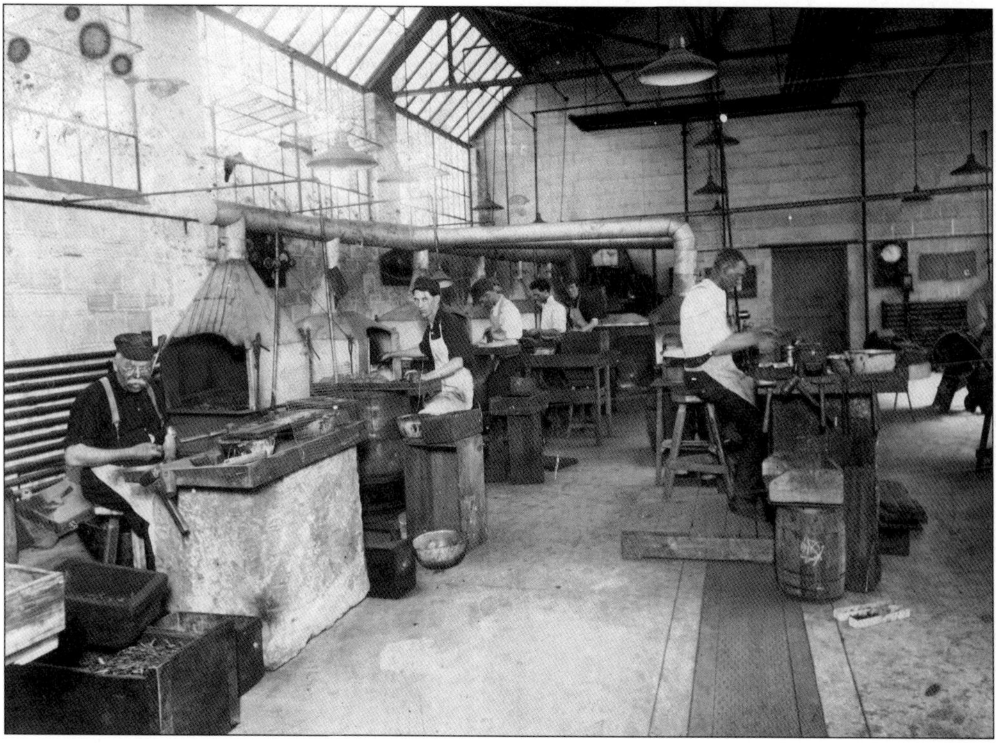

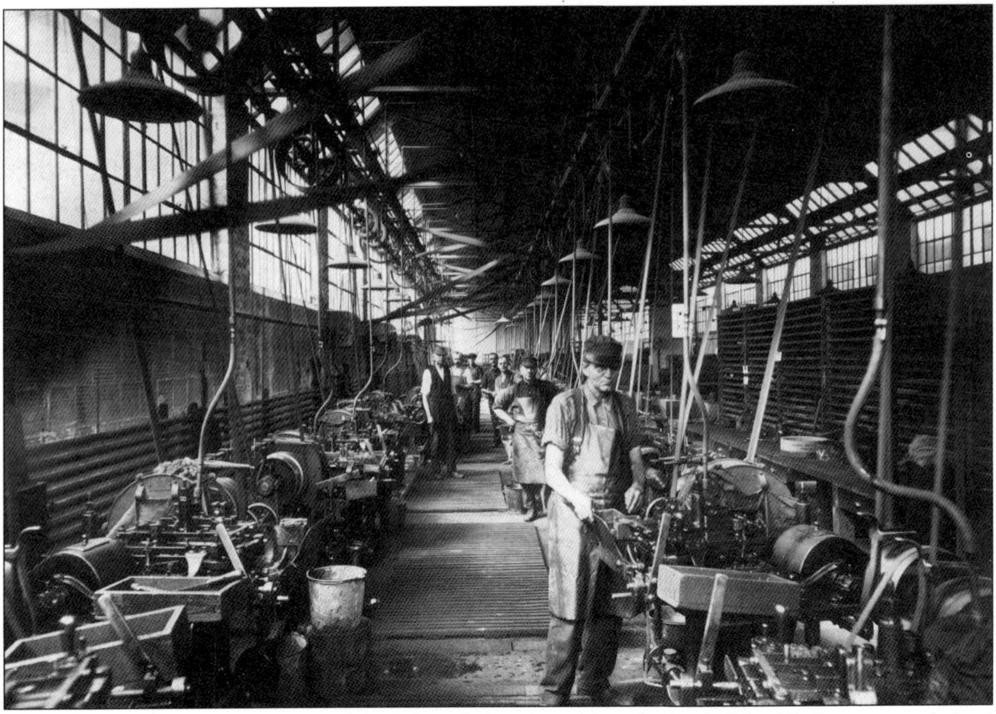

Shown *c.* 1910 are the polishers (above) and the assemblers (below). The blades were polished before the knife was assembled. Then, other workers placed the rivets in the bolsters of the knife after assembling the frame, the handles (scales), and the bolsters (caps). (Courtesy of the Walden Historical Society.)

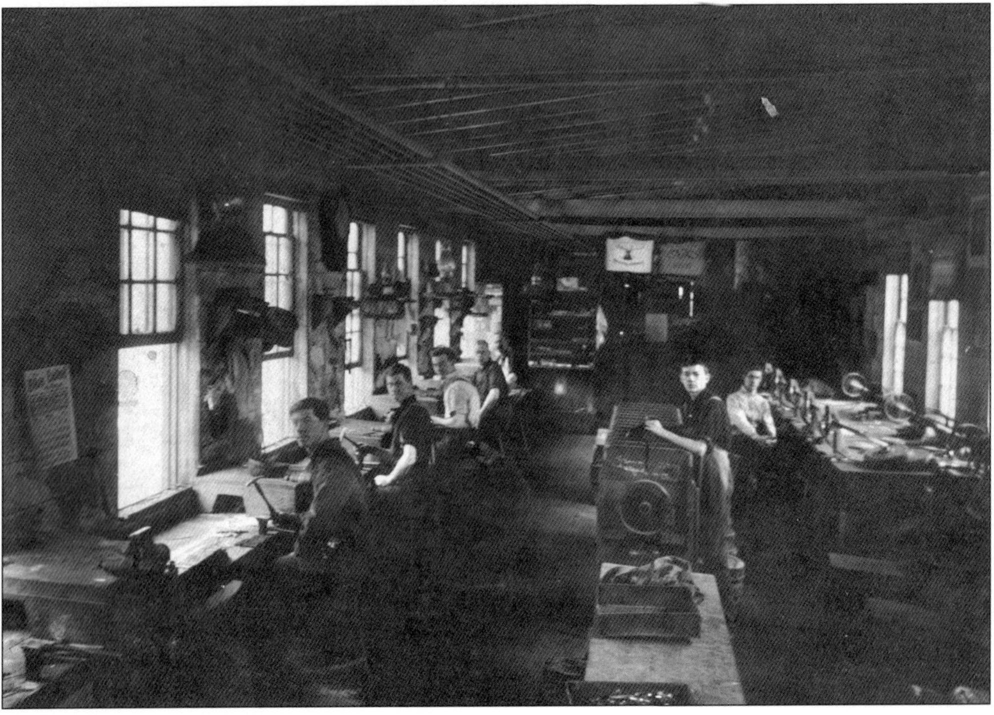

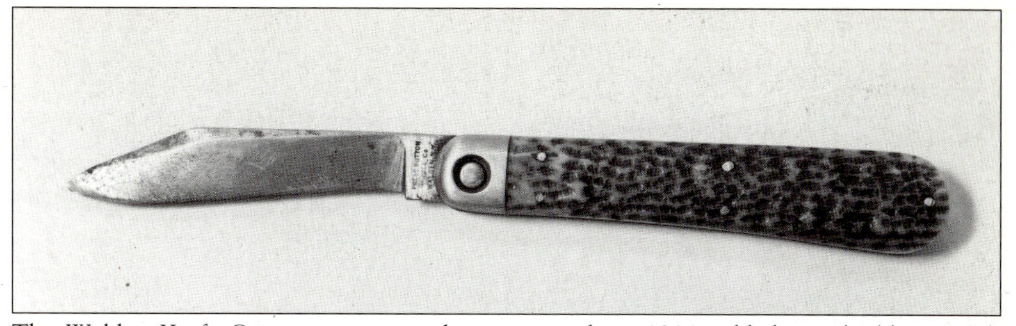

The Walden Knife Company continued to grow and, in 1914, added new buildings with electrical equipment. The new buildings were given the nickname "White Elephants." During World War I, the Walden Knife Company procured a government contract through the Department of the Navy. The company had created a large navy jackknife that was considered very popular and practical. During the 1920s, after orders for the jackknives decreased, the E.C. Simmons Company sold Walden Knife to Winchester Arms of Bridgeport, Connecticut. By 1927, Walden Knife Company was no longer in business. The only knife company that survived the Great Depression was Schrade Cutlery Company, originally known as the Press Button Knife Company. In 1903, inventor and scientist George Schrade of Sheffield, England, created the pocketknife, pictured here c. 1904. The knife ejected a large clip-point blade from the side. The blade locked into place in front of the bolster. With financial support from Shrade's father, Gottlieb Schrade, the Press Button Knife Company was established in Walden in 1904. (Courtesy of Marc Newman.)

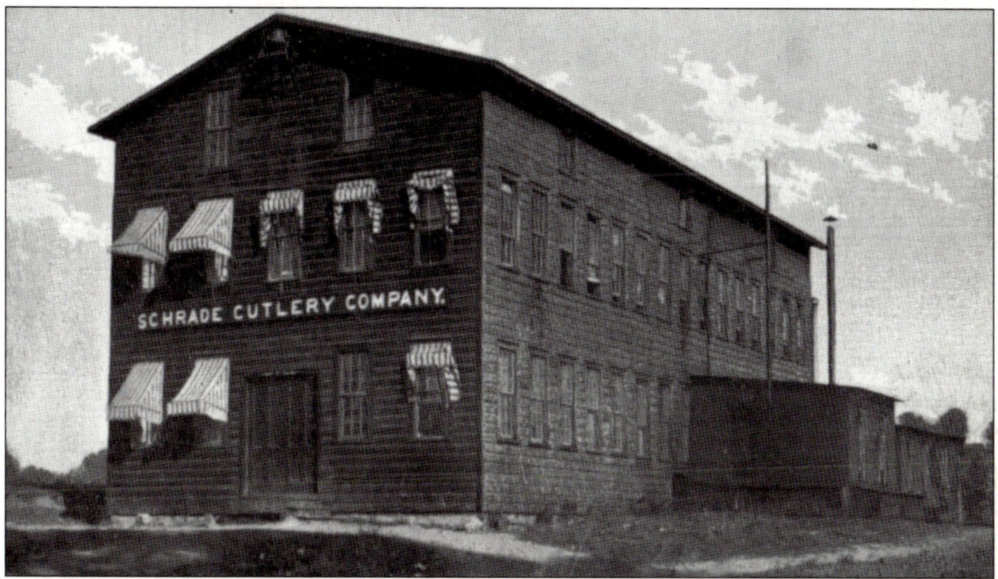

In the early years, company officers included George Schrade, president; Philip Hasbrouck, vice president; J. Louis Schrade, treasurer; and I.H. Loughran, secretary. The first building of the Press Button Knife Company was erected on East Main Street and was about 30 feet by 70 feet. By 1911, the company had changed its name to the Schrade Cutlery Company. During that year, the original building was expanded by 30 feet with a three-story addition. Many of the workers were English and Irish immigrants recruited by members off the Schrade family, for example Gottlieb Schrade and George Schrade, who were skilled as cutlers, having been employed in Sheffield, England, before coming to the United States. (Courtesy of Marc Newman.)

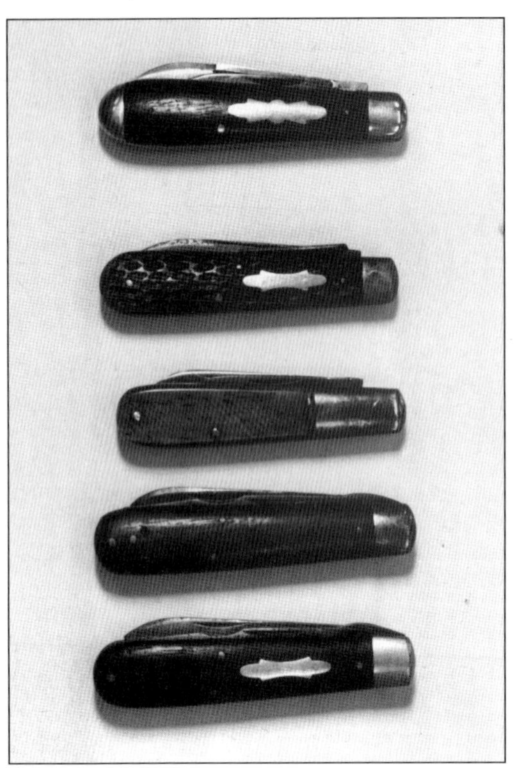

To make sure the company would have sufficient imitation stag handles, the Schrade Cutlery Company bought out the Walden Cutlery Handle Company. This company was originally created by all three of the knife companies to provide the most common style handle, or slabs: stag. This company was referred to as the Stag Shop. Shown are Schrade jackknives with stag and walnut handles, *c.* the 1920s and 1930s. (Photograph by Liz Bassett, courtesy of Marc Newman.)

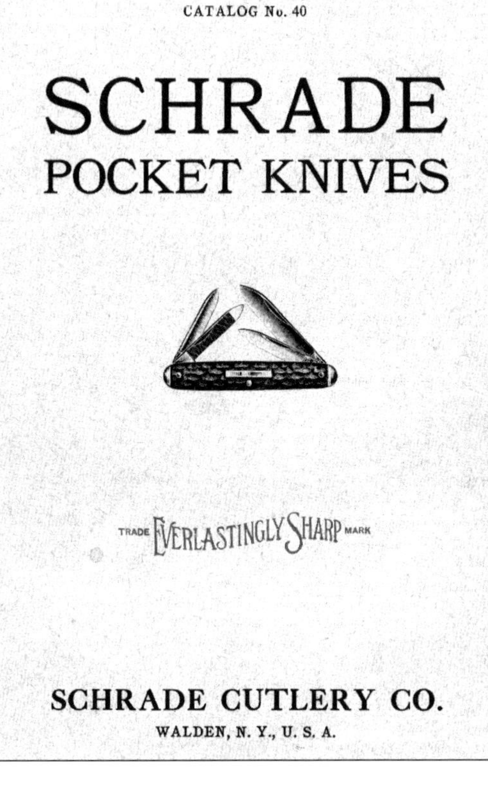

During the early period of development, George Schrade left the Walden company to create another Schrade Company in Bridgeport, Connecticut. He had developed a shielding device, which he manufactured, as well as knives stamped "Bridgeport." The success of the switchblade knife resulted in the full expansion of the company. J. Louis Schrade was elected president. With full use of electrical machinery, the company began to mass-produce knives to meet the growing national and international demand. The company logo was "Everlastingly Sharp," as seen here *c.* 1940. A lifetime warranty went with each knife produced; any customer dissatisfied with the blade or handle would receive a new knife as a replacement. (Courtesy of Marc Newman.)

Brochures and fliers, such as this one (right) from c. 1940, were printed to announce the full line of Schrade push-button knives. Knives were made in various sizes, from the small penknife with one blade to the two-blade switchblade. The company also manufactured a pull-ball automatic switchblade (below) c. the 1920s. (Lower photograph by Liz Bassett; both courtesy of Marc Newman.)

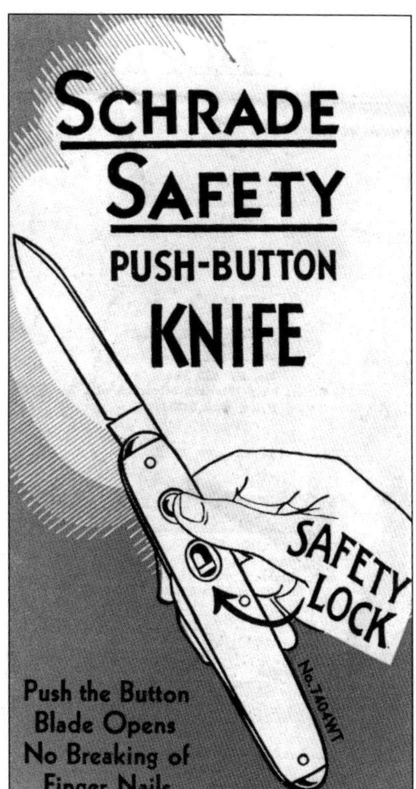

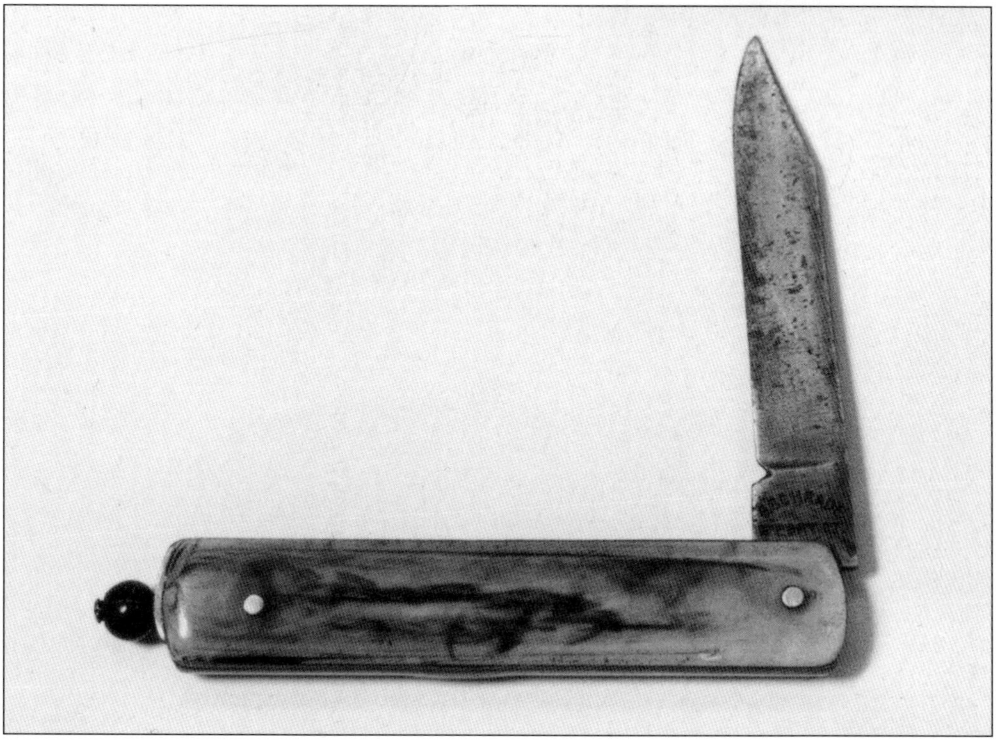

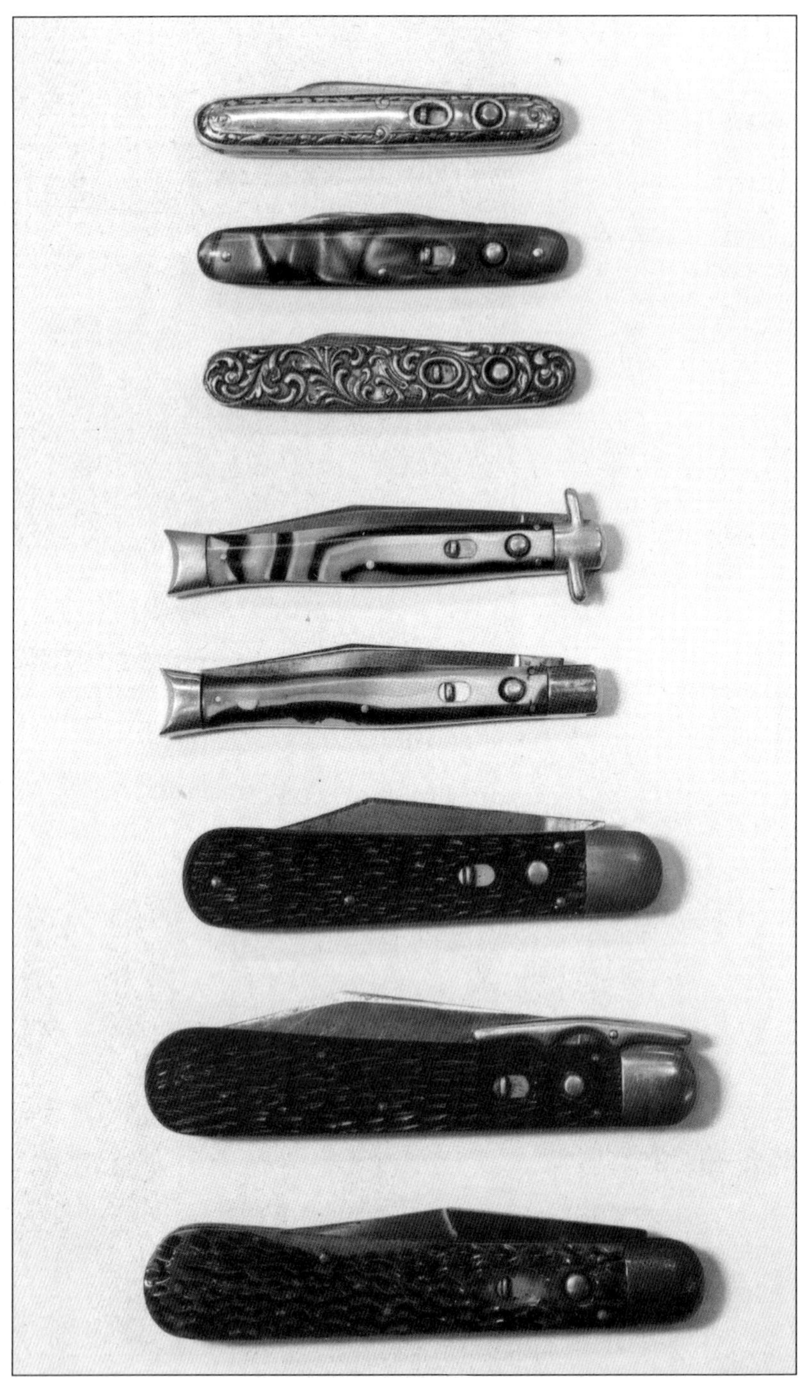

This photograph shows an assortment of Schrade Cutlery Company switchblades from the 1930s to the 1950s. They are, from top to bottom, a sterling silver double press-button knife, a celluloid double-press button knife, an engraved sterling silver double press-button knife, two celluloid press-button knives, a pocket press-button knife, a pocket press-button knife with double guard, and a hunting press-button knife. (Photograph by Liz Bassett, courtesy of Marc Newman.)

The Schrade Cutlery Company created thousands of different designs for many of its knives. Some knives were made with a company name on the scales, or handles, and were used by the company as a means of advertising to increase sales. Shown, from top to bottom, are examples of such knives, produced from the 1920s to the 1950s: Union Carbide Coatings Service; Newburgh Lodge 309 F&AM 35th Anniversary Class of 1920, E.H. Best & Company, Boston; and Knoxall Textiles. (Photograph by Liz Bassett, courtesy of Marc Newman.)

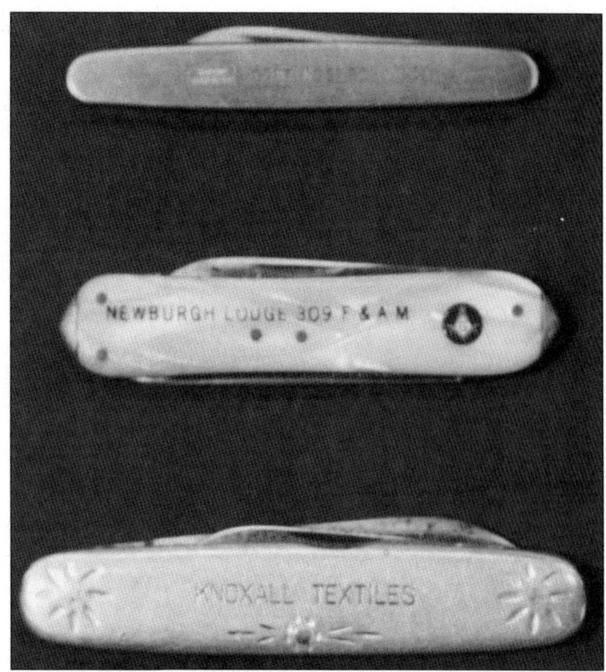

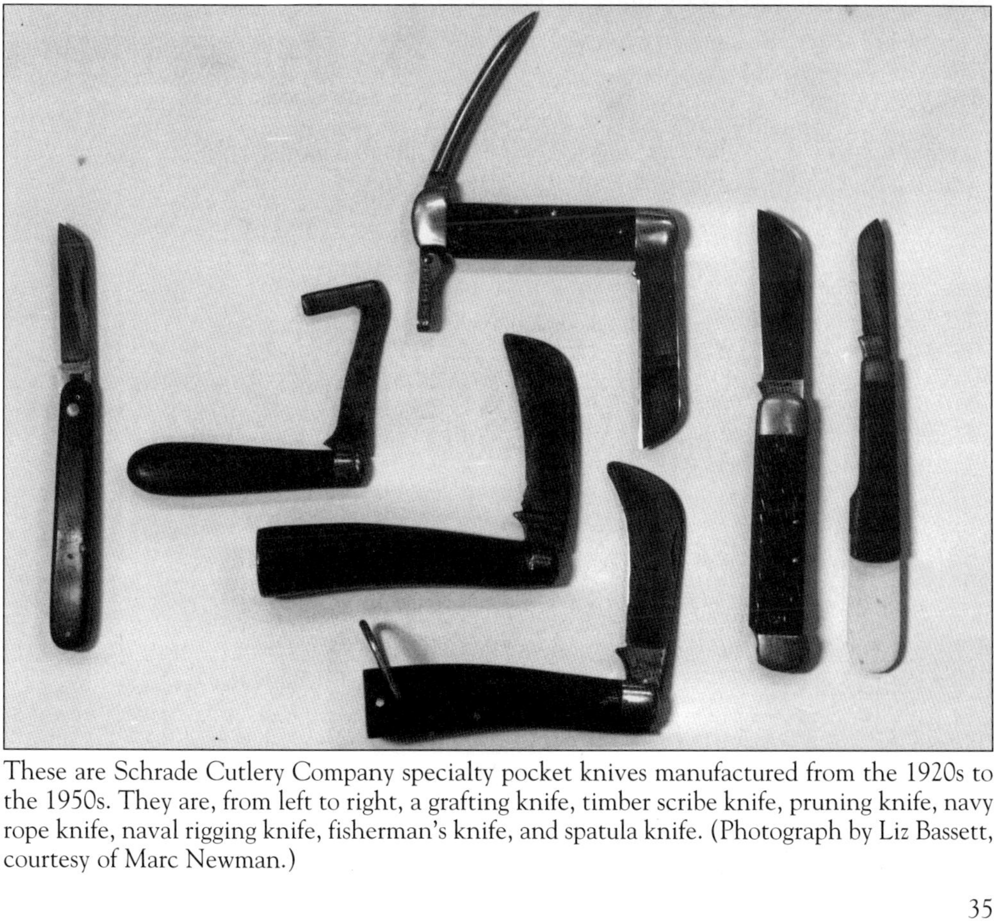

These are Schrade Cutlery Company specialty pocket knives manufactured from the 1920s to the 1950s. They are, from left to right, a grafting knife, timber scribe knife, pruning knife, navy rope knife, naval rigging knife, fisherman's knife, and spatula knife. (Photograph by Liz Bassett, courtesy of Marc Newman.)

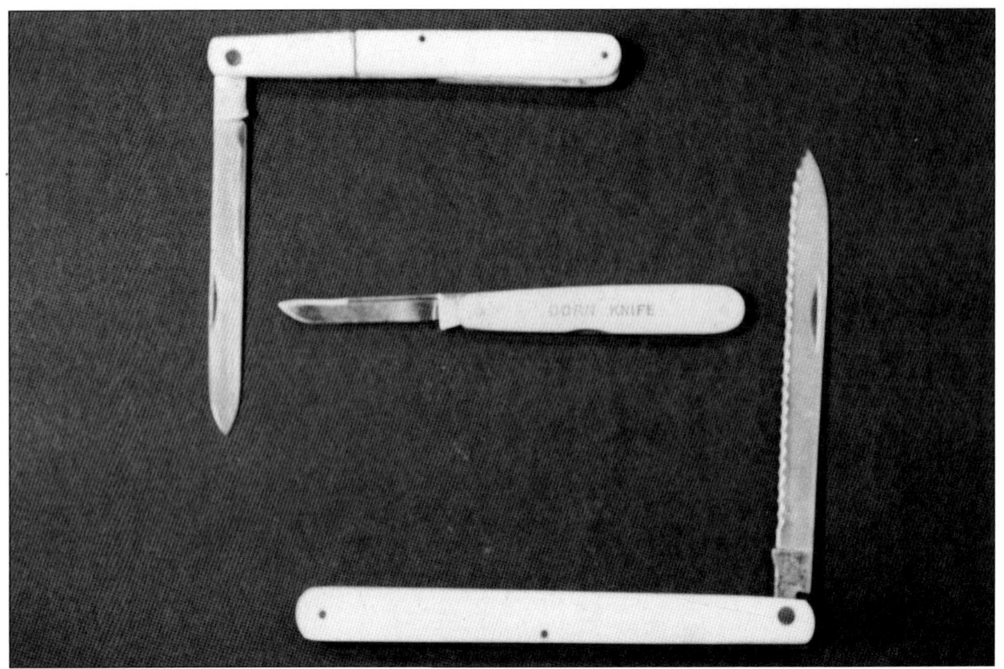

These Schrade Cutlery Company fruit and vegetable pocket knives were made *c.* the 1950s. Shown, from top to bottom, are a fruit knife, corn knife, and pineapple knife. (Photograph by Liz Bassett, courtesy of Marc Newman.)

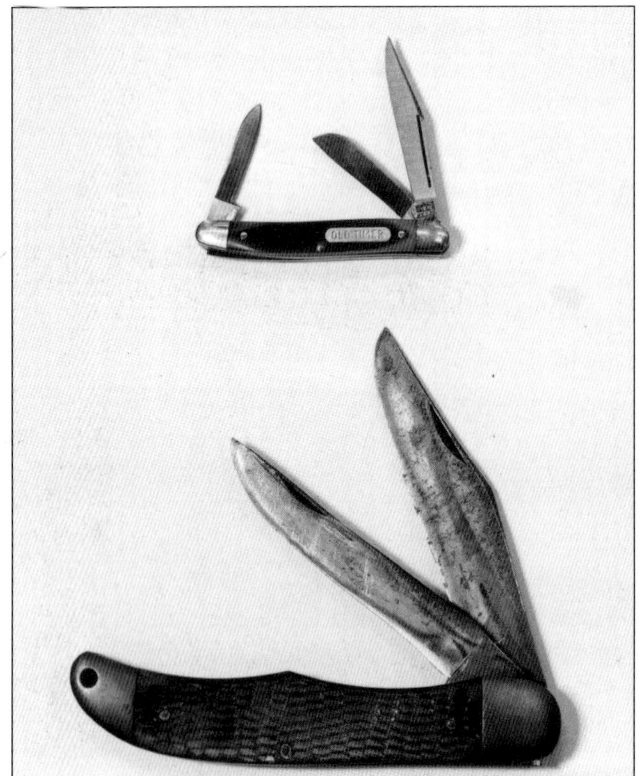

Some of the traditional Schrade knives produced in the 1950s and 1960s include the old-timer penknife and the Uncle Henry pocketknife. (Photograph by Liz Bassett, courtesy of Marc Newman.)

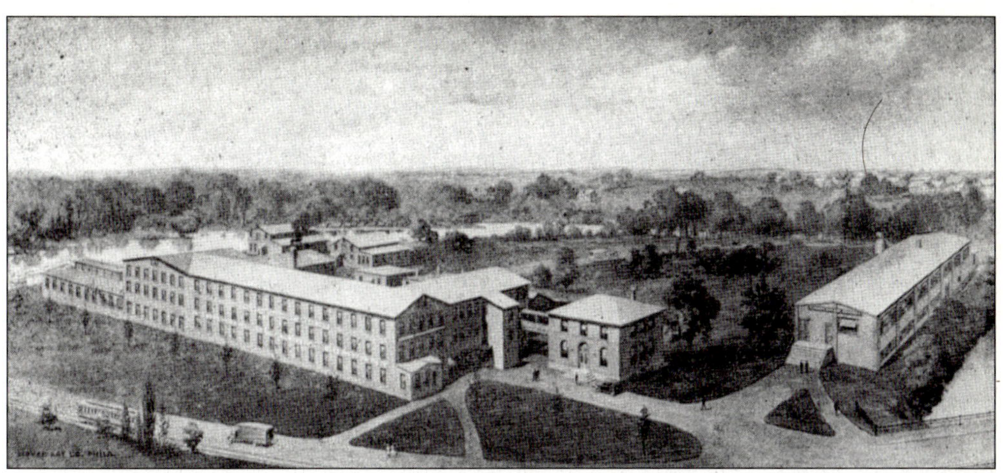

Over the years other family members were involved as officers in the Schrade Corporation: J. Louis Schrade (president), William Schrade (treasurer), Alfred V. Schrade (director) and Joseph Schrade (manager). By the 1920s and 1930s, Schrade Cutlery had expanded and opened a second production plant in Middletown, about 20 miles from Walden. The Walden plant (pictured, in the 1940s) had some 200 employees; the Middletown branch had about 75. (Courtesy of the Walden Chamber of Commerce.)

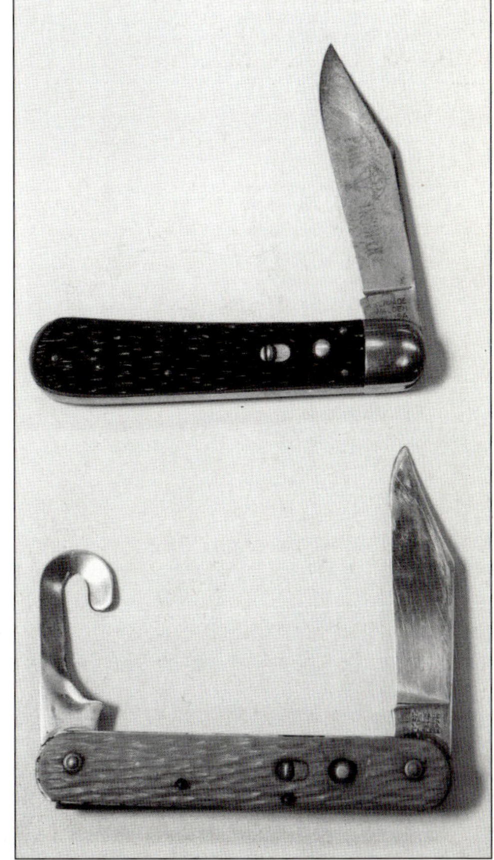

Many of the knives that were made by Schrade Cutlery Company were on contract for the army and navy during World War II. The switchblade with a safety lock (top) was stamped with the insignia "Paratrooper." The M2 survival switchblade (below) added a hook at the end of the knife. Using just one hand, a paratrooper could release the blade, lock it, and cut the parachute line. The knife was iridescent orange and hung from the harness on a hook. It continued in production during the Korean War, but like all switchblades it was banned from production and sale by the Kefauver Act. In 1947, J. Louis Schrade sold the Schrade Cutlery Company to Albert and Henry Baer, owners of the Ulster Knife Company. The designs and tooling did not change, but the logo of the knife was changed from "Schrade Cut Co." to "Schrade-Walden." The Walden Company closed in 1957 after a fire caused serious damage. Buses were arranged to transport the Walden employees to the company plant in Ellenville. By 1973, the logo was changed by the Imperial Knife Company to Schrade USA. Today, the company still exists in Ellenville, under new management and with the majestic title of Schrade Imperial Corporation. (Photograph by Liz Bassett, courtesy of Marc Newman.)

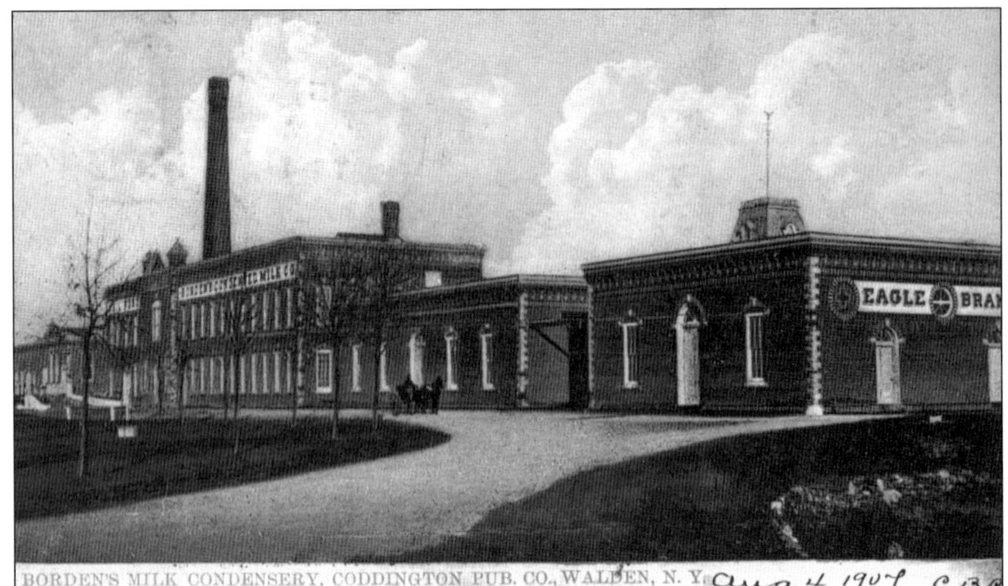

Many companies developed and prospered in and around the village. During the Civil War, in 1864, the Walden Condensed Milk Company was organized; it was later named the Highland Condensed Milk Company. The New York Condensed Milk Company was bought by the Borden family, later referred to as the Borden Milk Company. The company established its dairy farm north of the village. Some Walden residents worked on the farm. (Courtesy of Robert Kidd.)

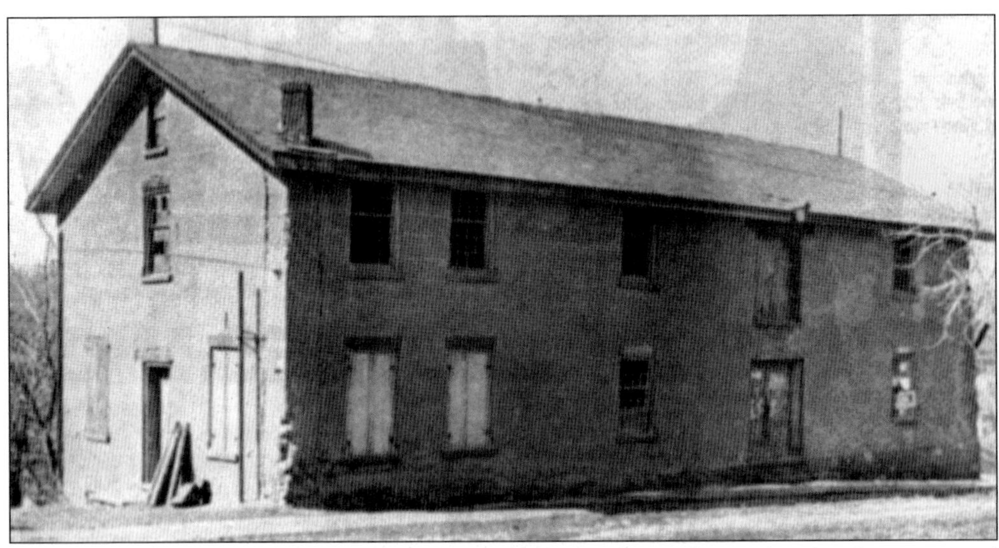

One major industry of the village was the Gowdy Brick Works, under the direction and ownership of James Gowdy. Many of the brick houses and businesses in the county and neighboring counties relied on the Walden Brick Yard to supply the necessary materials, including grout. Shown is the brickyard's grout building *c.* the 1880s. (Courtesy of the Village of Walden.)

Iron production developed in Walden during the 1840s. One company that was successful for many decades in producing iron was the Delameter Iron Works. The company was later redesigned for iron and steel hot-air engines. In 1870, the Rider-Ericsson Engine Company was incorporated. The chief engineer of the company was inventor and scientist John Ericsson (right), the man who developed the screw propeller used to generate speed to navigate ships. Ericsson created one of the most famous ships of the Civil War: the USS *Monitor*, the first ironclad vessel of the Union Navy. (*Battles and Leaders of the Civil War*, Vol. I, page 730.)

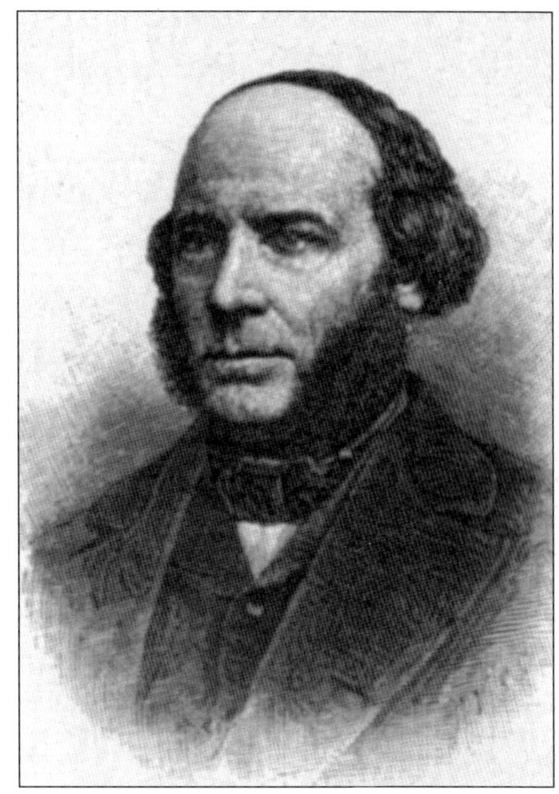

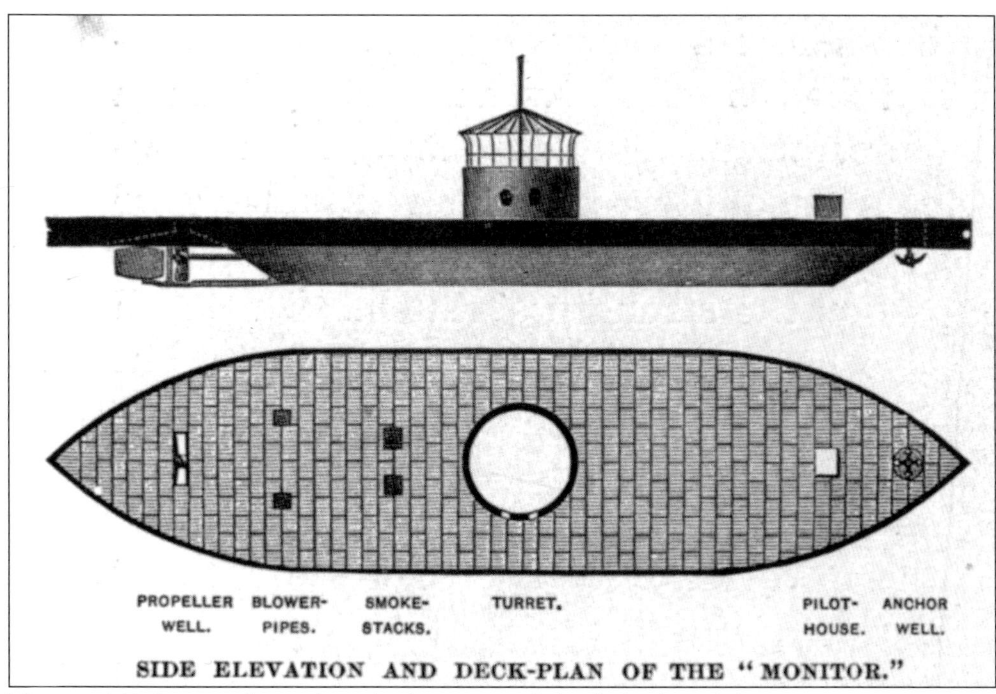

This *c.* 1860 diagram shows the side elevation and the deck plan of the USS *Monitor*.

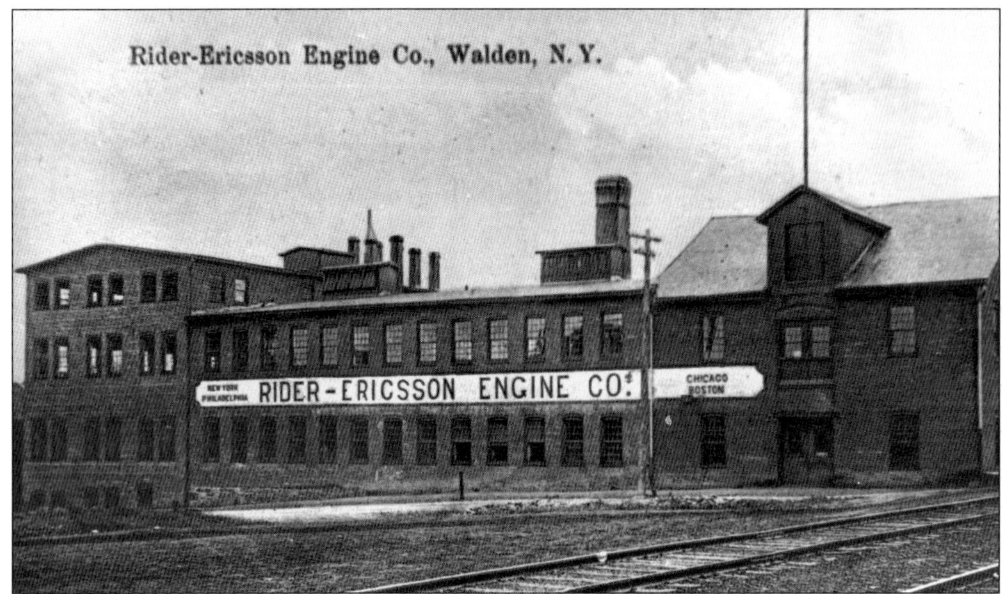

The Rider-Ericsson Engine Company (above, *c.* the 1870s) was purchased in 1917 and remained in the hands of business residents until 1939. Paulson Spence purchased the business and created Spence Engineering, which specialized in the manufacturing of the reduction valve. Other small businesses had thrived before and after the establishment of the knife companies. Textile Mills in Walden were highly successful in the decades prior to the Civil War. In the 1840s, Gyles Andrews created a woolen mill with housing for his workers (below, *c.* 1920s). His business was one of the largest producers of woolen goods in New York State. The Andrews Woolen Factory produced about one third of the woolen products made in Orange County. Other businesses that existed in the antebellum years included Homer Kidd's Soap Factory. (Courtesy of Marcus Millspaugh.)

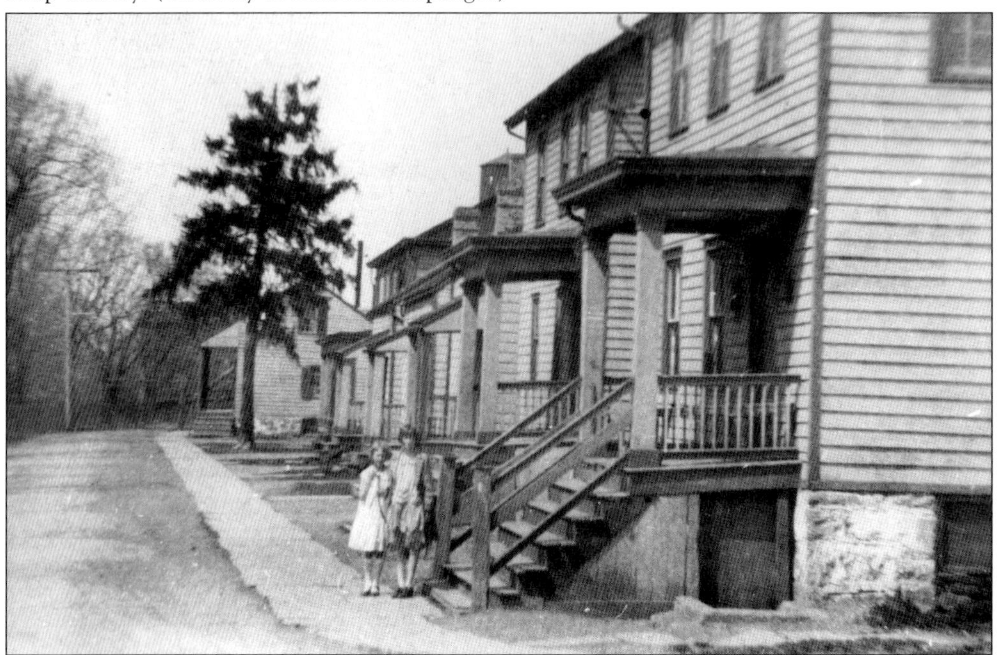

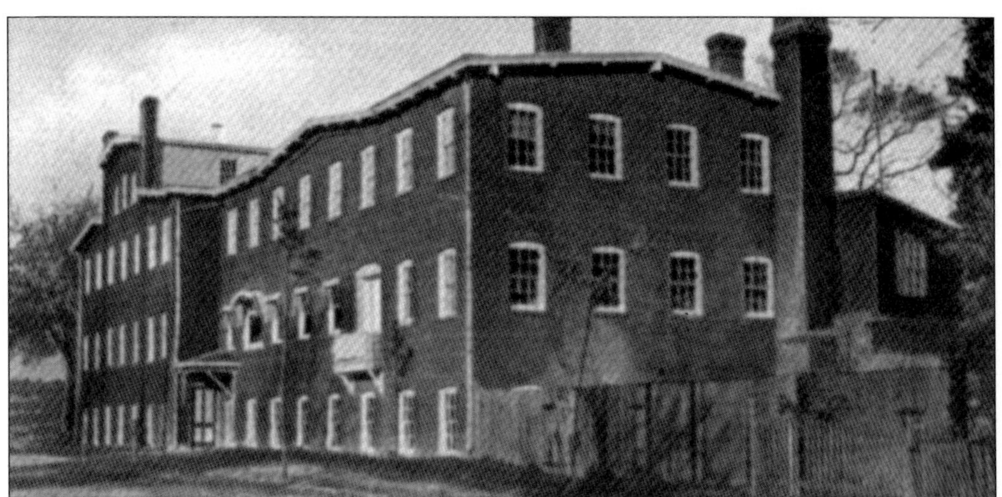

The major success of the knife companies and many profitable small businesses resulted in a period of expansion and development. Hiram Wooster created a special pair of overalls for factory workers in 1876. Wooster operated a general store for customers, but the success of the overalls led to expansion in 1882, when he took on a partner, George Stoddard. The Wooster Manufacturing Company, pictured *c.* 1906, was the second-largest manufacturer of overalls in New York State. Wooster Manufacturing first added other garments, such as hats and underwear, to its line; then, as business prospered *c.* 1900, it added furniture and some consumer goods to its inventory. Wooster Manufacturing was one of the most solvent and successful companies in Walden and was a source of employment for area residents. The company's success and the introduction of electrical power attracted other textile entrepreneurs, including the Gutman brothers and Louis Leis. (Courtesy of Robert Kidd.)

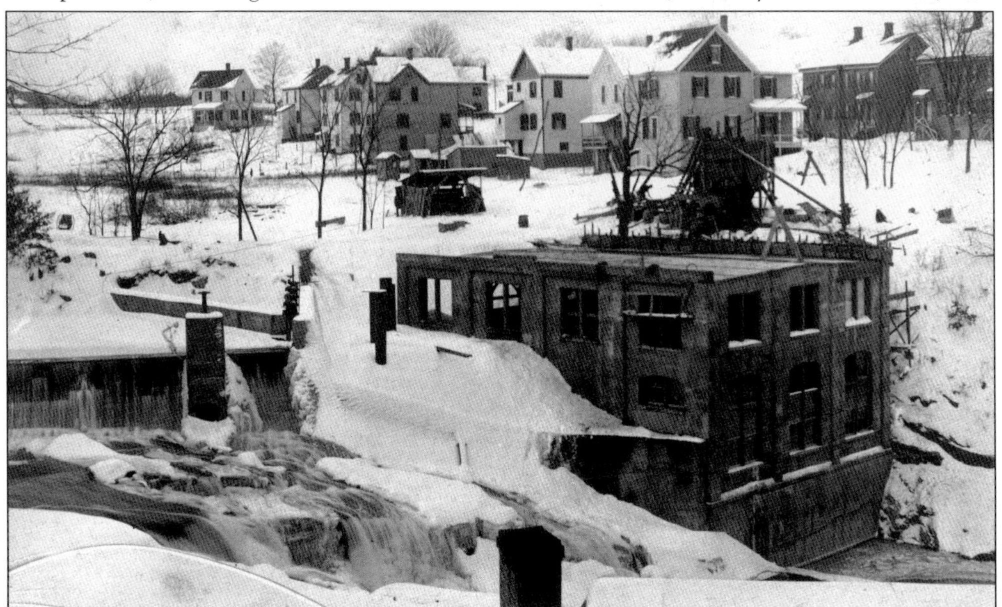

The construction of a hydroelectric plant at Walden Falls, pictured *c.* 1908, and the advent of gas and electric power brought more businesses into the community during the early 1900s. The Fowler family was instrumental in helping to electrify the village of Walden, replacing kerosene lights as early as 1893. (Courtesy of Marcus Millspaugh.)

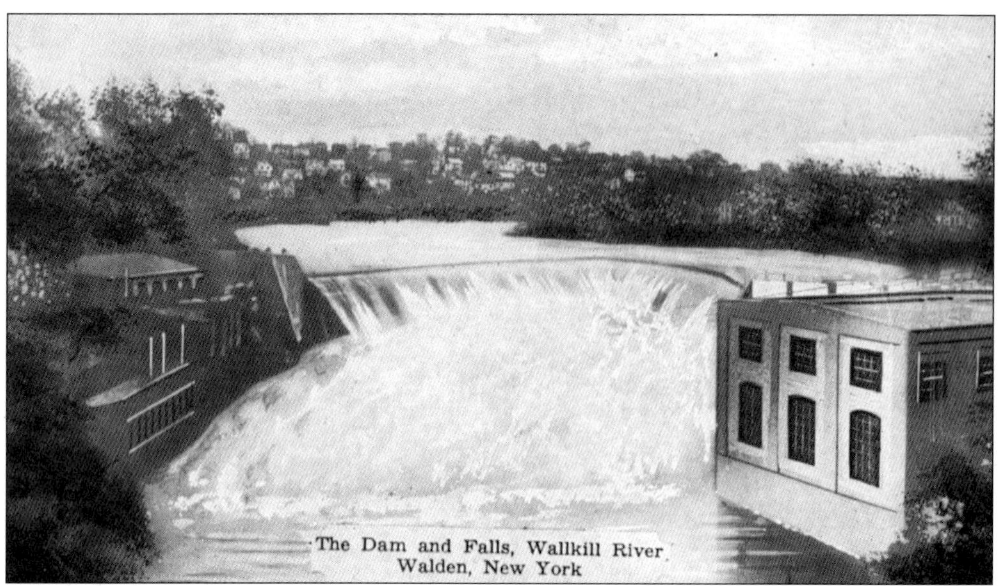

The hydroelectric plant at Walden Falls was completed *c.* 1910. Through electric lights and power, Walden transformed itself into a modern industrial center, with leadership in cutlery and textiles. (Courtesy of Marcus Millspaugh.)

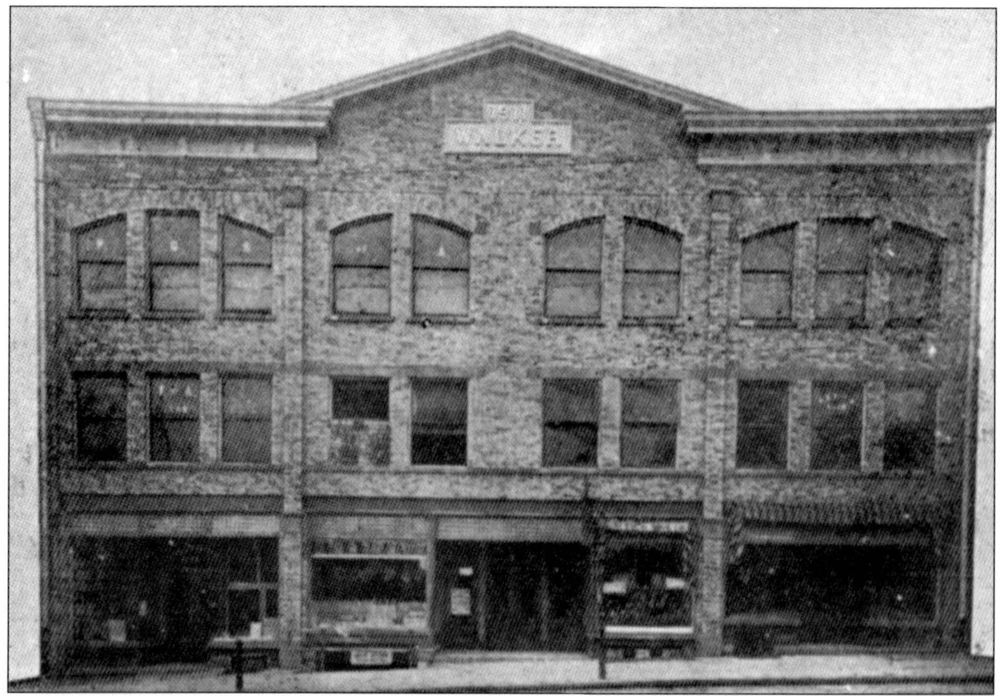

One of the largest manufacturing companies of ladies undergarments in New York City was Gutman Brothers, pictured *c.* the 1920s. The company decided to open a factory in Walden to manufacture muslin corset covers. Other Gutman Brothers factories were located in nearby Newburgh and in Butler, New Jersey. However, the Walden factory was highly successful and encouraged many other business in the textile industry to open their stores during the Roaring Twenties. (Courtesy of the Walden Chamber of Commerce.)

Cupid Underwear Company

Walden, N. Y.

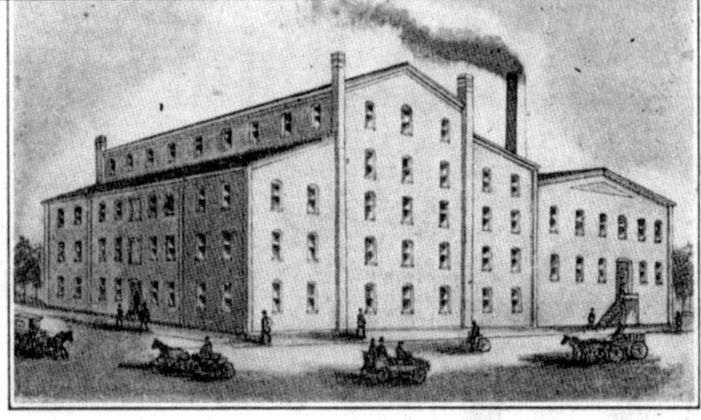

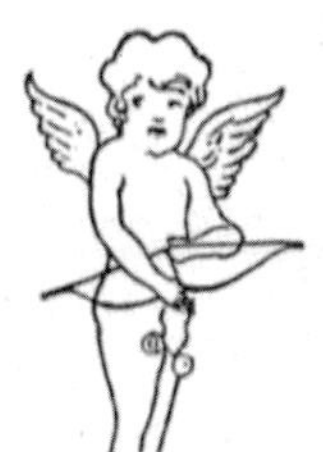

THE HOME OF

CUPIDSILK UNDERWEAR

The Wooster Building, on East Main Street, was the location of Gutman Brothers, one of many clothing and textile companies. Others included Garrison, Sweet & Company, Bobbi-Bell, Ina Dresses, Walden Manufacturing Company, Penrod Dress Company, Arrow Corset Company, White Swan Uniforms, Kitzes Dress Company, and Cupidsilk Underwear Company, pictured here *c.* the 1920s. (Courtesy of the Walden Chamber of Commerce.)

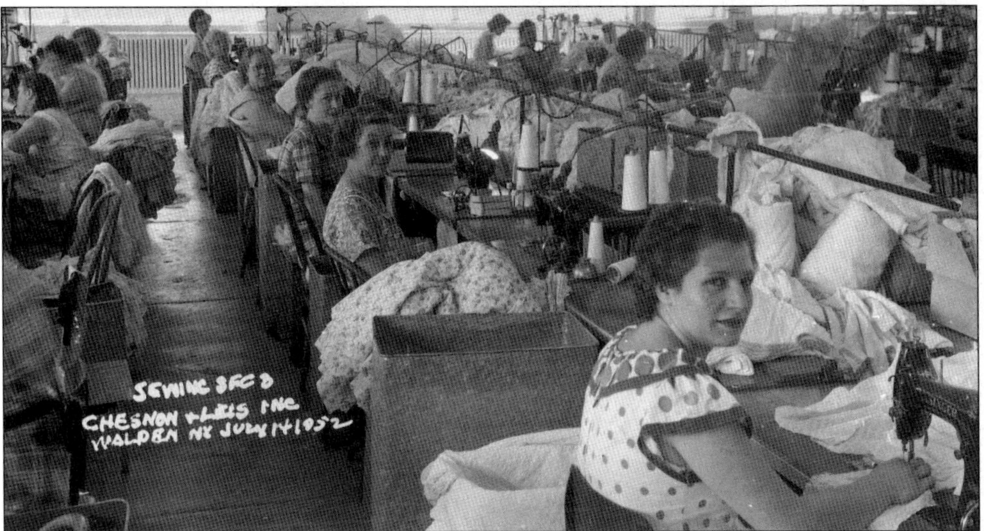

One of the most successful of the companies that was established in the mid-1920s was the Chesnin & Leis Company. Louis Leis had established his own company with Sam Chesnin of New York City in 1923. Throughout the 1920s, the Great Depression, and World War II, this company was a mainstay for the employment of many of the women of Walden. Through orders placed with Sam Chesnin in New York City, the company manufactured large quantities of garments, especially undergarments and nightdresses. Garments were made of cotton and silk. Shown are Chesnin & Leis Company workers at their sewing machines *c.* the 1950s. (Courtesy of Ella Orndorff.)

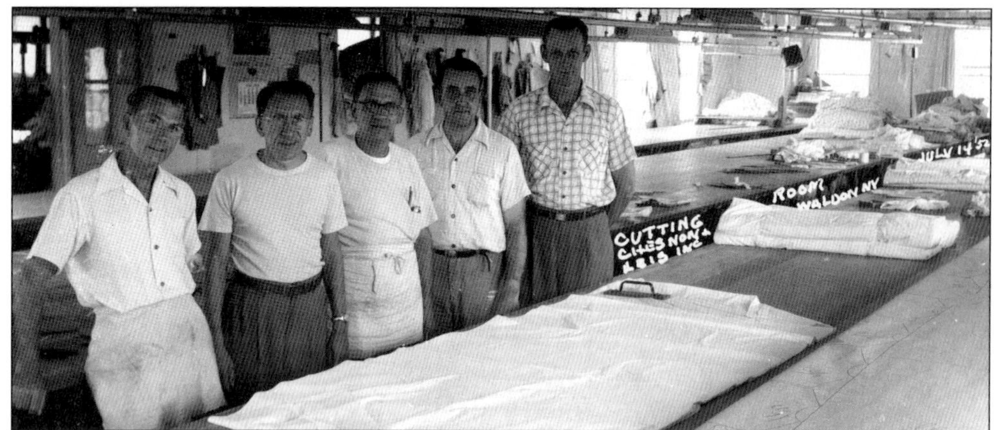

Silk was imported from Asia to Walden. Rooms were created to store the silk and for dying the material. During the Great Depression, women were hired to do piecework at home as part-time workers. Regardless of how menial the task, for example "adjusting buckles on slip straps," the money the residents earned helped them survive the Great Depression. Jobs were maintained for employees who had children to care for during the summers or who were on pregnancy leaves. The logo of the Chesnin & Leis Company was Love Lee. Many fashionable stores in New York City contracted with the company for its sleepwear products. Shown are Chesnin & Leis cutting room workers *c.* the 1950s. (Courtesy of Ella Orndorff.)

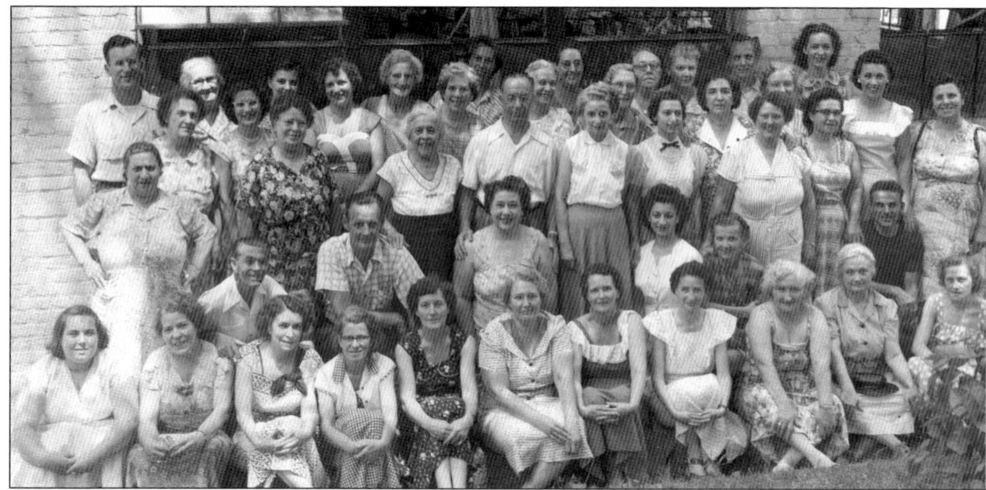

Louis Leis believed that businesses had a responsibility to give something back to their community. Under his auspices, numerous social and religious buildings were erected. During World War II, Leis converted the Old Grout Building into a canteen for teenagers and hosted social activities, both civic and school functions. During the early post–World War II years, the cutting room men of Chesnin & Leis created a Friendship Train food drive for the starving children of Europe. Pictured are Chesin & Leis Company workers outside the building *c.* the 1950s. Another business that was established in Walden was the Interstate Bag Factory, the beginnings of which date back to the early 20th century. The company specialized in paper shopping bags with handles on each side of the bag, known as the "bag with a handle." The company has supplied bags nationally and internationally to many businesses, especially leading department stores in New York City. The business boom of the late 19th century and early 20th century brought transportation, as well as numerous hotels and inns, to Walden. (Courtesy of Ella Orndorff.)

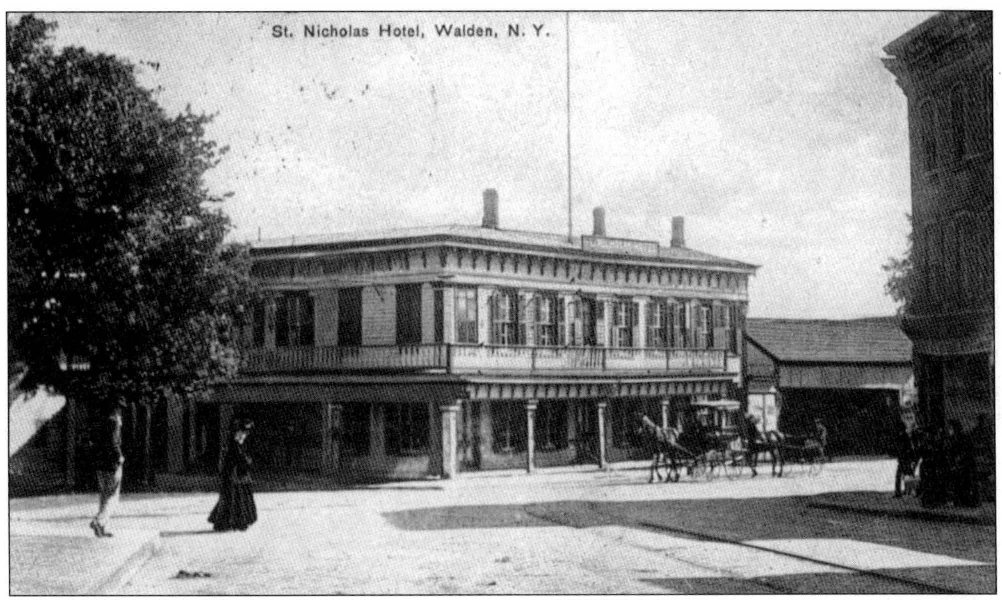

There were numerous hotels in Walden, located on and off Main Street. Some were majestic; many were erected during the Victorian age of the 1880s and 1890s, including the St. Nicholas Hotel (above, *c.* 1908), the Terrace Inn (lower left, *c.* 1911) and the Grand View House (lower right, *c.* 1912). (Courtesy of Robert Kidd.)

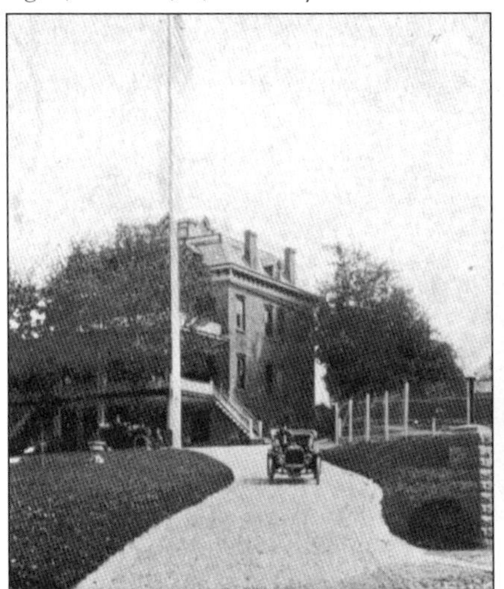

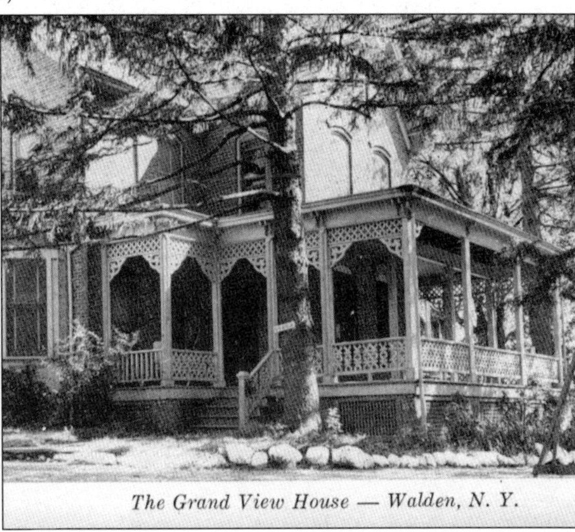

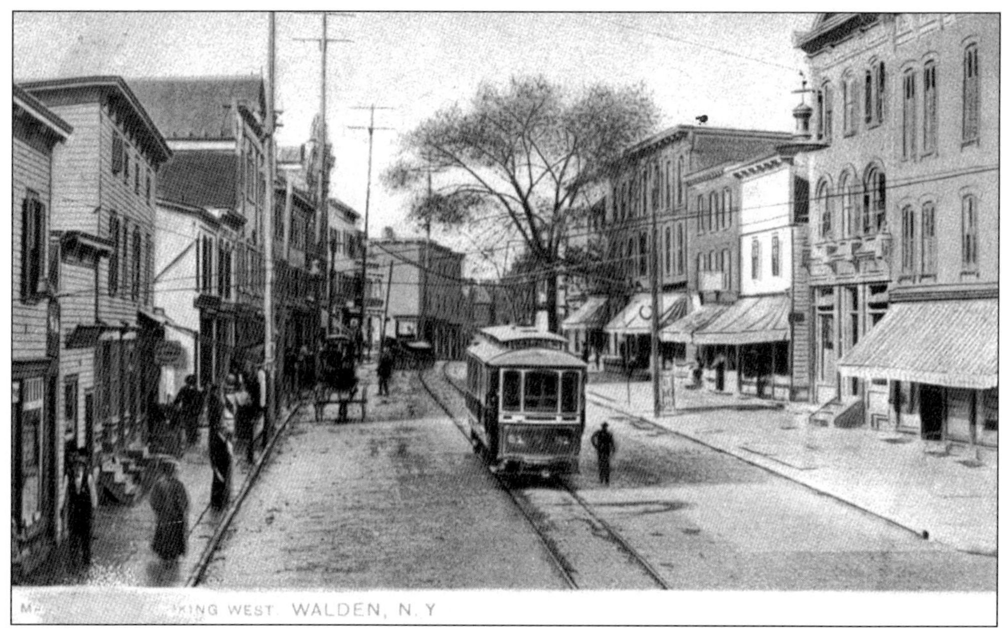

To accommodate workers and shoppers, a trolley car was established that transported people from and to Walden and Newburgh. This photograph shows the trolley on Main Street *c.* 1909. (Courtesy of Robert Kidd.)

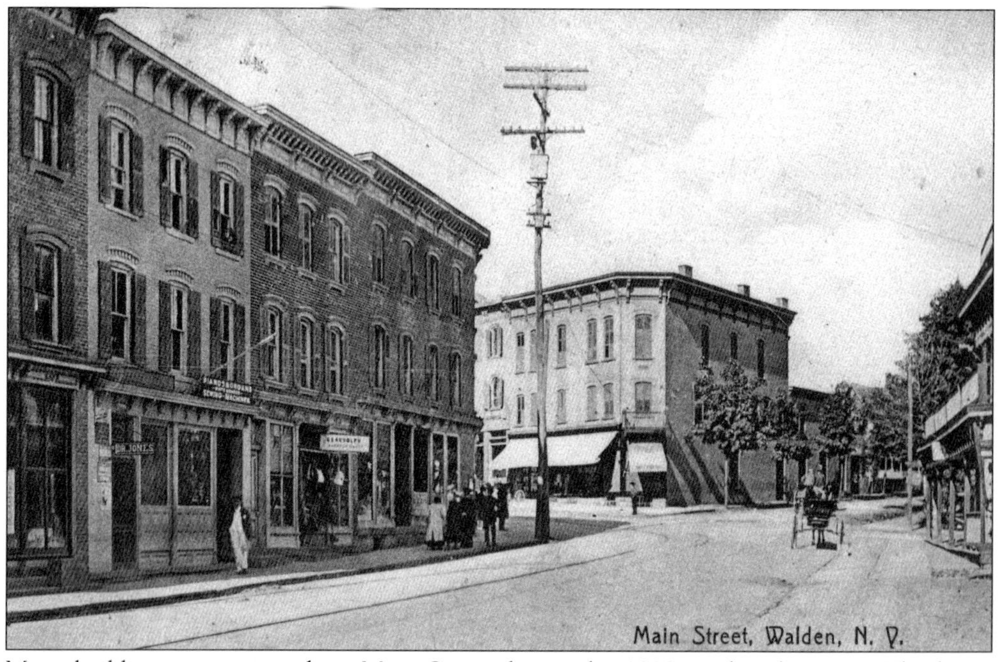

Many buildings were erected on Main Street during the 1890s and early 1900s. The horse and carriage was soon to give way to the automobile, as businesses and population continued to grow in the post–World War I era. This photograph dates from *c.* 1907. (Courtesy of Robert Kidd.)

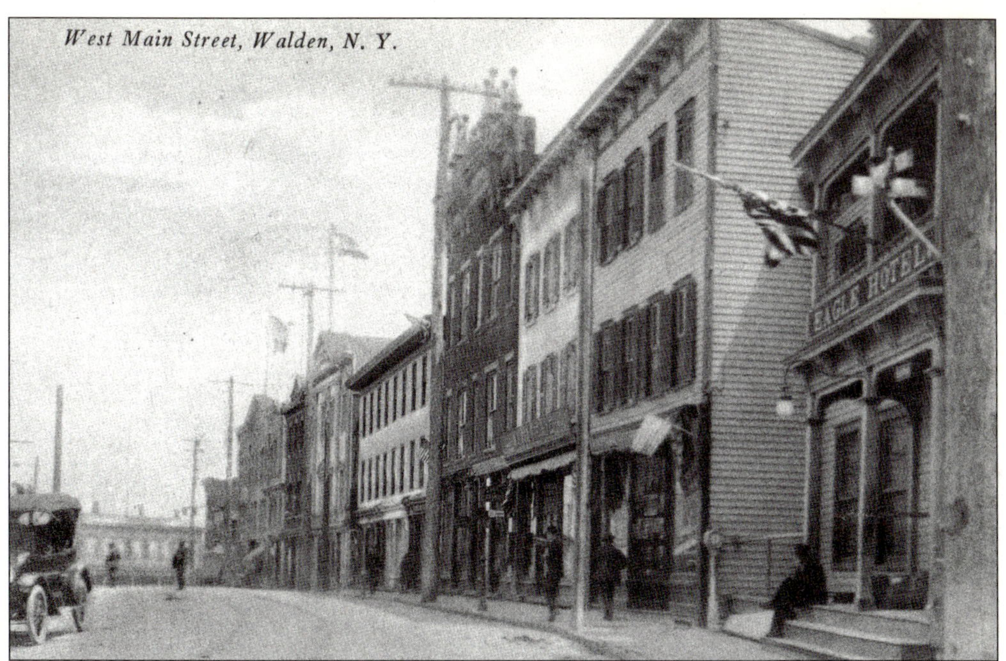

This photograph shows West Main Street *c.* the 1920s. (Courtesy of Jeff Sohns.)

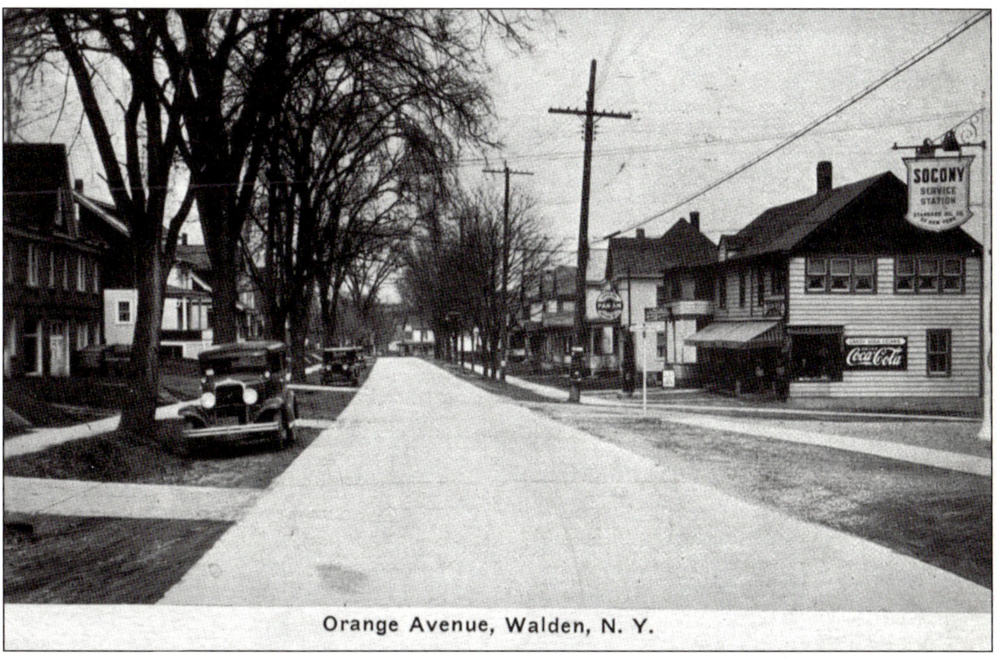

The area had grown and prospered in the 1920s. The Great Depression had forced many businesses into bankruptcy. However, some of the major companies such as Schrade Cutlery Company and Chesin-Leis continued to employ Walden residents. Millspaugh's Furniture Store, Ticks Clothing Store, Fowler's Insurance Company, Lustig's Department Store, Sohns, and other small family businesses were able to survive the Depression. Pictured is Orange Avenue *c.* 1934. (Courtesy of Jeff Sohns.)

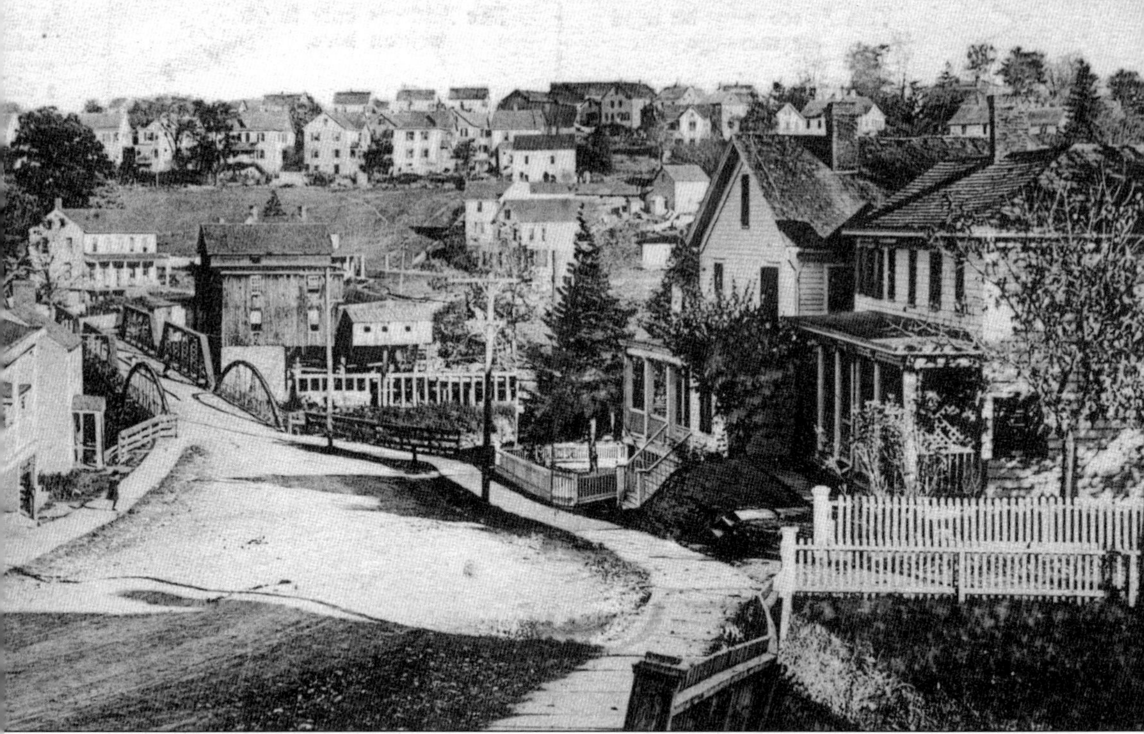

During the early 20th century, Walden expanded along its major avenues, Ulster and Orange, as well as its main streets. Prosperity brought businesses and residents, swelling the population to several thousand. Numerous homes were built along the east bank of the Wallkill River. This *c.* 1920 photograph shows the Lower Bridge and Walden Heights. (Courtesy of Marcus Millspaugh.)

Three
Social and Recreational Life

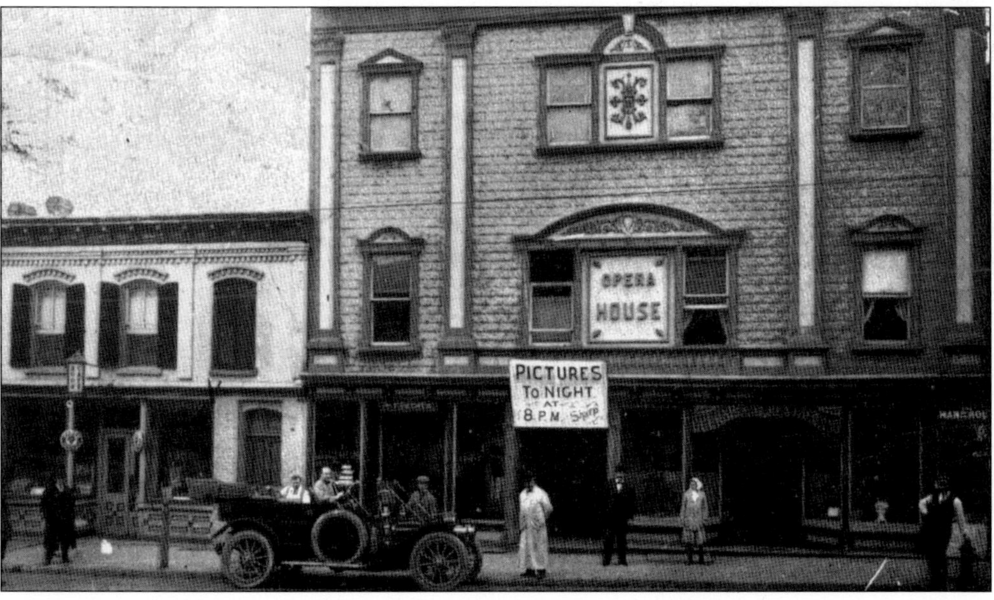

Many other companies opened factories in Walden during the height of the second industrial revolution. One entrepreneur was William Didsbury, who created the Walden Shear Company in 1895. This company specialized in tool production. The metal products were various types of shears that were used for sheep shearing. In the decades that followed, an opera house was built on Main Street, shown here *c.* 1911. Named the Didsbury Opera House, it was also called the Didsbury Theater, and it was the major social center for the arts, as well as a place for people to visit and play a game of bingo. Many concerts and shows were performed at the Didsbury Opera House. Aside from local and professional minstrel shows, the theater was host to some of the most renowned entertainers and instrumentalists of the day. The great Italian tenor Enrico Caruso gave a concert at the opera house, and John Philip Sousa and his Marching Band performed, as did other bands, orchestras, and fife, drum, and bugle corps. From the 1920s to the early 1970s, motion pictures were shown in the little theater.

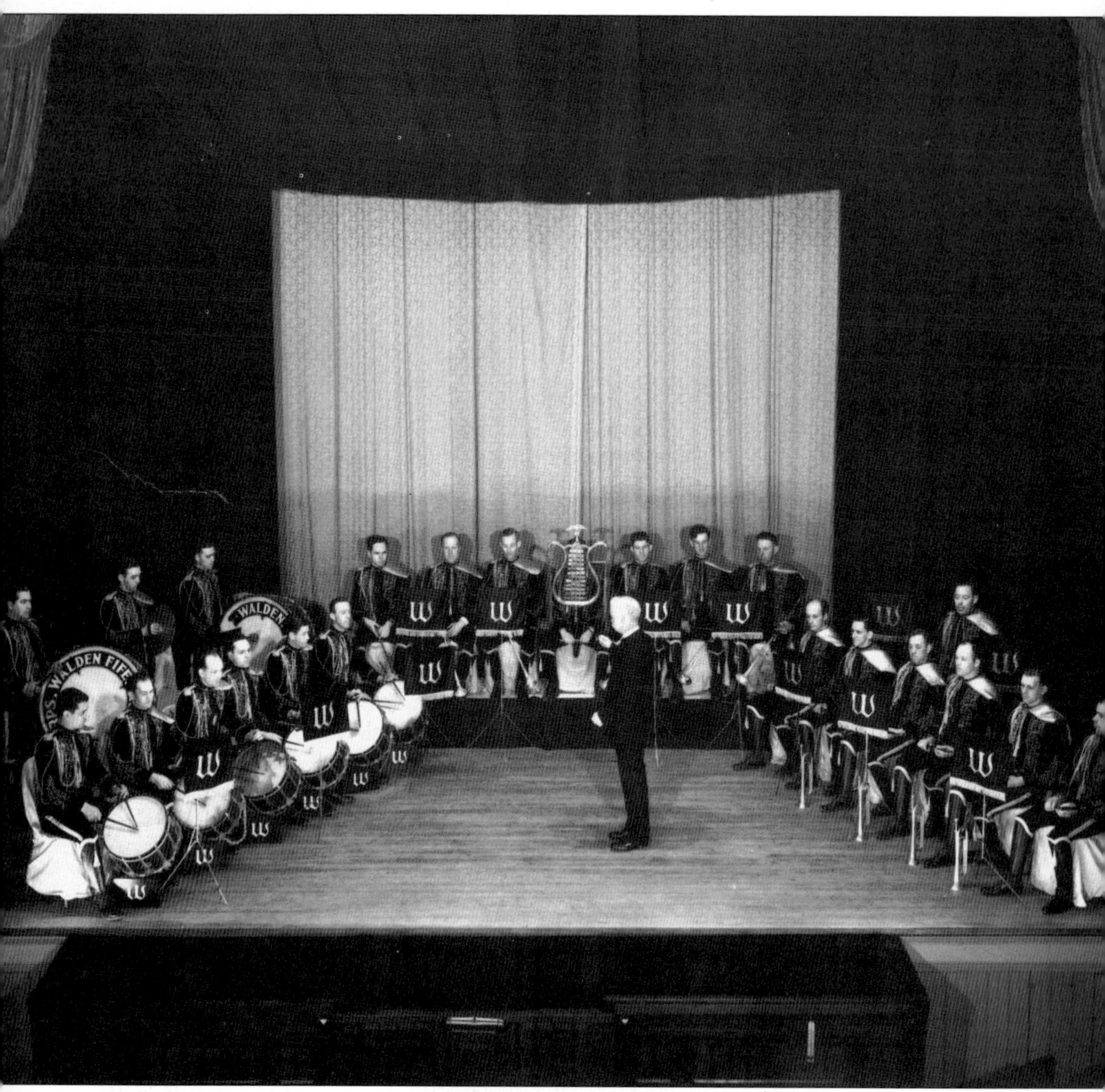

J.A.A. Sohns was one of the community's most gifted directors of instrumental music. Known as the Music Man, he is shown with the Walden Fife, Drum & Bugle Corps Band in the Didsbury Theater *c.* 1920. Sohns was a businessman who sold musical instruments. Each of his children was an accomplished instrumentalist. The family company sold musical instruments, sheet music, and eventually electronic equipment such as records, phonographs, radios, and televisions. (Courtesy of Jeff Sohns.)

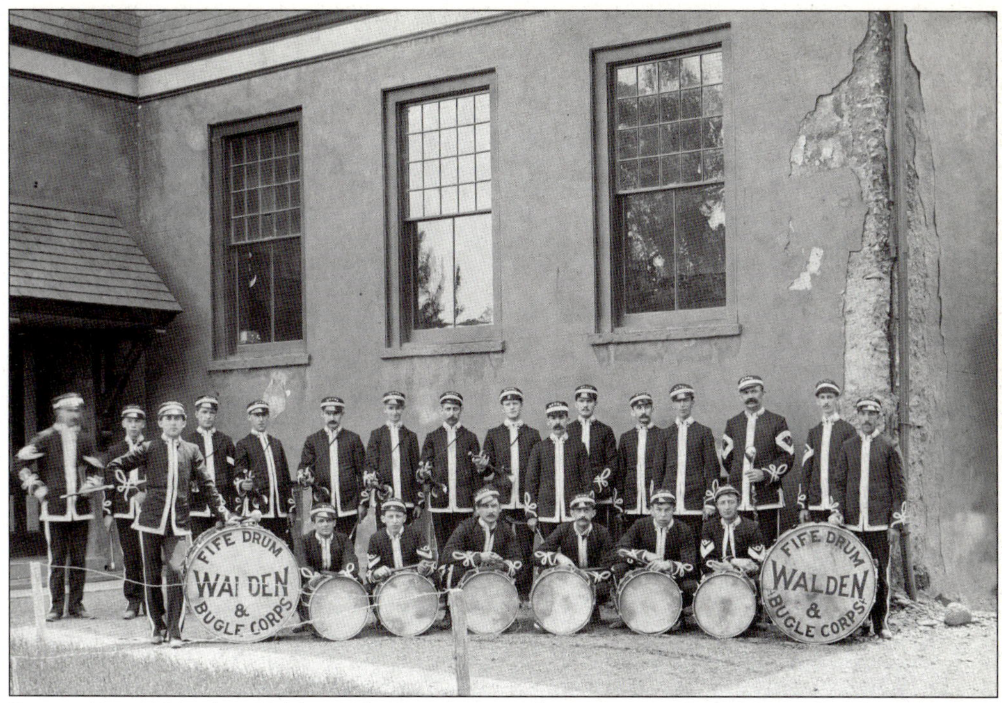

Pictured *c.* 1890, the Walden Fife, Drum & Bugle Corps Band was formed and entertained residents of the community decades before the construction of the Didsbury Opera House. (Courtesy of the Walden Historical Society.)

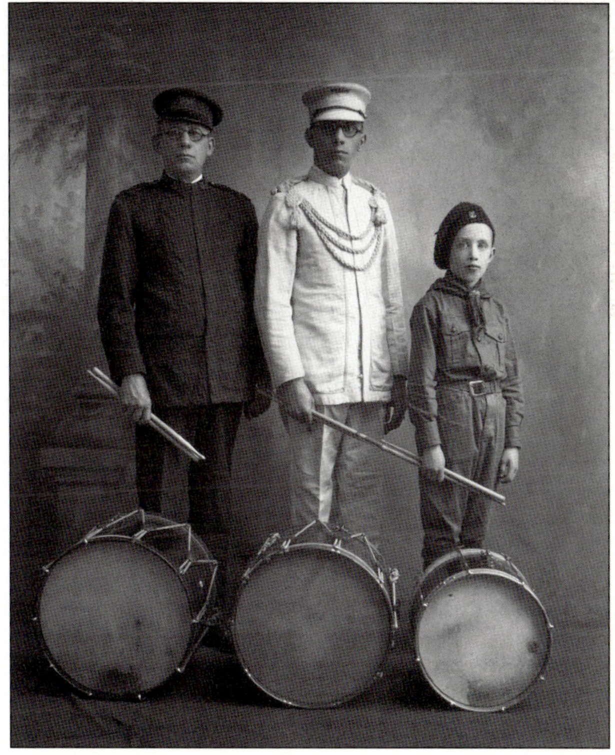

Members of the Conklin family included three generations of instrumental drummers who, over the course of four decades, played in the Walden Fife, Drum & Bugle Corps Band. The youngest one was Clifford Conklin, shown in the Boy Scout uniform *c.* the 1930s, who later became the music director of the West Point Band. (Courtesy of the Walden Historical Society.)

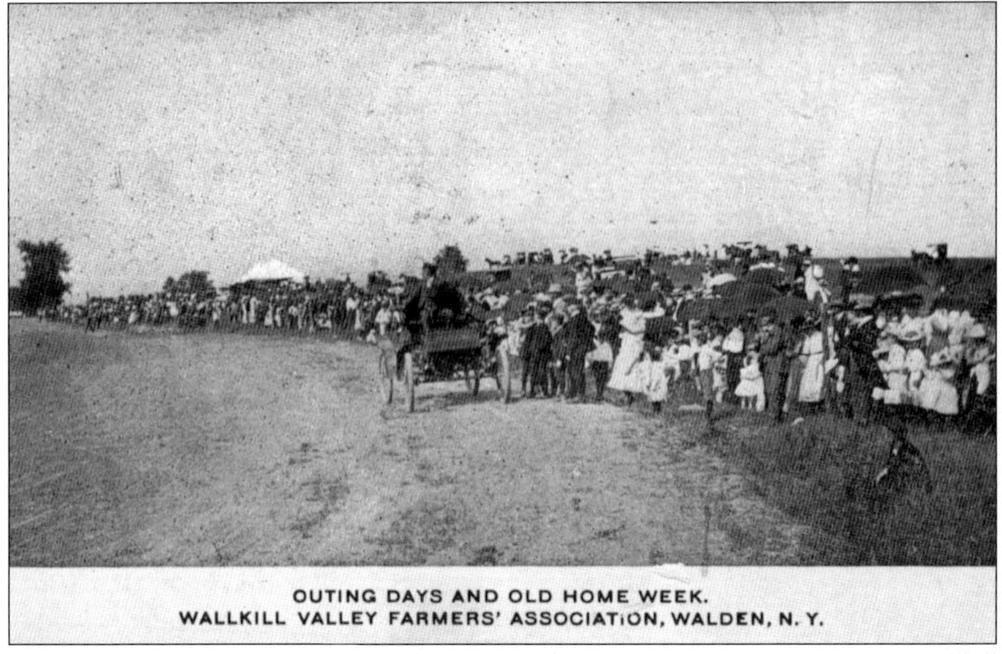

This is a 1903 view of the annual Old Home Week and Outing Days picnic of the Wallkill Valley Farmers Association. (Courtesy of Robert Kidd.)

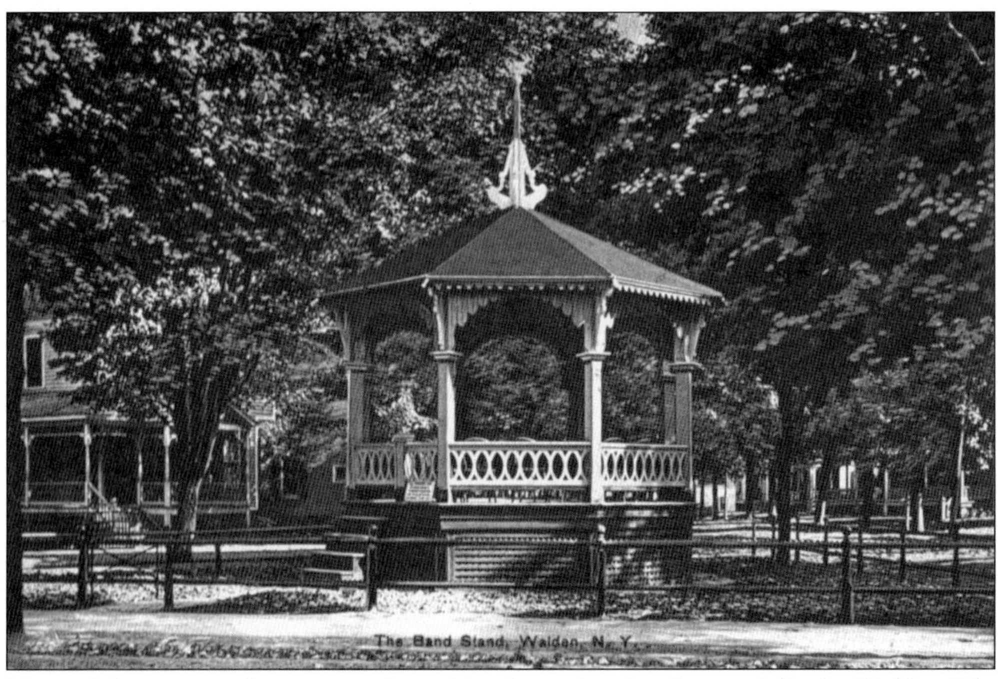

Many of the concerts that were performed by the various bands, especially the Walden Fife, Drum & Bugle Corps, were given outdoors on the Walden Bandstand, shown c. 1920. (Courtesy of Robert Kidd.)

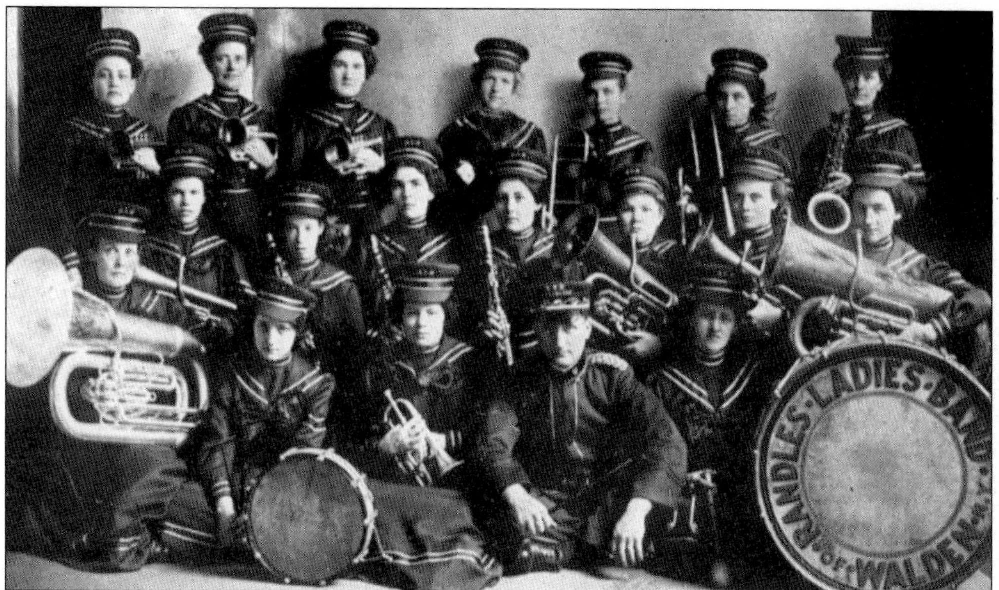

Women in Walden formed their own concert band. J.W. Randles was the director of Randles Ladies Band, pictured *c.* 1911. The band performed at the Old Home Week and Outing Days of the Wallkill Valley Farmers Association. One such outing was held at the Borden Farm in Wallkill. (Courtesy of Robert Kidd.)

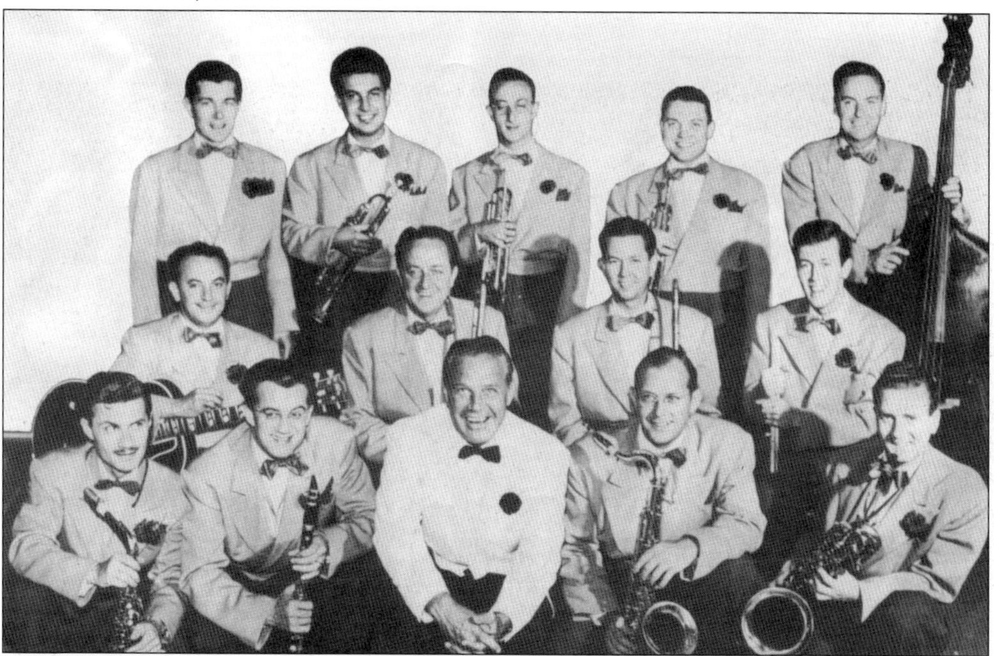

Adeline Sohns, the daughter of music proponent J.A.A. Sohns, was an accomplished musician and a schoolteacher. She married musician and bandleader Horace Heidt. Heidt's band, the Musical Knights, pictured *c.* 1940, held national and international prominence, appearing on radio, on stage, and in the movie *Pot O' Gold*, starring Jimmy Stewart and Paulette Goddard. The Heidts lived in Van Nuys, California, and were instrumental in developing the music that was popular from the late 1930s through the 1940s: swing. (Courtesy of Jeff Sohns.)

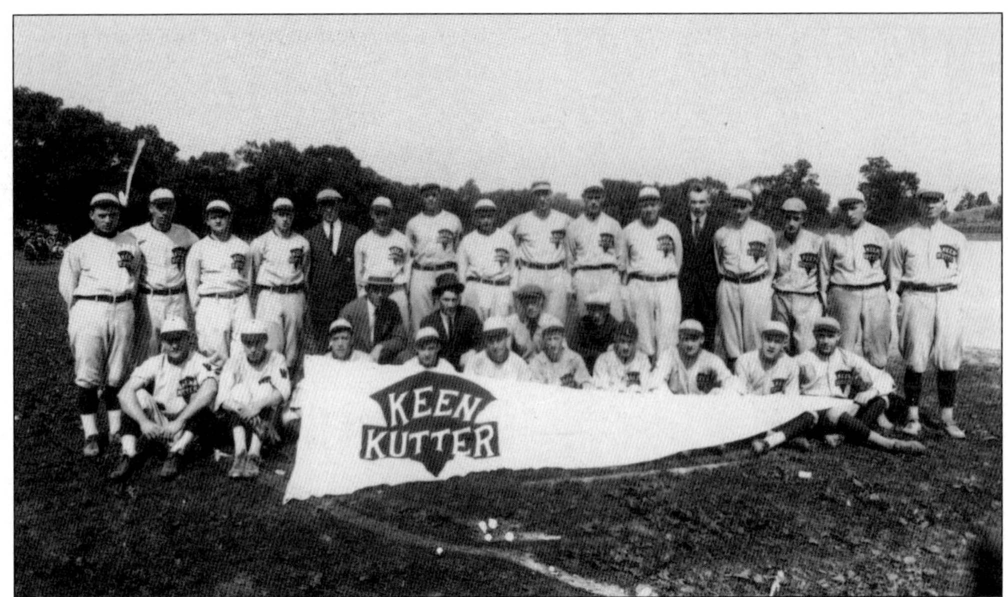

Athletic competition between the different factories, as well as the high school teams, was part of village life in both Maybrook and Walden. Semiprofessional teams in several sports developed during the first half of the 20th century. Pictured is the Walden Knife Company Keen Kutters baseball team *c.* 1918. After baseball became the major sport in the United States in the 1920s, Walden and Maybrook school districts allocated money for equipment, uniforms, and coaches. (Courtesy of Marcus Millspaugh.)

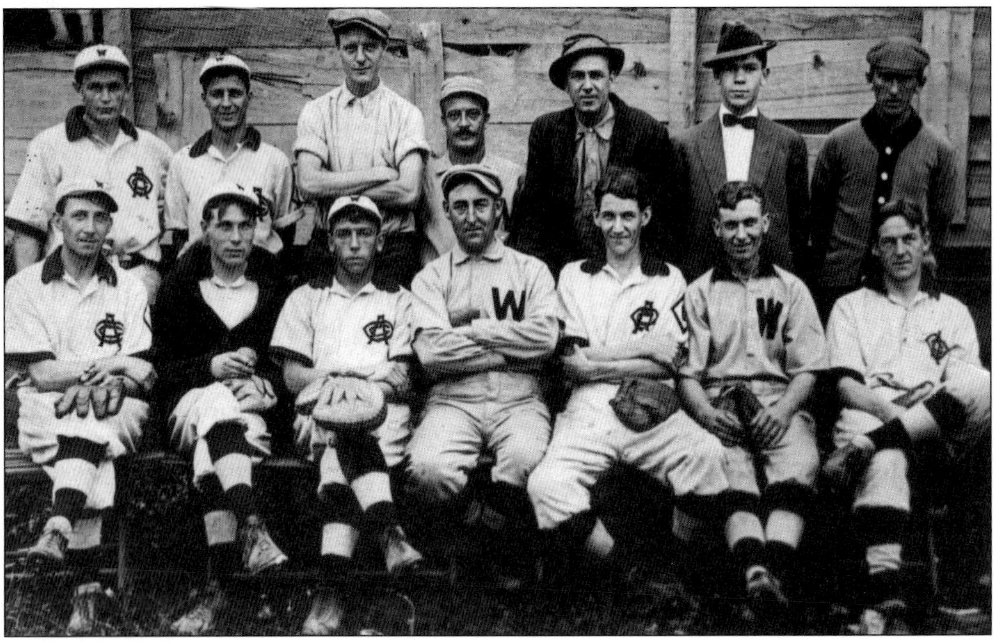

Toward the end of the 19th century, local baseball teams were created throughout portions of the Hudson Valley. In 1895, a championship game was played between Walden and Newburgh. Walden fielded one of the best teams, shown here *c.* 1930. It had men on the diamond such as Heck Millspaugh, Lew Decker, Ed Stickles, and Dave Kaiser. (Courtesy of the Walden Historical Society.)

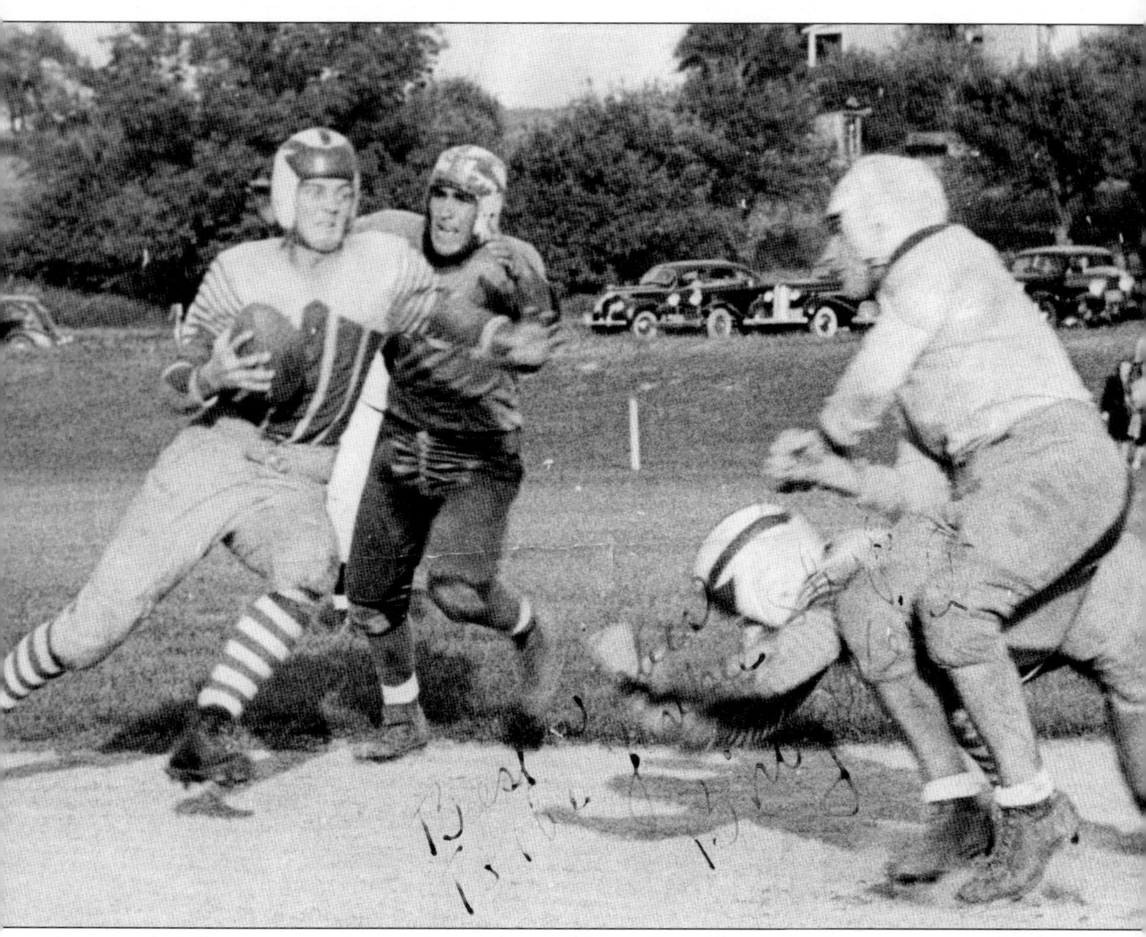

In 1944, Frank Geignas brought a baseball franchise to the village through the newly created North Atlantic Baseball League. The Humming Birds was one of the semipro teams established in the league, but after a year the franchise expired and the movement toward professional baseball died. The local knife companies formed football teams as well as baseball teams. In the late 1800s, football teams were established at the high school level in Walden, Montgomery, and Maybrook. Some of the founding fathers of the Walden High School football team were Abner Birch, Marshall Allison, Leighton Andrews, Harry Brown, and Lawrence Didsbury. At the beginning of the Great Depression, George Scofield, later known as "Mr. Football," was the Walden High School coach. He created a dominant team in the region and gained a reputation as being one of the finest football coaches in the Hudson Valley. Some of the players of 1933, were Doug Stickles (center), Bull McKay (guard), Bill Sharp (quarterback), and Fred Cryer (fullback). The semipro team the Walden Red Tigers, pictured here *c.* the 1940s, was established in the 1930s. Funded and organized through the assistance of Jane Johnson and G.R. Bartlett, it was one of the top teams under the direction of Scofield. It won the Hudson Valley League championship in 1937. (Courtesy of Sam Phelps Jr.)

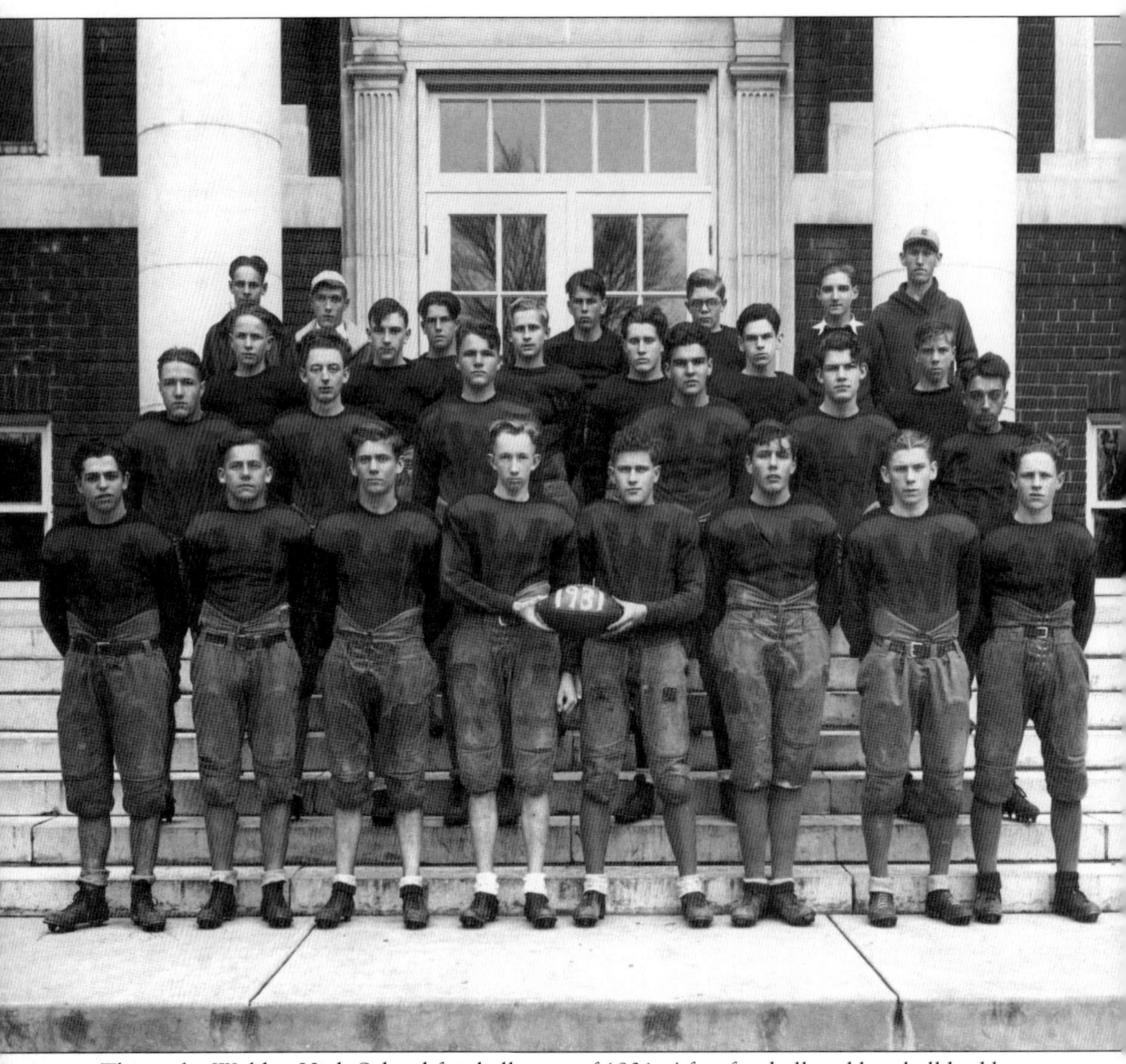

This is the Walden High School football team of 1931. After football and baseball had become rooted in the village, other teams were organized under the auspices of Walden High School, including basketball and track and field. (Courtesy of Marcus Millspaugh.)

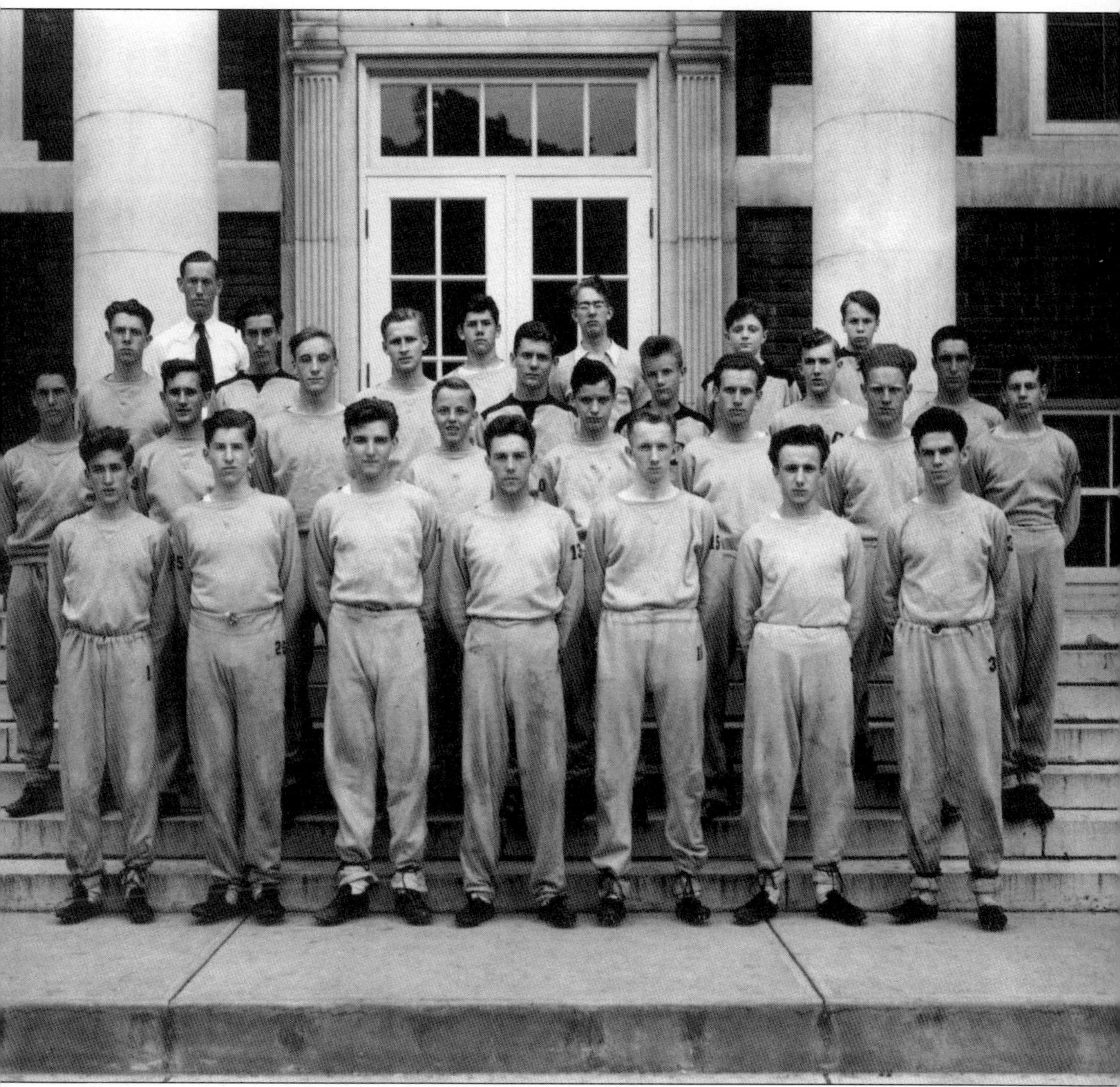

Basketball and track and field events contributed to the leisure enjoyment of the village residents. The early teams and athletes were created from the organization and membership of the fire companies of the village, such as Bradley Hose and Orange Hose. Basketball games were usually held on Saturday night, with a community dance after the game. Shown is the 1931 Walden High School track and field team. (Courtesy of Marcus Millspaugh.)

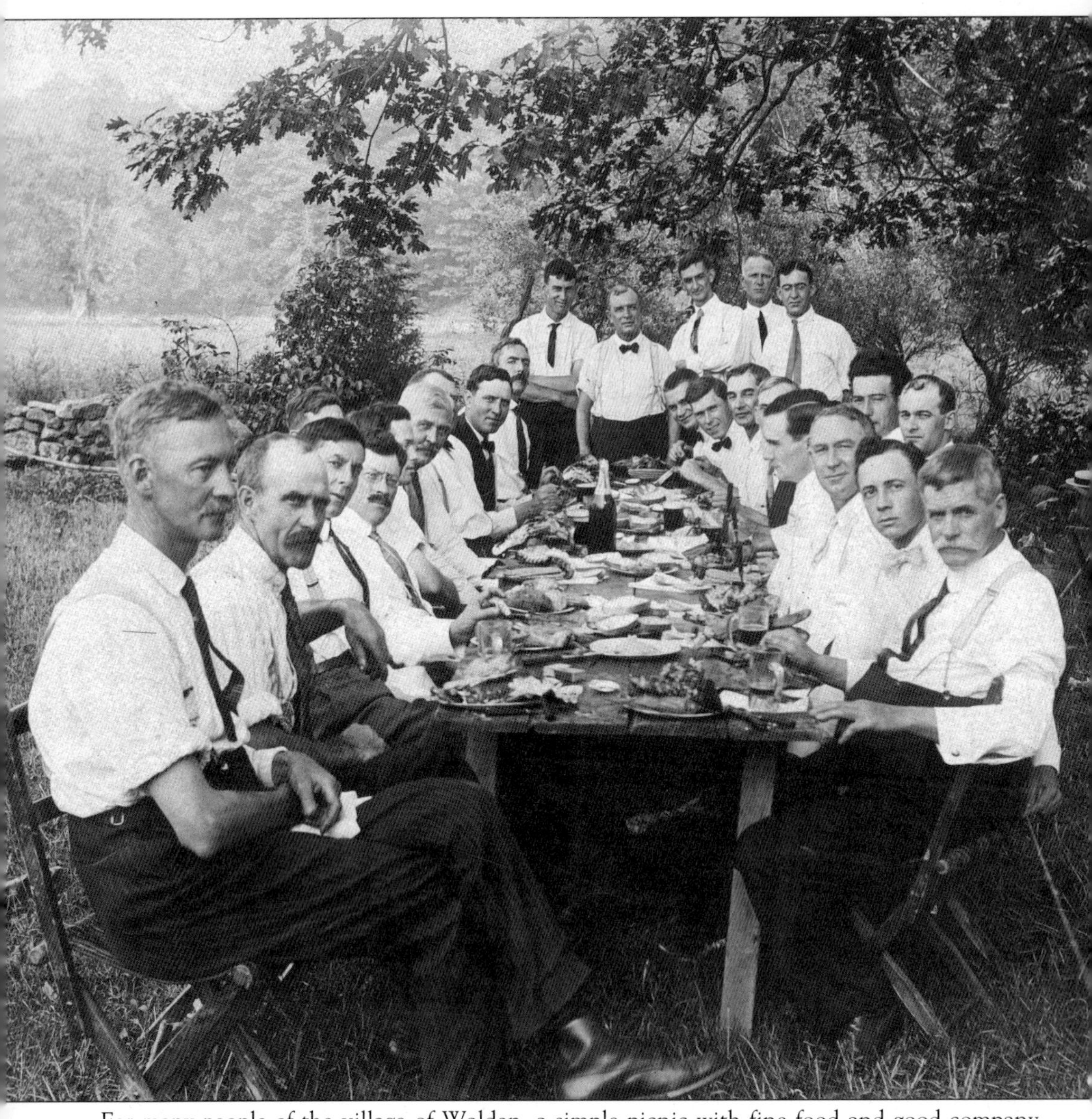

For many people of the village of Walden, a simple picnic with fine food and good company would satisfy any appetite. Clambakes were very popular for families and for employees of the New York Knife Company, as shown in this *c.* 1900 photograph. (Courtesy of the Walden Historical Society.)

Four

MEMORIES

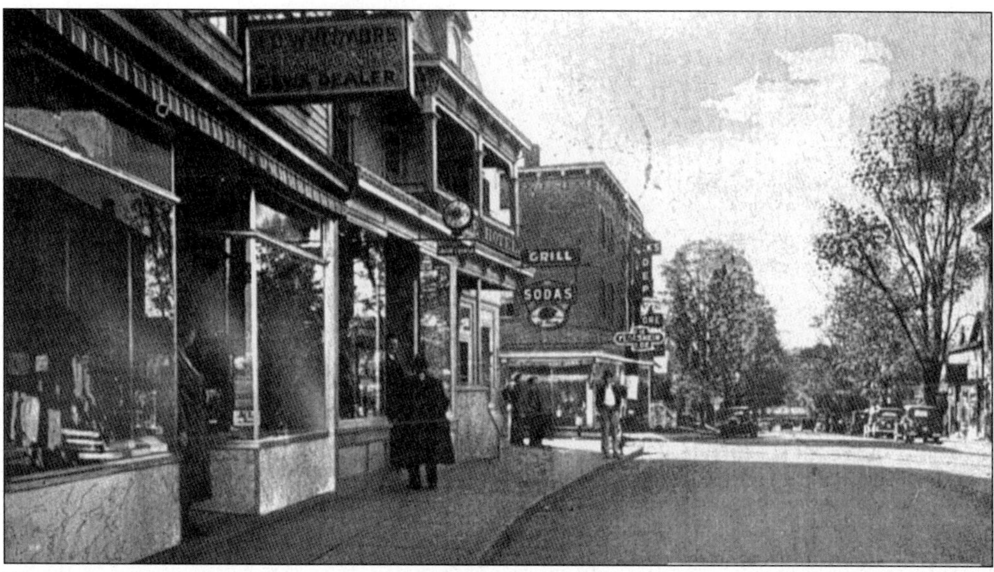

The Roosa family has spent more than 80 years as jewelers in New York State. Jacob Isaac Roosa, shown outside his store with a friend in the 1930s, began the family business in 1919. During the winter of 1917, Jacob Roosa walked across the frozen Hudson River and traveled on foot from Newburgh to Scotts Corners. He was able to get a ride to Maybrook and then a train to Goshen to be reunited with his family for Christmas. He married Ruth Dayton in 1920 and, by 1928, had four children. From 1920 to 1934, Roosa's Jewelry Store remained in Monroe. The Great Depression had a terrible affect on many small businesses, including jewelry stores. Roosa decided to leave Monroe to work in the village of Walden. The family relocated in 1934 and ran its jewelry business on West Main Street in the Eagle Hotel Building until 1951. (Courtesy of Walter Roosa.)

The youngest son, Walter Roosa, joined his father's business after being trained in jewelry and watch repair. When the store was relocated on Main Street, the building was the Caleb Birch Shoe Store. The company was called J.I. Roosa and Son. The son continued to maintain the business long after his father retired in 1960. Thirty years later, Walter Roosa retired, leaving the business to his son, Paul Roosa, who carries on in the tradition of his grandfather started more than 80 years ago.

—Walter Roosa

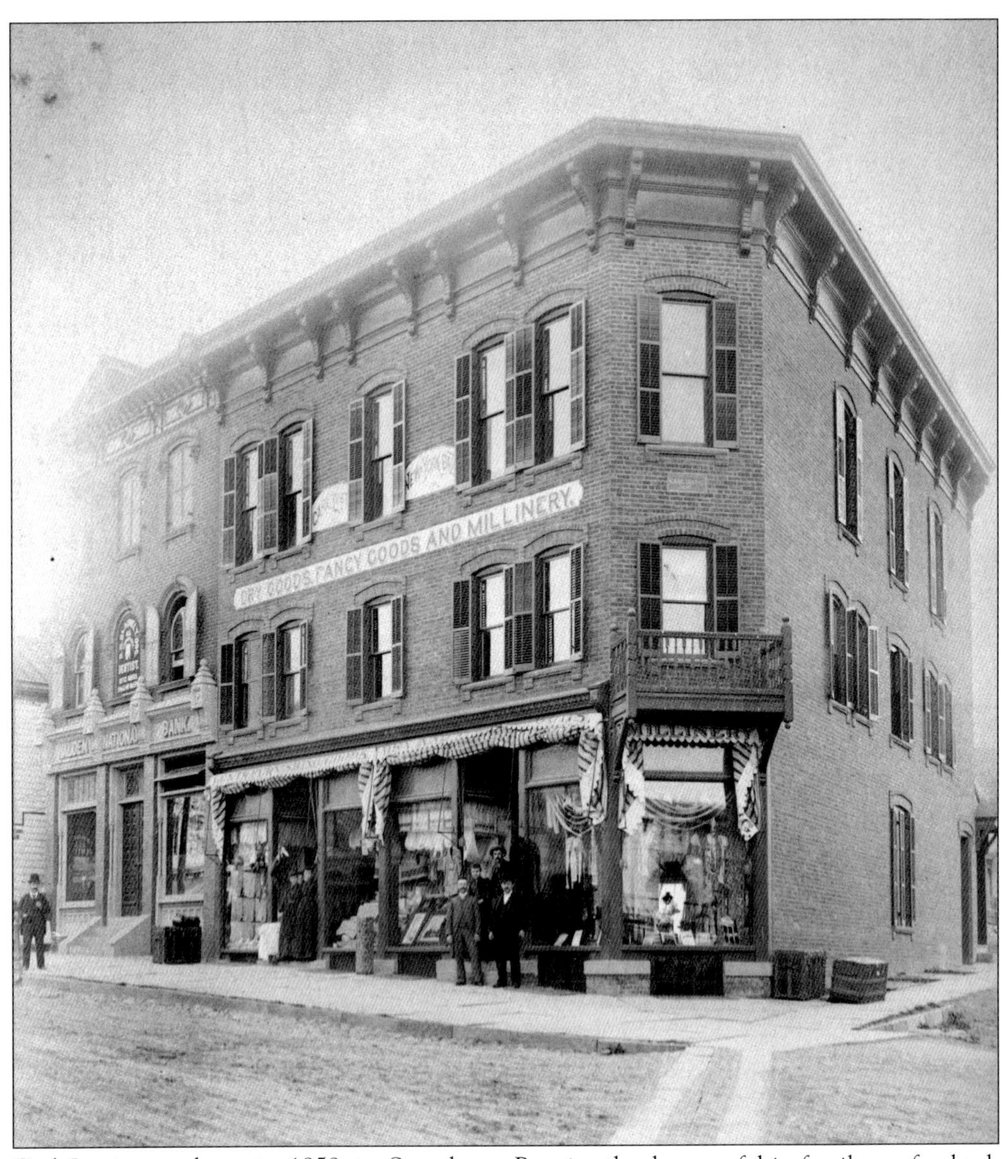

Carl Lustig was born in 1859 in Strassburg, Prussia, the home of his family as far back as the 1790s. He came to New York and worked in a department store in Chatham. He peddled dry goods peddler using a horse and wagon. During one of his excursions, he met Gale Borden of the Borden Condensery Milk Company. During a friendly game of poker, Borden suggested that Lustig settle in Walden because of the great success of the New York Knife Company and the Wooster Manufacturing Company. Lustig took the suggestion, settled in Walden, and opened the New York Bazaar, pictured *c.* 1892. The store sold ladies' millinery products, corsets, and hoopskirts. In 1885, Lustig married Bertha Namm, whose father was the founder of Namm's Department Store of Brooklyn. Within five years, Lustig was able to erect a three-story building on Main Street. During the 1940s the store was known as Lustig's Department Store. The son, David Carl Lustig, took over the business after his father died in 1942, assisted by his son, Dave, and daughter, Arlene. Dave Lustig married Violet Rosenblum and together they continued the tradition established by his grandfather.

—Dave Lustig

During the late 18th century, the area that extended from Scotts Corners to the Wallkill River was known as Kidd Town. The Kidd family came from Northern Ireland. James Kidd was a successful businessman who owned a gristmill at the High Falls and a local tavern. Shown is Alexander Kidd *c.* 1914. (*In a Beautiful Country*, page 76.)

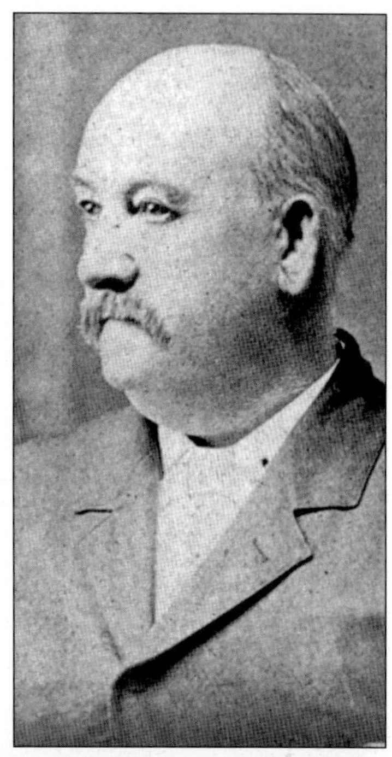

Many of the members of the Kidd family were farmers who owned large tracts of land. Homer Kidd owned a soap factory in Walden. Alexander Kidd was director of the St. Nicholas Hotel in Walden. According to Robert Kidd, son of the local iceman, Pres. Lyndon Johnson made a specific visit to the village of Walden during the presidential campaign *c.* 1964. A large crowd was assembled near the Walden Municipal Building to catch a glimpse of the candidate. Robert Kidd, who was an auxiliary policeman, stopped one woman moving in front of the small barricade and escorted her back toward the crowd. The woman turned to him, smiled, and said a quiet "thank you." It was very clear that she was in the wrong area, and Kidd allowed Lady Bird Johnson to join her husband and the other dignitaries during the festivities.

—Robert Kidd

The Eberhardts originally came from Alsace-Lorraine, France. In 1922, Al Eberhardt moved to Walden. A professional musician, he established the Rainbow Orchestra in 1928 with local musicians. Eberhardt married Ella Clineman, a descendant of Thomas Clineman, whose family settled in Walden's in the mid-1700s. The Clinemans were sheep and livestock farmers who purchased a 167-acre farm during the Colonial era. The Eberhardts opened a gas station and garage in the mid-1920s while continuing to entertain with with instrumental music. Shown is a business card for Al Eberhardt and the Rainbow Orchestra. (Courtesy of Ella Orndorff.)

One major company that opened a chain store in the village was the Grand Union Company. During the 1930s, it employed some of the local residents. Many small businesses, such as the Walden Bakery, met the basic needs. Walden High School offered sports programs for women and hosted several women's teams to compete against some of the other schools in the area. Oda Rogers coached the women's intramural teams that played Maybrook, Montgomery, and Tuxedo. The local attitude toward sports was a strong sense of fair play and the enforcement of rules and regulations for competition. Athletes were censored by their coach for violating a rule regardless of whether the umpire or the referee had called a penalty for the infraction.

—Ella Eberhardt Orndorff

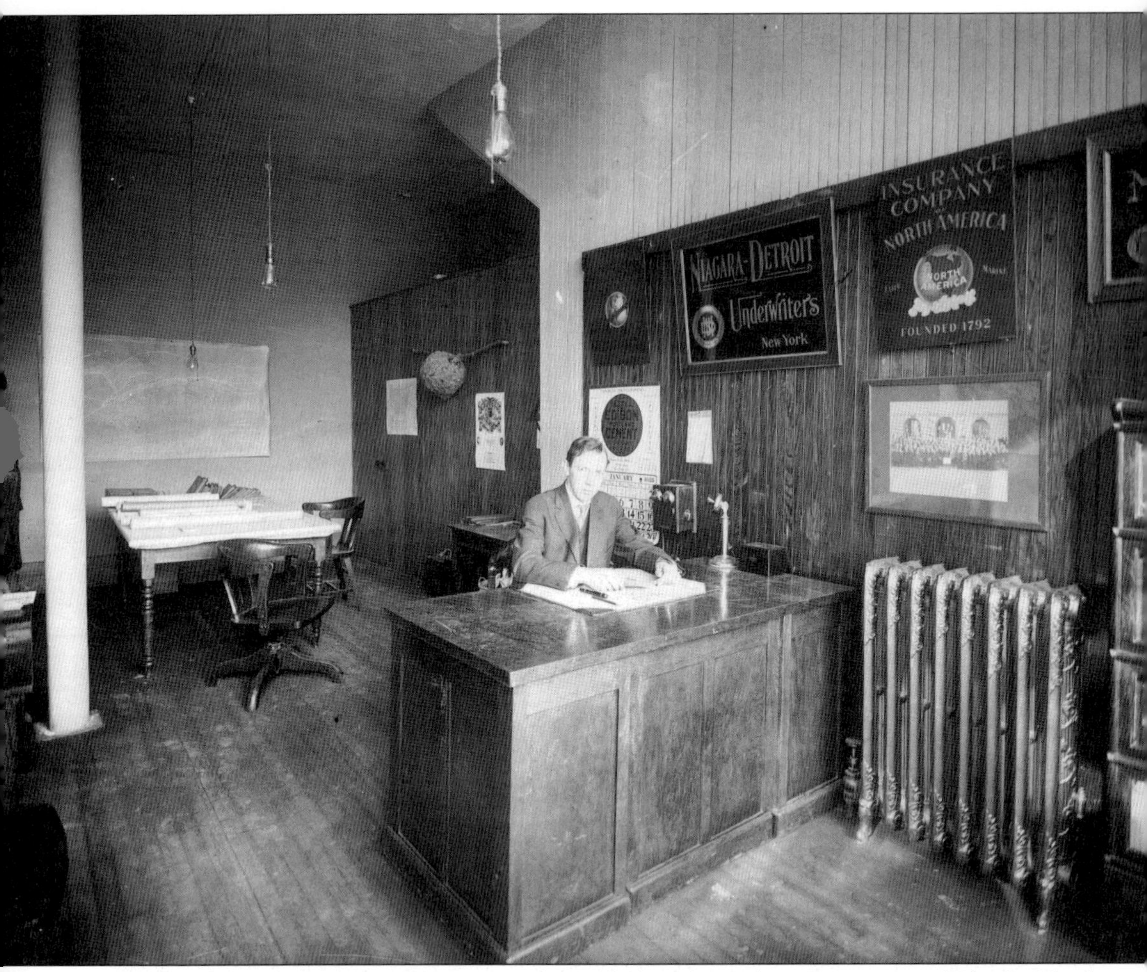

The Fowlers were Prussian immigrants who settled in the Colonial province of Rhode Island during the 1650s. They arrived several decades after Roger Williams established the colony as a haven for political dissidents from the Plymouth Colony. Members of the Fowler family migrated to New York and settled in Westchester; some, such as Isaac Fowler, migrated north to Middlehope. Dr. Charles Fowler settled in Montgomery during the Revolutionary War. His descendant Nicholas J. Fowler created the power company at the Great Falls. Shown is a *c.* 1920 interior view of the Fowler Insurance office at the Fowler Building. (Courtesy of Marcus Millspaugh.)

The Fowler family had a hardware store, originally named Fowler Hardware Company and later called Westerman's Hardware Store. The creative genius of the family was C. Fred Fowler, who created a telephone line between the Fowler Hardware Store and the Fowler House, on Ulster Avenue. This led to the development of the Walden Telephone Company, which extended to Pine Bush, Wallkill, and Montgomery. Later enterprises included the Walden Insuring Agency and the Walden Federal Savings and Loan, maintained through the strong leadership of C. Fred Fowler.

—Joe Fowler

The Millspaughs were German Palatine immigrants who settled as farmers in the town of Montgomery *c.* the 1720s. Skilled cabinetmakers, they built furniture and sold it locally. In the 1850s, the family opened a furniture store. Theron L. Millspaugh, pictured *c.* 1858, helped establish the business. Today, a sixth generation of the family maintains the enterprise at two locations, east and west of the Hudson River. (Courtesy of Marcus Millspaugh.)

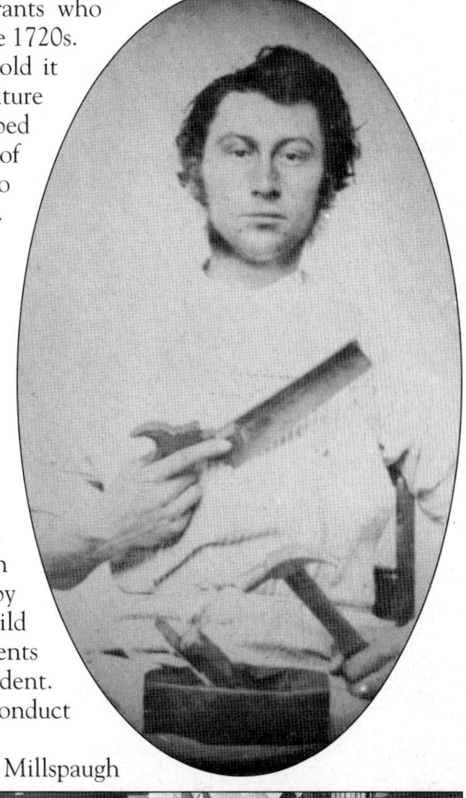

As early as the 1880s, there were clubs such as the Women's Broom Society, who drilled with brooms as if they were rifles. Young people growing up in Walden in the 1940s also had clubs and activities to keep them occupied after school—sports teams, the Science Club, and the Beta Tau History Honor Society, established by social studies-history teacher Helen Hoke in 1943 and still in existence today. There were three Boy Scout troops within the village, and the local churches had numerous activities for the children of the community. Everyone knew the children by name and know where each one lived. If a child created a problem in or out of school, the parents would be contacted before dinner by an area resident. Students usually conformed to a positive code of conduct because of this relationship among the residents.

—Marcus Millspaugh

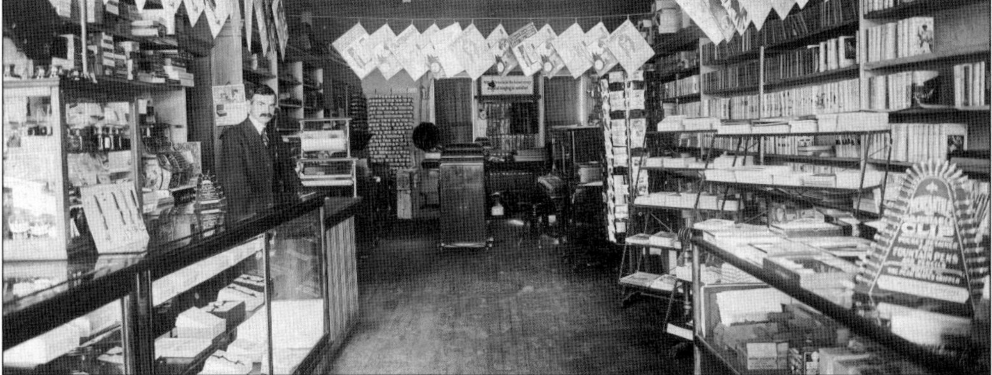

The Sohns family came to New York City from Germany, settled in Walden *c.* 1907, and opened a music shop. At first the shop sold guitars and violins along with sheet music. By the 1920s, it was selling music boxes and soon thereafter, phonographs and radios. In 1939, it carried one of the first commercial televisions. Four generations of the family have continued the music and appliance business. Pictured is J.A.A. Sohns inside Sohns Music Emporium *c.* the 1920s. (Courtesy of Jeff Sohns.)

The Sohns family performed chamber music on violins, cello, and base fiddle. Mr. Sohns Sr. also played in a dance band. J.A.A. Sohns was active in the Walden Fife, Drum, and Bugle Corps. Concerts were held in the Didsbury Opera House and at the Walden Bandstand. Sohns, a specialty business, has maintained its "Main Street–USA" appearance and personalized service.

—Jeff Sohns

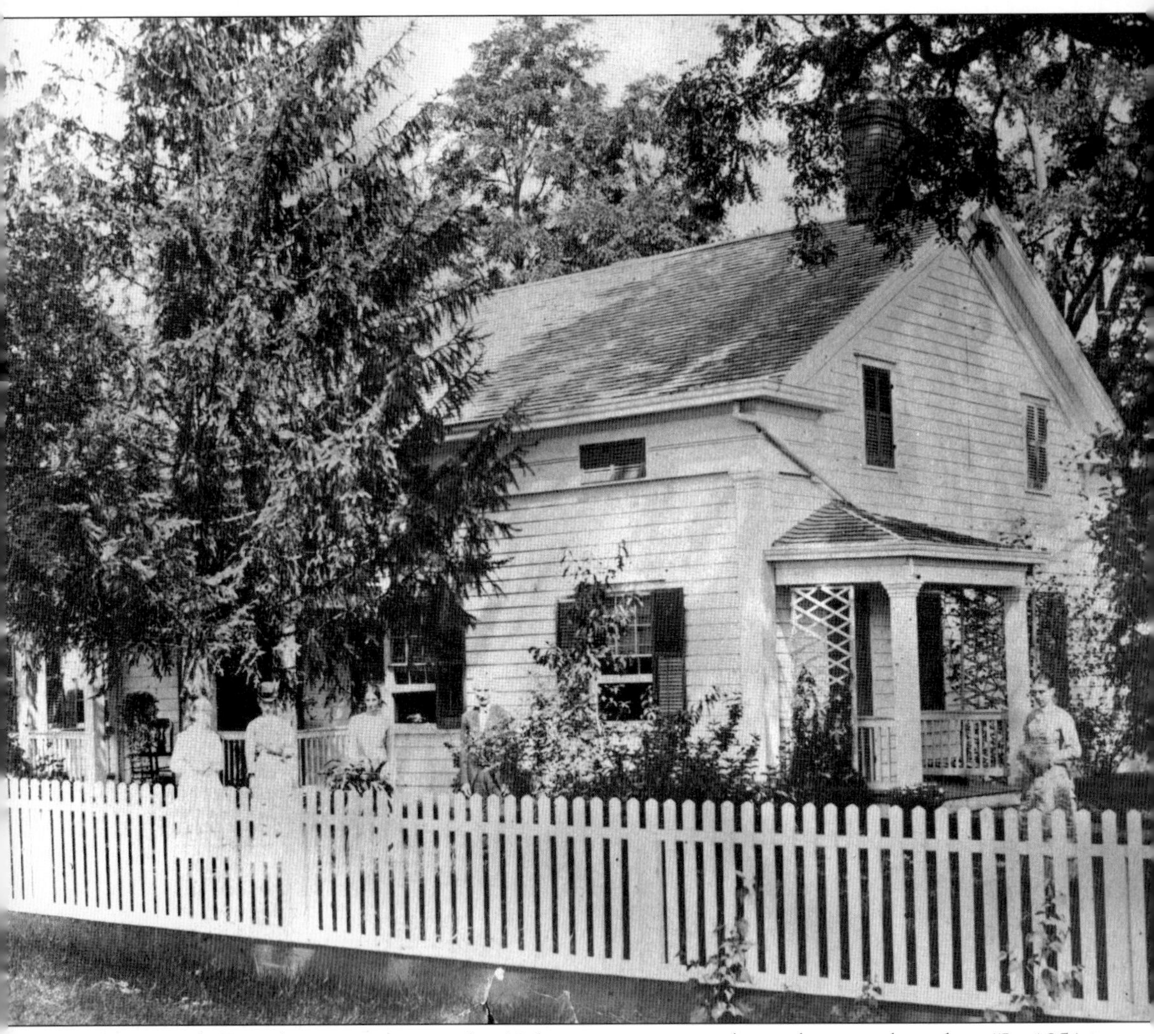

Riverside Farm has its origins in the 18th century, as noted on a historical marker: "In 1851 it was purchased by Nathaniel Dubois who added and remodeled [it] into the Greek Revival style. The Phelps family acquired the farm in 1922." The Phelps family can trace its origins back to England during the Colonial era. Several generations of the Phelps family have been farmers. The DuBois-Phelps Farmstead is a working farm. The Wallkill River borders the property on its eastern boundary. The southern half of the farmhouse dates back to the Colonial period and has a keeping room in its basement with a large cooking hearth and a beehive bake oven. The farmhouse is pictured here *c.* 1910. (Courtesy of Sam Phelps Jr.)

Sam Phelps Sr. was a cabinetmaker in New York City, as was his father before him. The two men were well known for cabinet making and furniture carving. The Phelps family left New York and worked on Indian Springs Farm in Port Jervis. After Sam Phelps Sr. died, the farm remained a working farm, producing apples, chickens, cows, and crops under the ownership and care of Sam Phelps Jr., one of the few remaining farmers in the Walden area. After 70 years as a farmer, he writes a news column for the local newspaper, giving advice and opinions about agriculture and life on the farm. He has been the subject of a television documentary and remains a strong advocate for conservation and a dedicated environmentalist. He is Walden's embodiment of the American farmer.

—Sam Phelps Jr.

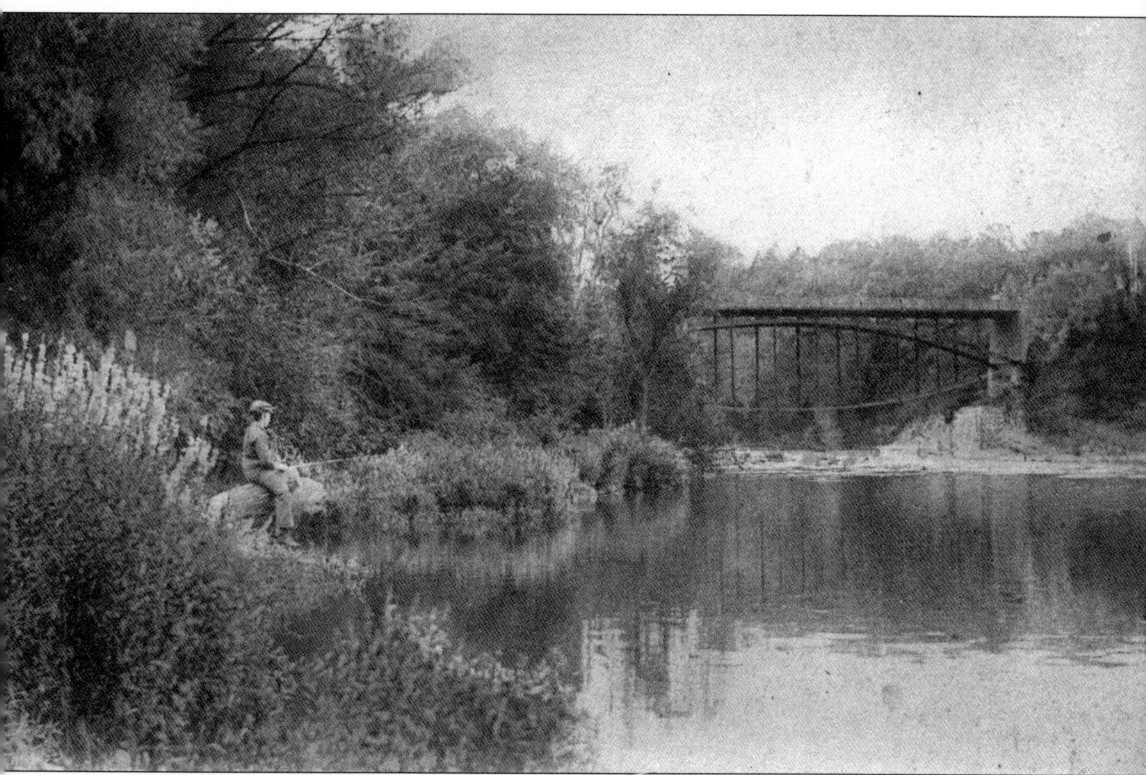

The Clarks originally came to New York from England. In 1886, the family bought a barn and 10 acres of land for $900 and became farmers. During the early 20th century, the head of the family worked in a meat market to supply food and income for the family. John Clark worked for several years for the New York Knife Company as a hefter.

One of the humorous tales told at the New York Knife Company was "Pulling the Cat across the Canal." A new and inexperienced worker was told that cats had a strong fear of the water and would gain great strength if threatened with drowning. To test the theory, the new worker had to stand on one side of the river embankment with a rope around his waist and the other end tied around a cat. A large extended piece of rope was tied from the cat below the embankment to four or five workers. Those workers were hidden from the view of the young worker. With his back to the "river," the young worker pulled the rope and started to move up the embankment. After a minute, the squad of workers "yanked" together on the rope and pulled the young worker off the ridge and into the river for a "dunking." As he surfaced, he noticed from the distance that the cat had not moved at all and was quite calm and peaceful as if nothing had happened.

Clark later became an employee of the New Haven and Hartford Railroad in Maybrook. He began repairing a Model T Ford as a hobby and then used the automobile to transport rail workers from Walden to Maybrook. His success in repairing the car resulted in his finding employment as a mechanic and maintenance engineer for several of the car dealers in the vicinity. While maintaining a successful career as an excellent mechanic, there was always time to go fishing in the "mighty Wallkill." This routine has continued for almost 75 years, as Clark has surpassed his 100th birthday. The photograph depicts fishing in the Wallkill River c. 1907. (Courtesy of Jeff Sohns.)

—John Clark

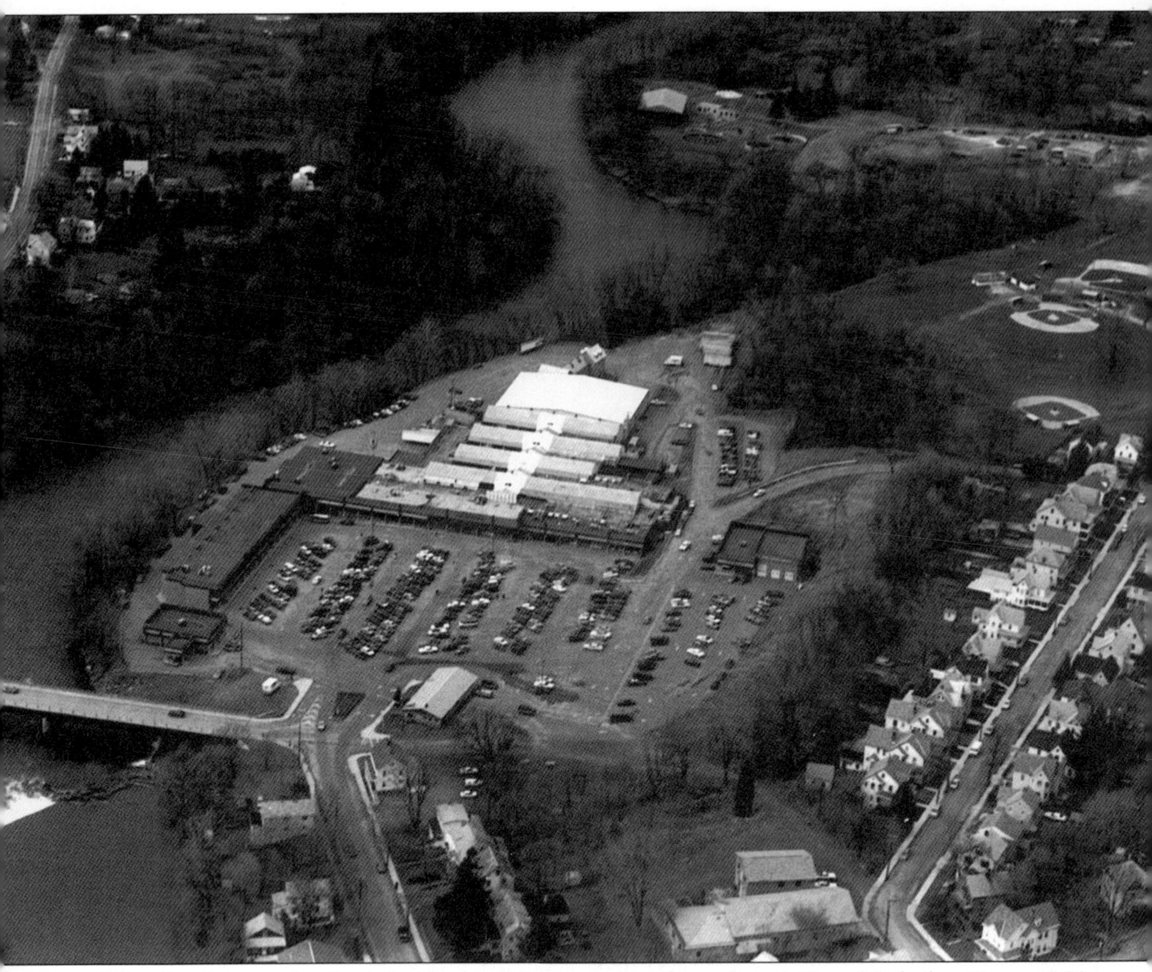

The Jacobowitz family left Czarist Russia under the rule of Czar Nicholas II *c.* 1900. The pograms and Jewish ghettoes forced many Russians to leave their homeland during the last few decades of the 19th century. Members of the Jacobowitz family arrived in Ellenville and became farmers. The produce and crops they grew were sold to the public at their Fruit Exchange in Ellenville, which was established by Meyer and Lillian Jacobowitz in 1924. The family moved to Walden and opened a business on Main Street: the National Self Service Market, selling meats, fruits, vegetables, and groceries. As the business grew and expanded, it was necessary to enlist the aid and support of daughter Joyce Jacobowitz Concors and her husband, Arthur Concors. Shown is the Thruway Market *c.* the 1980s. (Courtesy of the Concors-Jacobowitz family.)

As Walden's population grew in the early 1950s, the Jacobowitz family business continued to prosper. The need to expand led Arthur Concors and Meyer Jacobowitz to purchase the land and buildings that were the original Walden Knife Company. When the New York Thruway was constructed from New York City to Albany, the Jacobowitz-Concors family opened a new business, the Thruway Food Market and Shopping Center. The shopping mall has an expanse of 186,000 square feet. The third generation of the Concors-Jacobowitz family maintains the business under the direction of Les Concors, president, and Bruce Concors, vice president. In the future, a fourth generation may become involved in maintaining the business begun by an immigrant from Russia more than 100 years ago.

—the Concors-Jacobowitz family

Five
HISTORIC SITES AND MONUMENTS

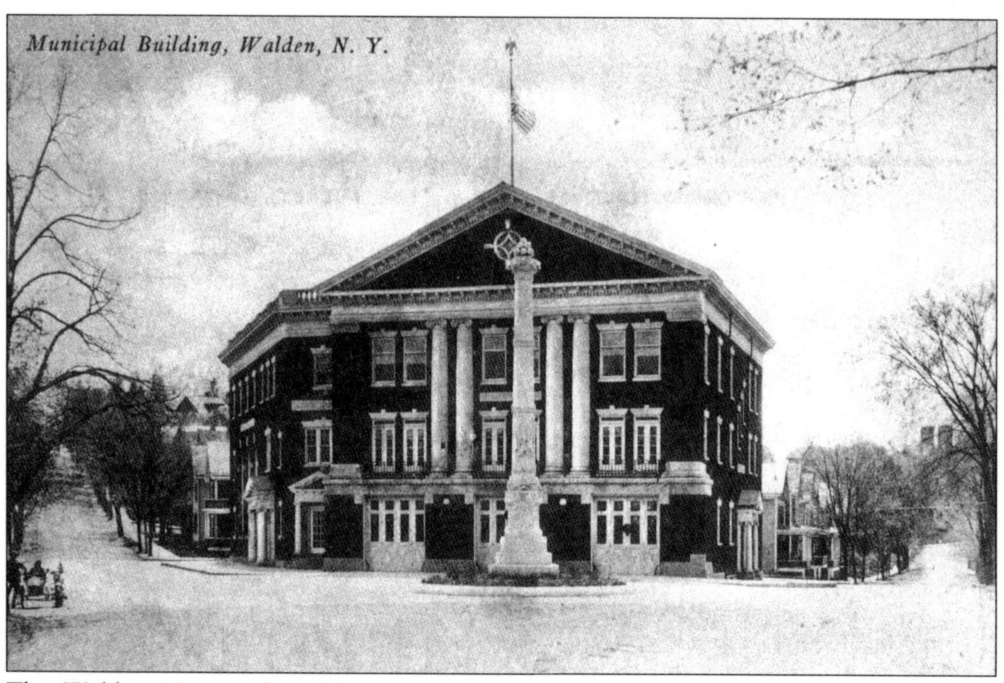

The Walden Municipal Building was erected with financial support from Col. Thomas W. Bradley. The building was used as a firehouse, municipal government building, and public library, named after Josephine Bradley, wife of Thomas Bradley, and their daughter Louise Bradley, Josephine-Louise Public Library. The Soldiers Monument *c.* 1890 stands before the building and honors those who served the nation in U.S. Army and Navy. (Courtesy of Robert Kidd.)

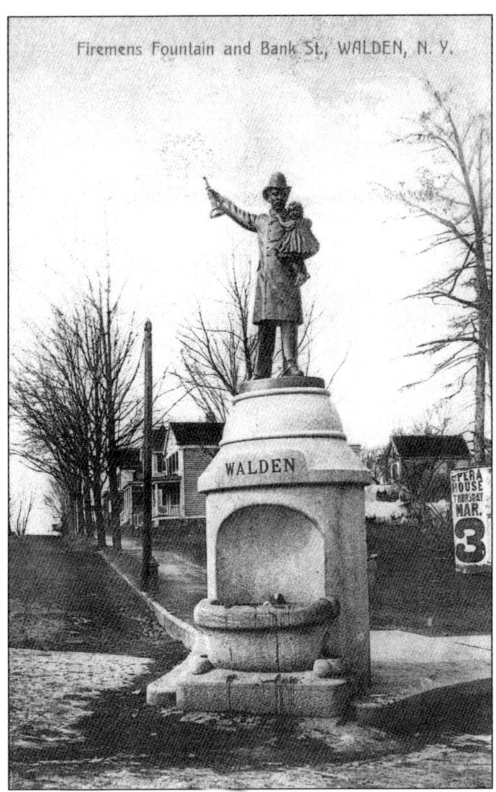

The Fireman's Monument, pictured *c.* 1909, was erected as a memorial to a Walden fire chief who saved the life of a young girl. The water trough was used for the watering of horses that pulled the fire carriages and wagons, as well as for the horses of those residents and businesses. (Courtesy of Robert Kidd.)

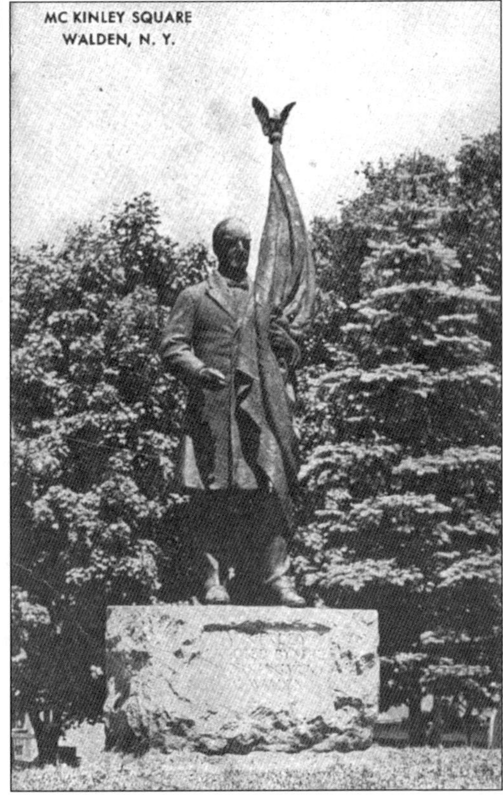

Pictured *c.* 1924 is this statue of Pres. William McKinley, funded through the will of Col. Thomas W. Bradley as a gesture of friendship and gratitude. McKinley was instrumental in creating the higher protective tariff that protected the cutlery business from competition from knife makers in Solingen, Germany. The statue was modeled after a 1901 portrait photograph by Frances Benjamin Johnston, known as the Mother of American Photo Journalism. The photograph was taken at the Buffalo Exposition just before McKinley was shot and killed. Three statues were created to duplicate the photograph. The other two were for Canton, Ohio, and Philadelphia, Pennsylvania. (Courtesy of Marc Newman.)

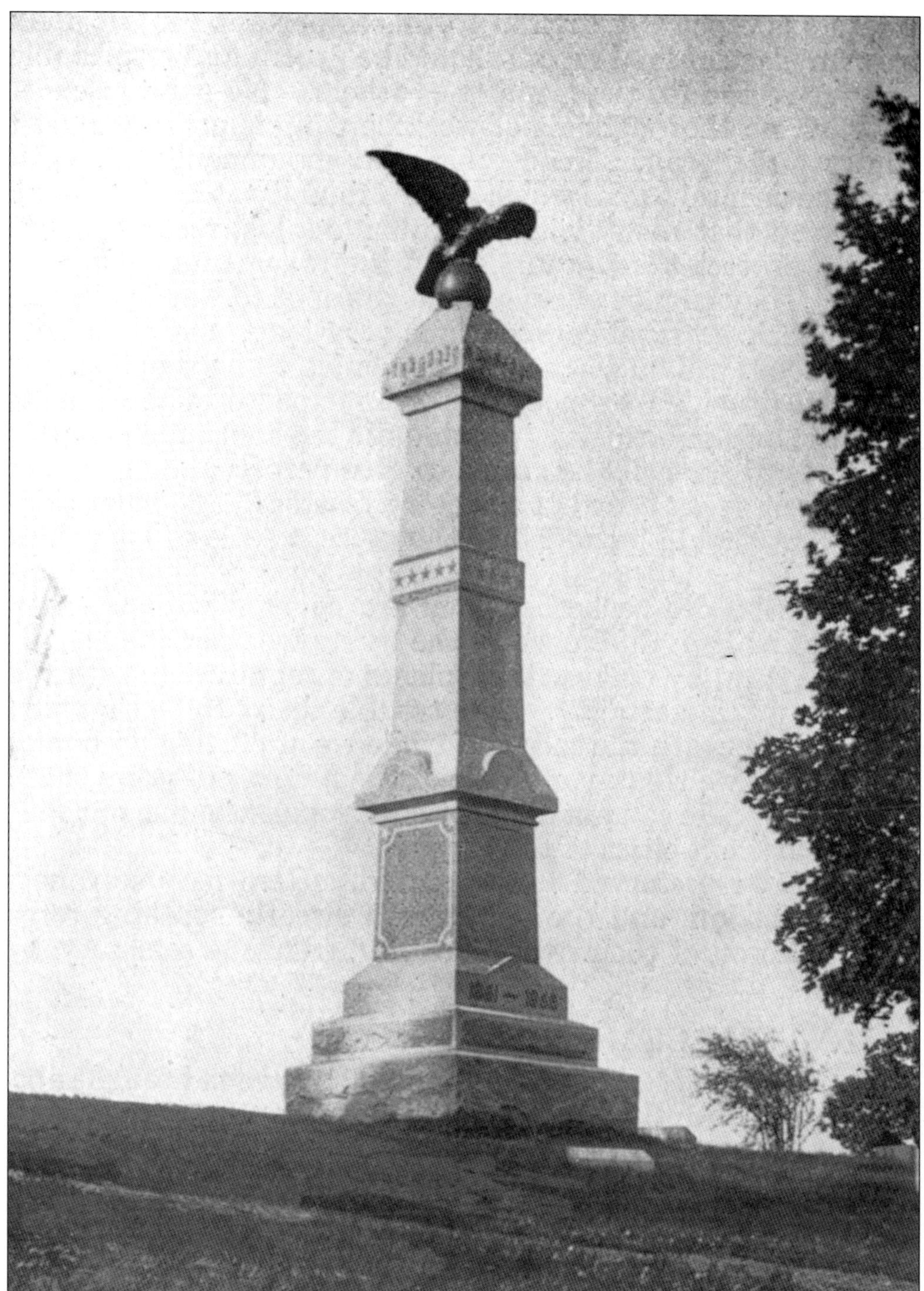

This monument was erected by the Fairchild Post No. 564 of the Grand Army of the Republic and the Fairchild Women's Relief Corps. No. 84 in "Memory of Our Soldier Dead." The monument, pictured in 1902, was created as a tribute to the men who served the Union army during the Civil War. A major portion of the cost was financed by Col. Thomas W. Bradley. (*Walden and Its Environs*, page 146.)

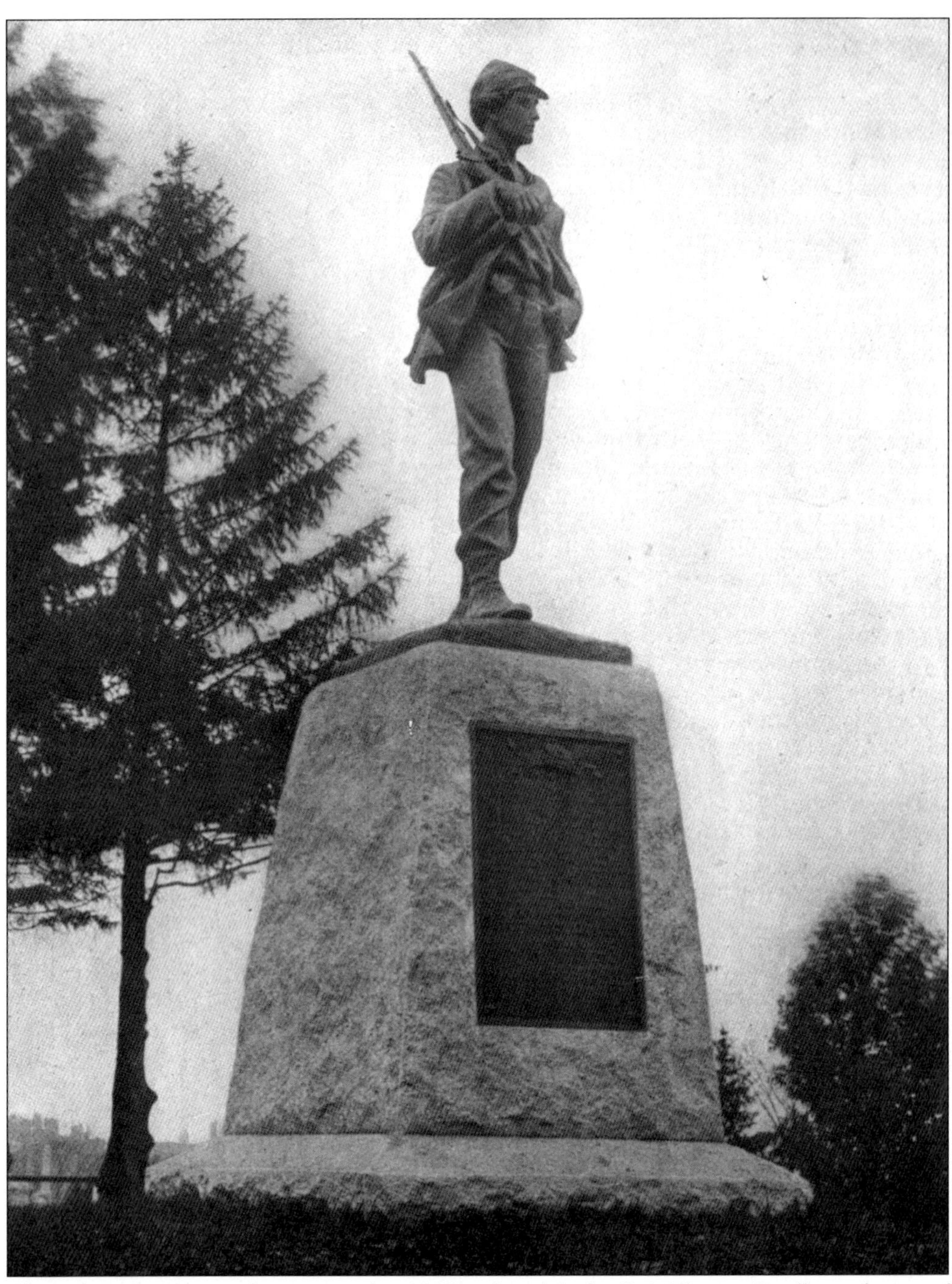

The Volunteer Memorial was erected *c.* 1905 and paid for by Col. Thomas Bradley in honor of the service dead of Company H, 124th New York State Infantry. The men of the 124th were called the "Orange Blossoms" and served during the Civil War, from 1862 to 1865. The regiment was organized at Goshen and became part of the Army of the Potomac. It served in major engagements including Fredericksburg, Chancellorsville, Gettysburg, Wilderness, Spotsylvania, Petersburg, and Appomattox. (*Walden and Its Environs*, page 148.)

Six
Early History

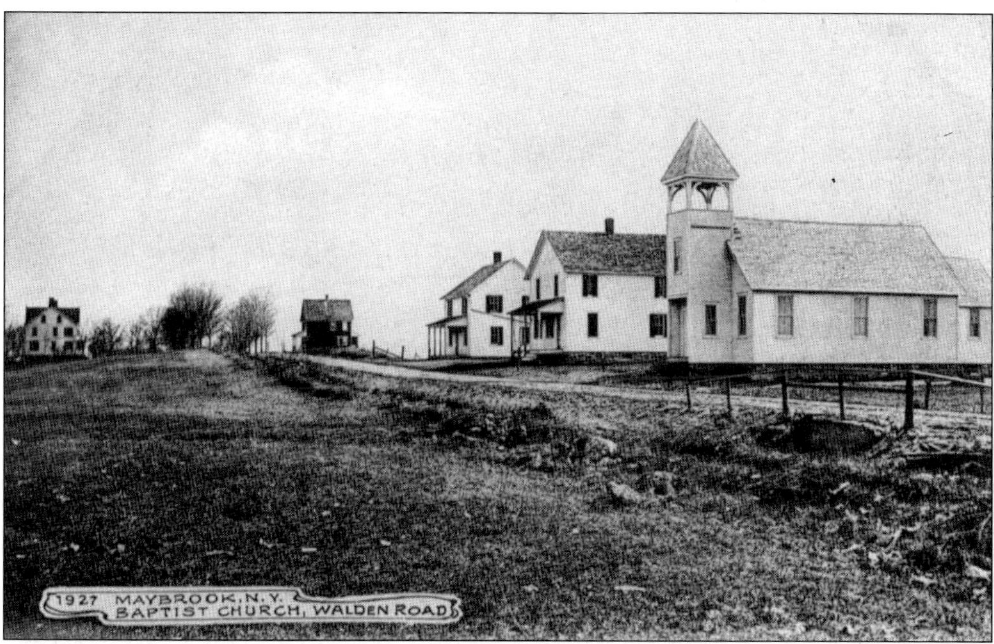

In 1926, more than a century after the village of Montgomery was established, the village of Maybrook was incorporated. Thus, during the height of the Roaring Twenties, Maybrook became the last of the three villages to be incorporated. It was unlike the village of Walden, whose Wallkill River became a catalyst for early gristmills, textile mills, and knife companies along the banks of the Great Falls. The Maybrook area was made up of sparse settlements of Colonial dwellings on large tracts of land that eventually became the rail center of the Hudson Valley and the rail link that connected the western and Middle Atlantic states to New England—a transcontinental railroad. Its roots were so deeply embedded in the early Colonial period of the 18th century, a deed was granted for land extension from the town of Shawangunk to the town of Goshen, which was the county seat of Orange County. In the area was a settlement of land in the 1730s belonging to Adam Graham. The Graham House became a meeting place for travelers and area residents. It eventually became the Goodwill Church. The route or road extension south of Walden, shown here *c.* 1927, was referred to as Walden Road and later Homestead Avenue and Route 208. (Courtesy of Eric Kruger.)

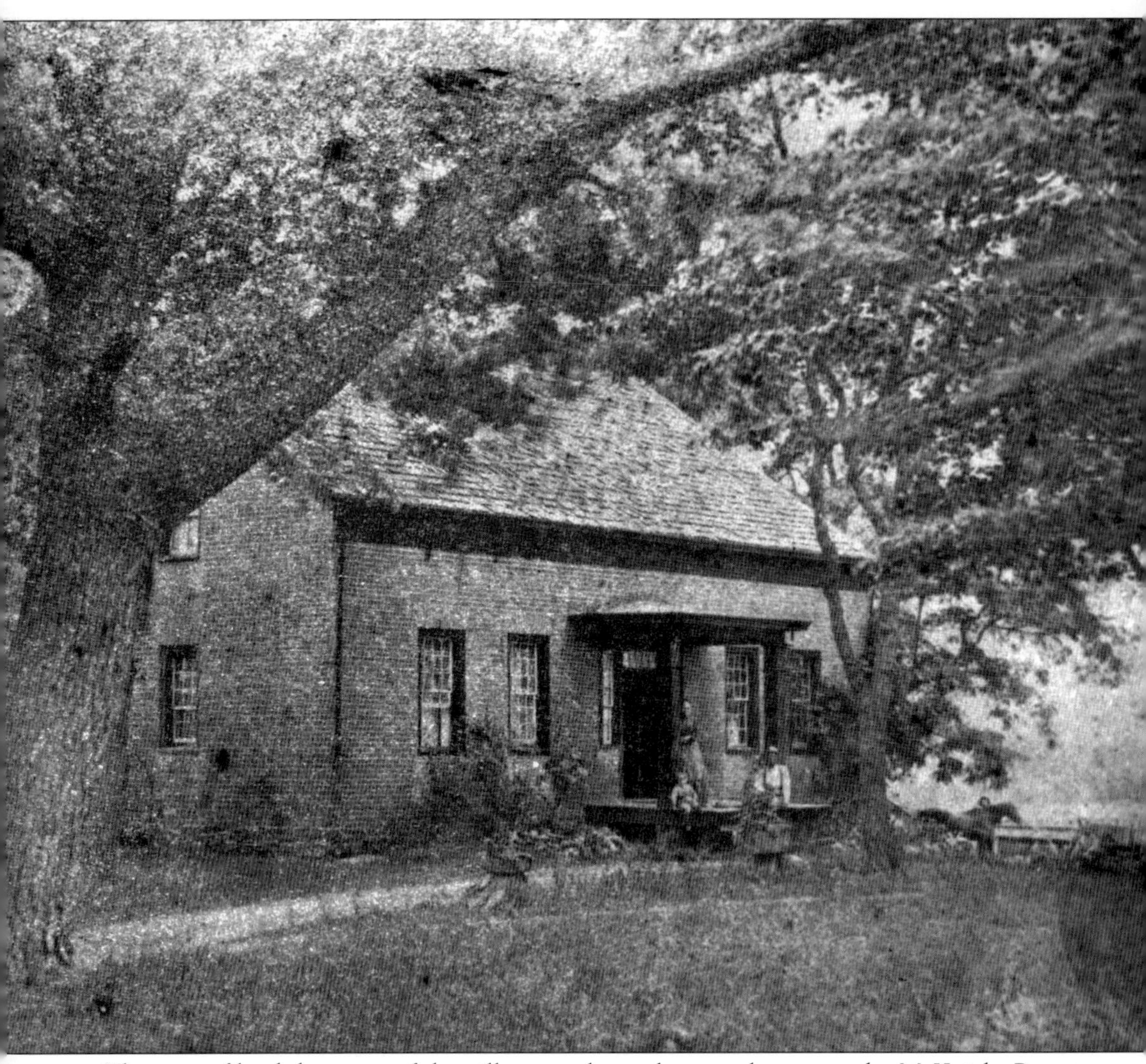

The tract of land that most of the village was located on was known as the McKnight Patent. John Blake Jr. received a land deed for 200 acres of land from that patent, originally bought from Cornelius Clapper of New York City for the fee of 224 British pounds and 10 shillings. The Blakes were in-laws of the Bull family of Hamptonburgh and Montgomery. Elsie Eager, the granddaughter of William Bull and Sarah Wells, was the first white woman in Orange County. She married John P.M. Blake. John Blake Jr., as an early founding father, was heavily involved in politics. In 1793, he was named deputy sheriff, and five years later he was elected to the New York State Assembly. When his term expired, he was elected sheriff of the county and served from 1800 to 1805. During the next decade, Blake served for several terms as New York State assemblyman, two terms as a member of the House of Representatives, and as a judge of New York Common Pleas Court. No individual in the history of the county had held so many positions on both state and federal levels of government. Pictured is the John Blake Homestead c. the 1890s. (Courtesy of Nancy Mitchell.)

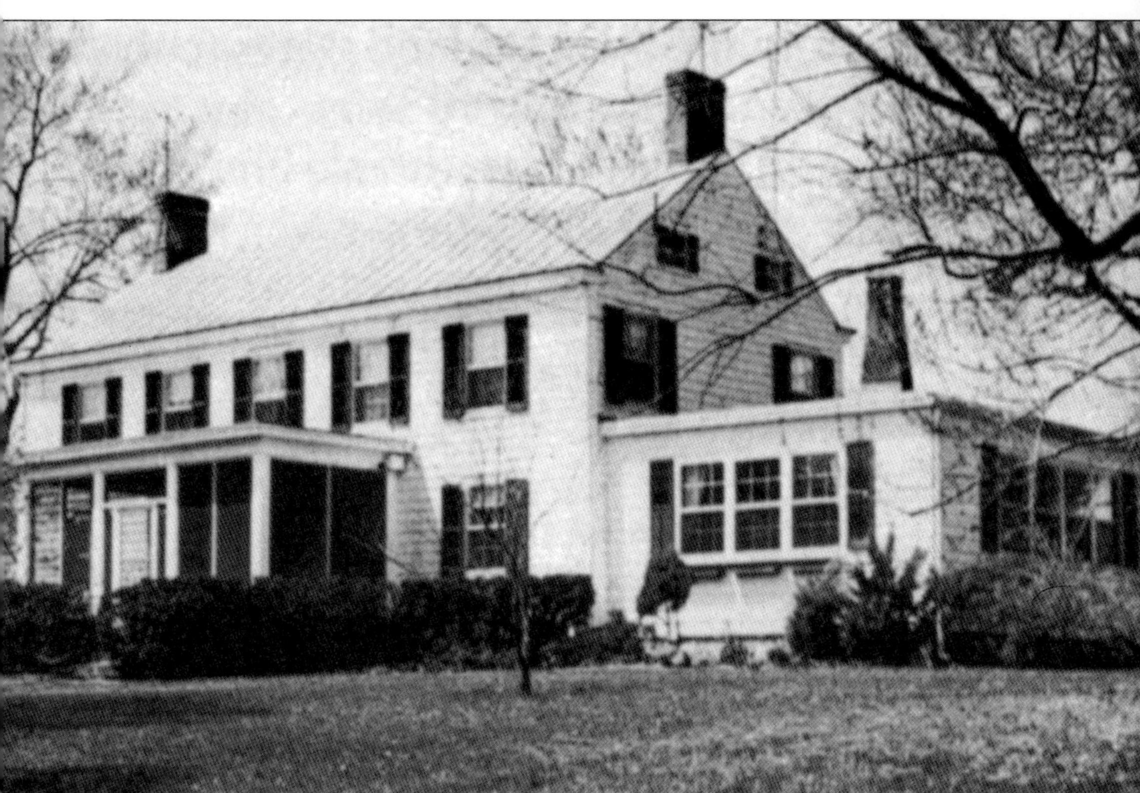

Another large landowner who purchased several hundred acres under the McNight Patent was John Nicholson. When the Revolutionary War began in 1775, Nicholson was the provincial congressman from Ulster County. During the Canadian campaign, he served as a captain of a volunteer company of the New York militia under Gen. Richard Montgomery in 1775. His courage in the Canadian campaign resulted in his being promoted to the rank of major and later lieutenant colonel. His regiment served from 1777 to 1778 under Gen. Israel Putnam. At the end of the war, he was appointed assemblyman in Poughkeepsie in 1782 and a year later in the same position as a member of the New York State Legislature in Kingston. The Nicholson Farm had two burial grounds; one was for the family members, and the other was a burial site for slaves. In the years prior to the American Revolution, Orange County had more than 300 African slaves. Shown is the Col. John Nicholson House, which dates from the 1770s. (Courtesy of the Maybrook Golden Jubilee Committee and Carole Brown Jennings.)

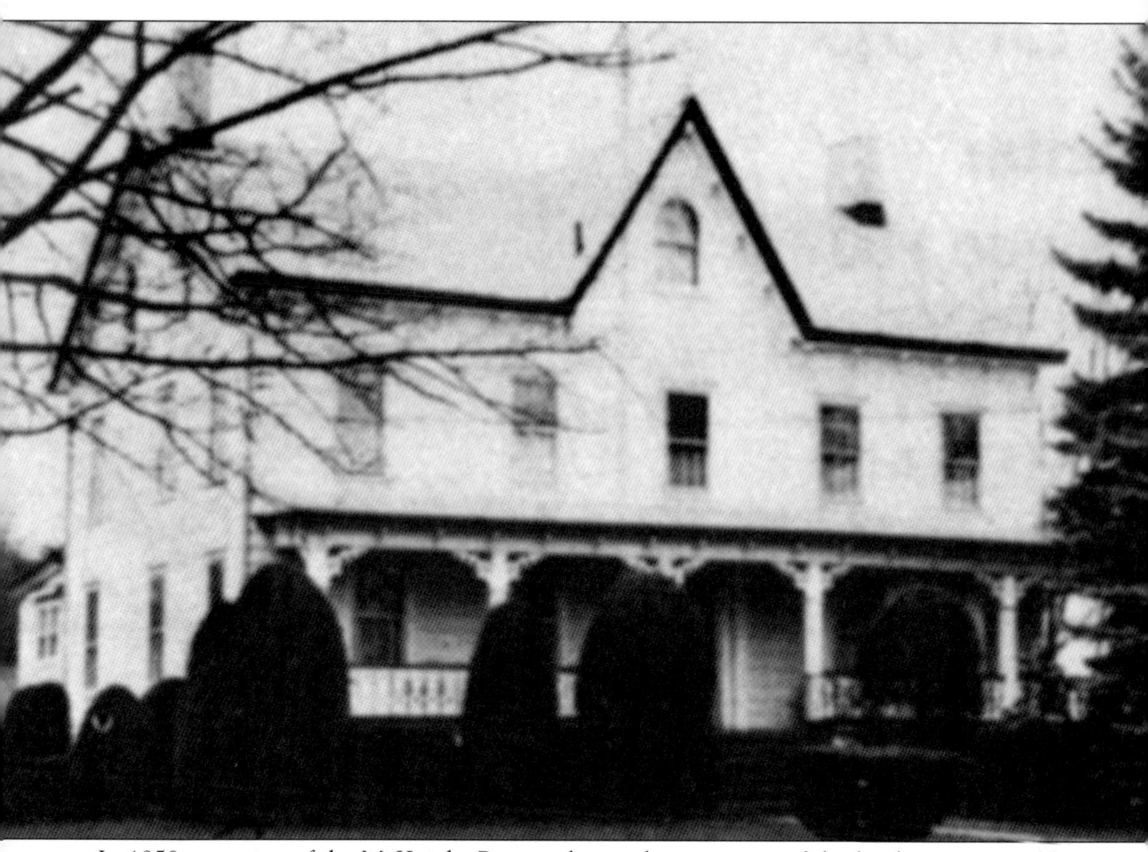

In 1858, a portion of the McKnight Patent, the southern portion of the land tract, was sold to Daniel Jewell and his wife, Cornelia Newkirk, the first of Maybrook's teachers. Pictured is the Daniel Jewell House *c.* the 1860s. By the early 19th century, dozens of homes with large tracts of land were constructed within the area of Maybrook. Some of these homes were used for farming; others were used for the breeding of livestock, especially trotting horses. However, during this early period, Maybrook was the least developed community within the town of Montgomery. A century later, it became the major rail center of the Hudson Valley and the gateway for passenger and freight service from Pennsylvania through to the New England states. (Courtesy of the Maybrook Golden Jubilee Committee and Roby Petzold.)

Seven

INDUSTRIALIZATION AND MASS TRANSPORTATION

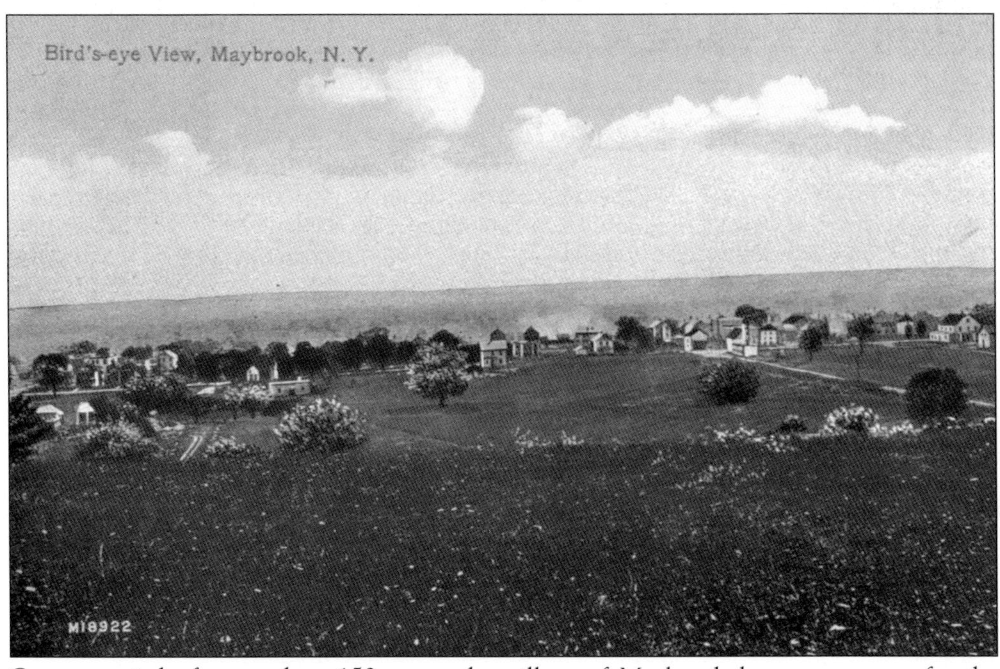

Over a period of more than 150 years, the village of Maybrook became an area for the development of three means of travel, the first of which was the breeding of racehorses during the second half of the 19th century. This is a bird's-eye view of Maybrook c. 1915. (Courtesy of Eric Kruger.)

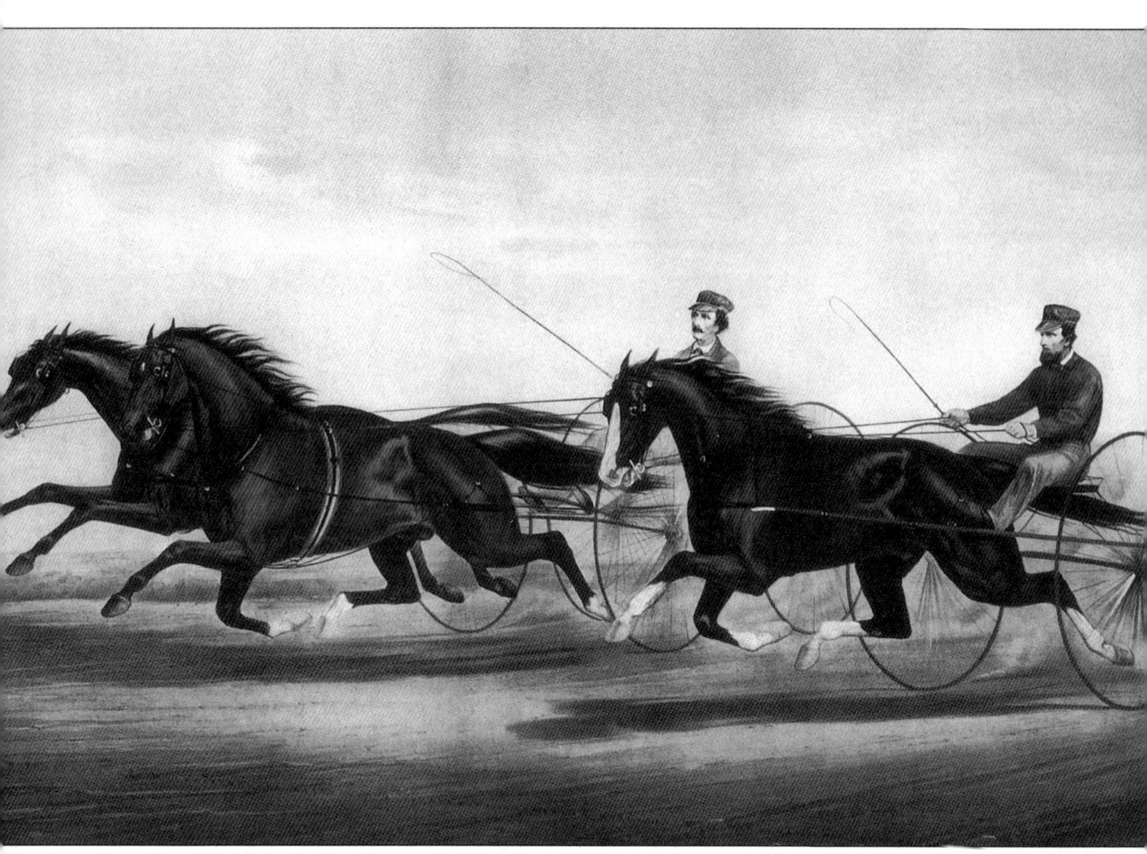

Jonathan Hawkins built a horse farm with stables in a major portion of Maybrook. Dexter, one of the champion trotting racehorses of the region, was foaled on this farm. He is shown here c. the 1860s, when he earned $67,000 (which would be well in excess of $1 million today). In 1864, he was considered the greatest trotting champion horse of his era and ran in 50 races, winning 46 of them. He was so famous that he was the subject of a Currier & Ives lithograph painting. He was sold for $35,000 and ran his last race in 1867. His lineage included a sister, Nellie, and a half brother, George Wilkes. All three horses were considered the best of the champion lines of that era, with Dexter having the fastest track time of the three, 2:17:14. Dexter's sire was William Rysdyks Hambiltonian, known as the grandfather of the modern standardbred horse. His dam was Clara, who was foaled from American Star. (Courtesy of the Harness Racing Museum & Hall of Fame.)

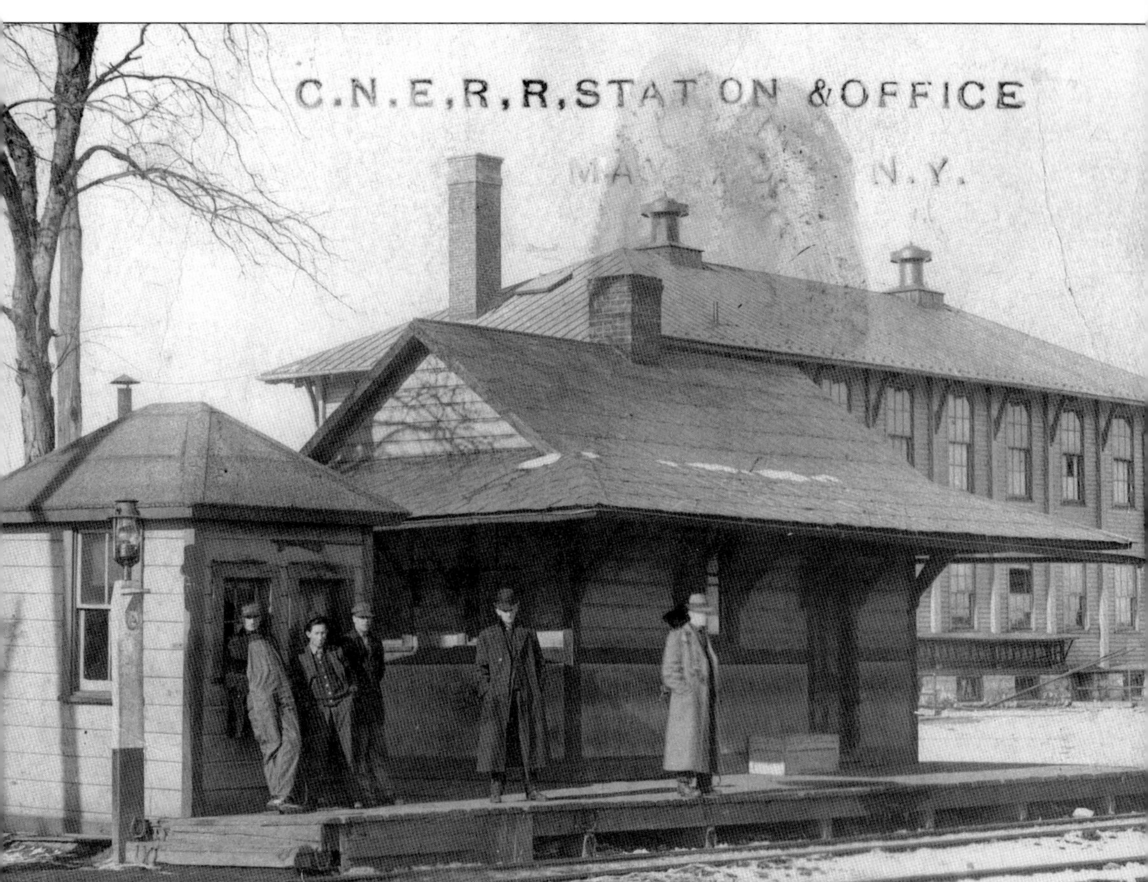

Most of the railroad lines were built in the northern and northeastern states—for example, the New York Grand Central Railroad and the Baltimore and Ohio Railroad. In 1862, the United States contracted with both the Central Pacific Railroad and the Union Pacific Railroad to build a transcontinental railroad by 1869. In less than 25 years, four other transcontinental railroads were constructed to connect the East to the West: the Northern Pacific, the Southern Pacific, the Atchison, Topeka, and Santa Fe, and the Great Northern. New York had several railroads upstate and in New York City. The railroad boom in neighboring states and the nation led to land surveys in the Wallkill Valley aimed at creating a line that would connect with neighboring railroads in New York and Pennsylvania. Before the 1880s, there were numerous rail lines that existed in New York and New England, but the two largest railroad companies were the Philadelphia and Reading Railroad and the Central New England Railroad. Since the Hudson River separated the Middle Atlantic states from New England, a railroad bridge over the river was built on the eastern side of the Hudson River at Poughkeepsie to reach what was then referred to as Orange Junction. The Poughkeepsie Bridge was completed in 1888. Originally, the junction was under the control of the Philadelphia, Reading, and New England Railroad, which directed operations from Highland to Orange (Maybrook) Junction. Ten years later, the Central New England Railroad took over the management and control of Maybrook Junction, from 1905 to 1910. Shown is the Central New England Railroad Station and office in 1910. (Courtesy of the Maybrook Historical Society and Railroad Museum.)

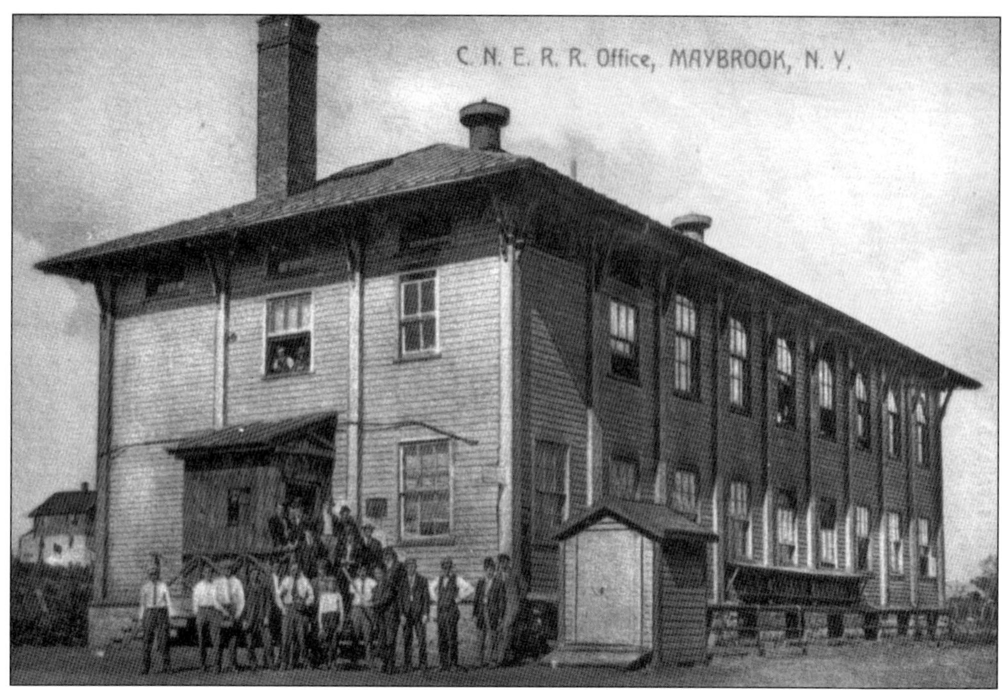

The Central New England Railroad administration office was created *c.* 1910 at the end of Main Street in Maybrook to direct the rail operations for westbound and eastbound freight and passenger cars. (Courtesy of Roby Petzold.)

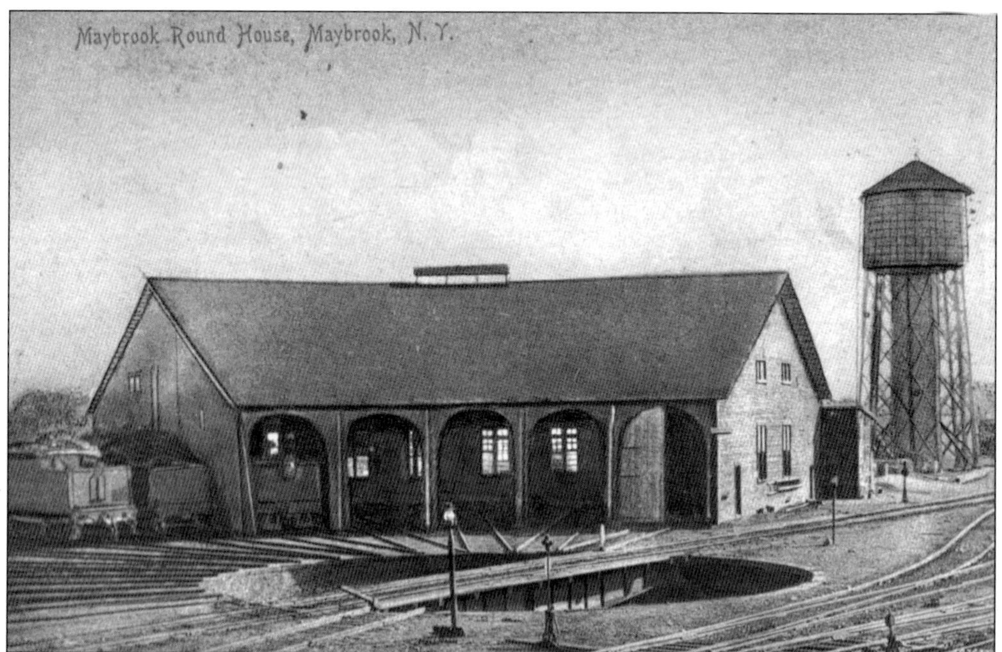

Pictured *c.* 1910 are the roundhouse and turntable built by the Central New England Railroad. It was here that the engines were turned around and shifted from one track to another. (Courtesy of Eric Kruger.)

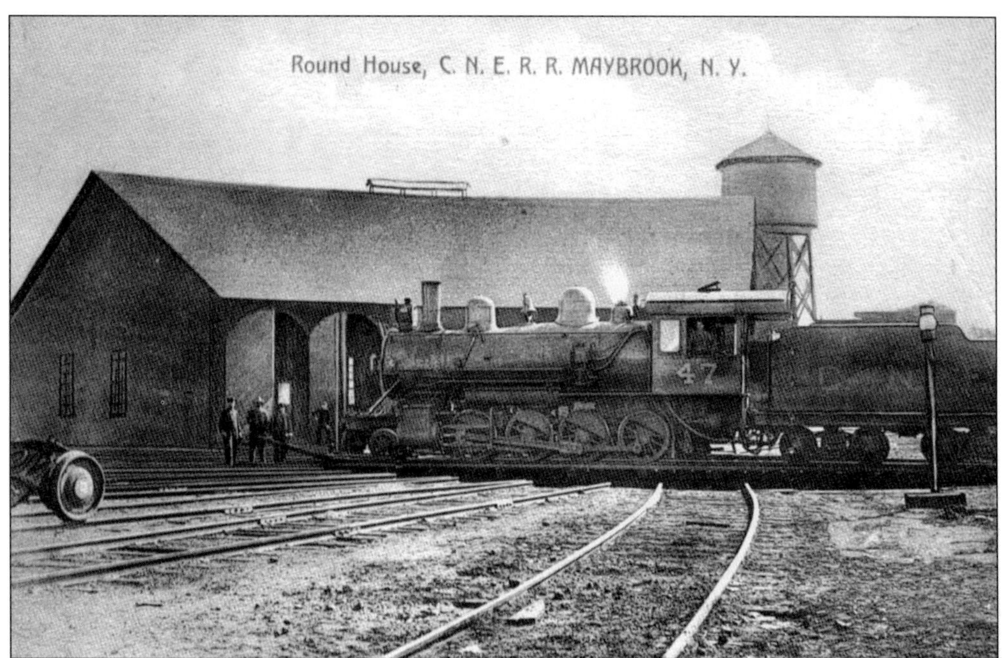

This *c.* 1910 view shows the Central New England engine and the roundhouse. (Courtesy of Robert Kidd.)

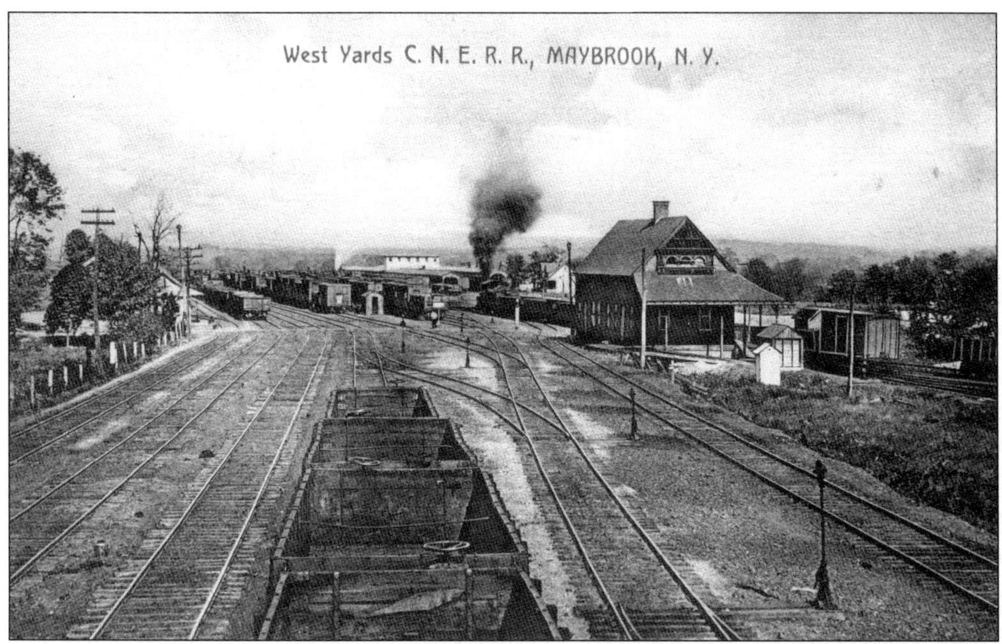

The Central New England Railroad Terminal in Maybrook had a few liner tracks that serviced the rail lines that were moving to the western portion of the United States across the Hudson River. Shown are the west yards of the Central New England Railroad *c.* 1910. (Courtesy of Robert Kidd.)

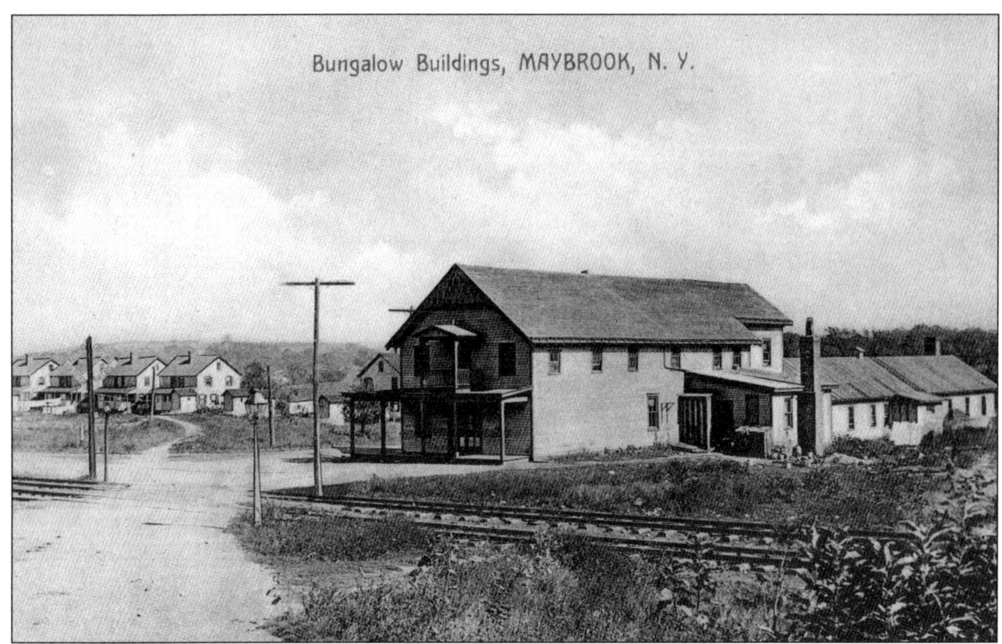

Some small housing was built to accommodate employees who needed a place to stay while transferring from one train to another. These are the bungalow buildings *c.* 1915. (Courtesy of Roby Petzold.)

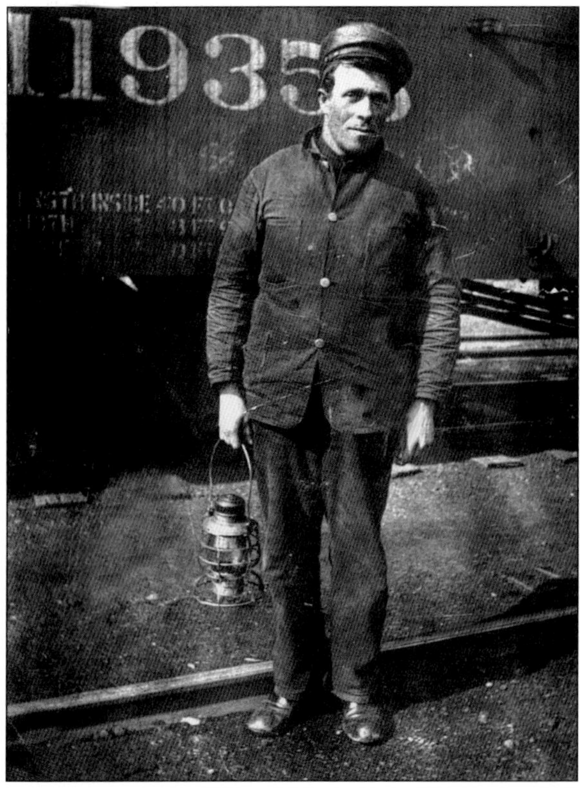

Morris Bailey, a brakeman of the Central New England Railroad, is shown *c.* 1915. (Courtesy of the Maybrook Railroad Historical Society & Museum.)

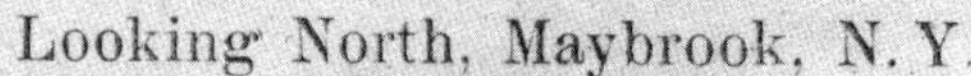

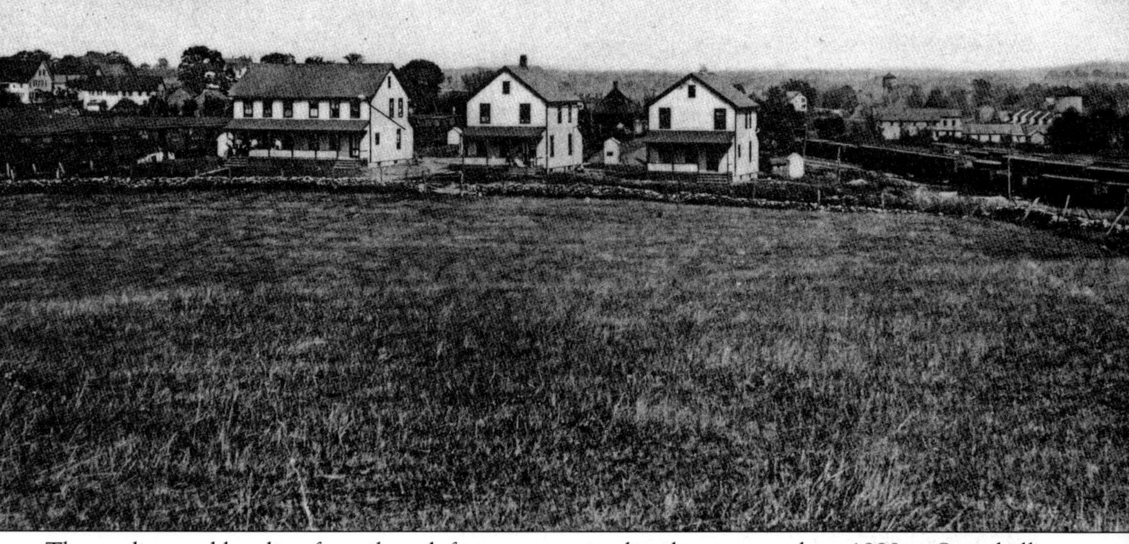

The grading and leveling for rail track for a connecting line began as early as 1888 in Campbell Hall, on the outskirts of Maybrook. Engineers and construction workers resided in the immediate area of Maybrook. Some of them were given sleeping accommodations at local farms, such as the Jonas Hawkins House and the John Blake House. Maybrook became a depot for men and materials in the construction of this rail line. In the years that followed, it was called Maybrook Junction and, later, Maybrook. During period of about 10 years, the railroad yards and the rail line expanded. The Orange County Railroad increased its real estate holdings by purchasing farmland that was parallel to the expansion track. Farms in the surveyed route were purchased and leveled over a period of three years. This view looks north toward Walden c. 1908. (Courtesy of Eric Kruger.)

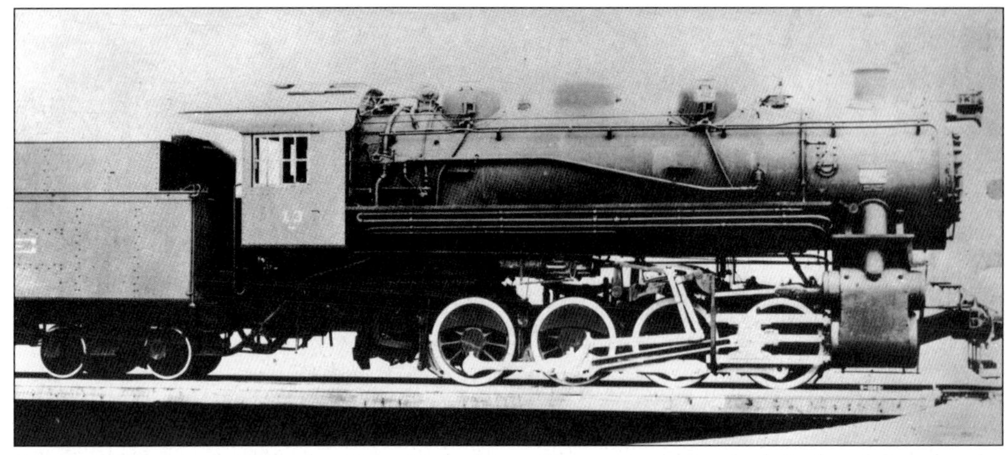

Between 1910 and 1927, the New York, New Haven, and Hartford Railroad bought the controlling stock of the Central New England Railroad and began to transform Maybrook Junction into the largest switching terminal in the Northeast. The trains kept the Central New England markings until 1927. (Courtesy of the Maybrook Historical Society & Museum.)

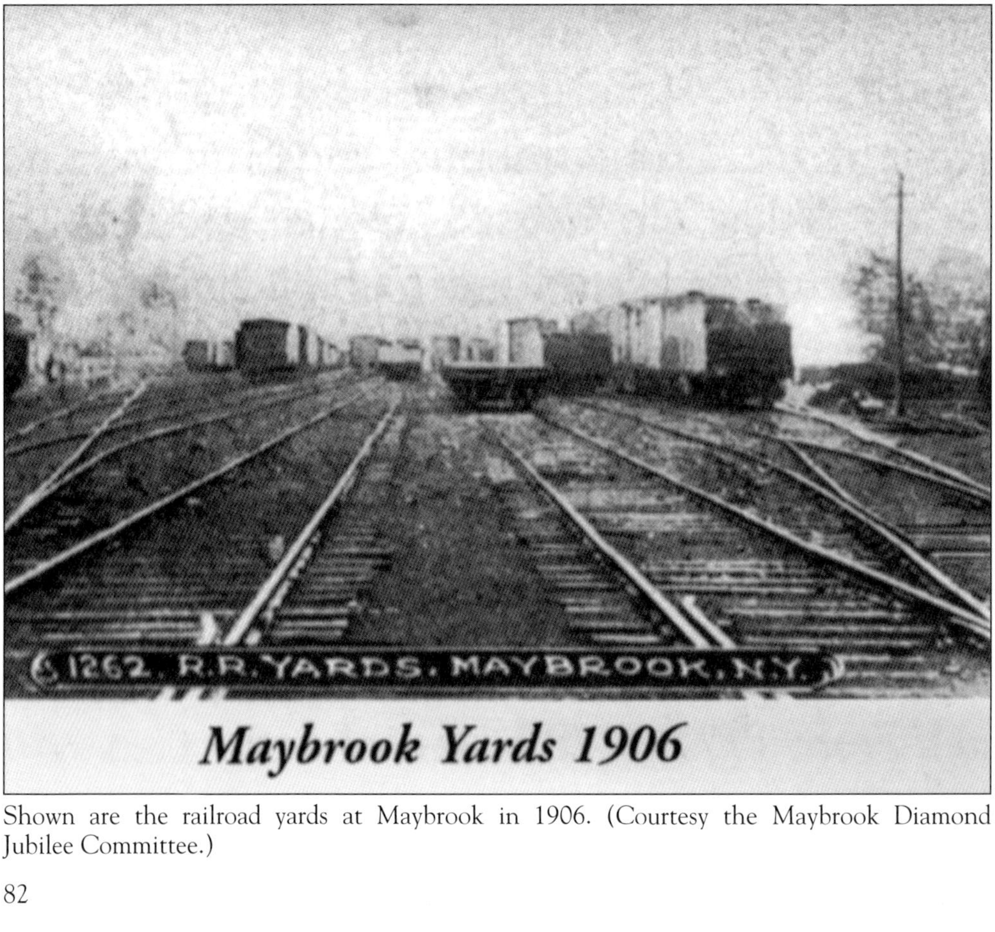

1262. R.R. YARDS. MAYBROOK, N.Y.

Maybrook Yards 1906

Shown are the railroad yards at Maybrook in 1906. (Courtesy the Maybrook Diamond Jubilee Committee.)

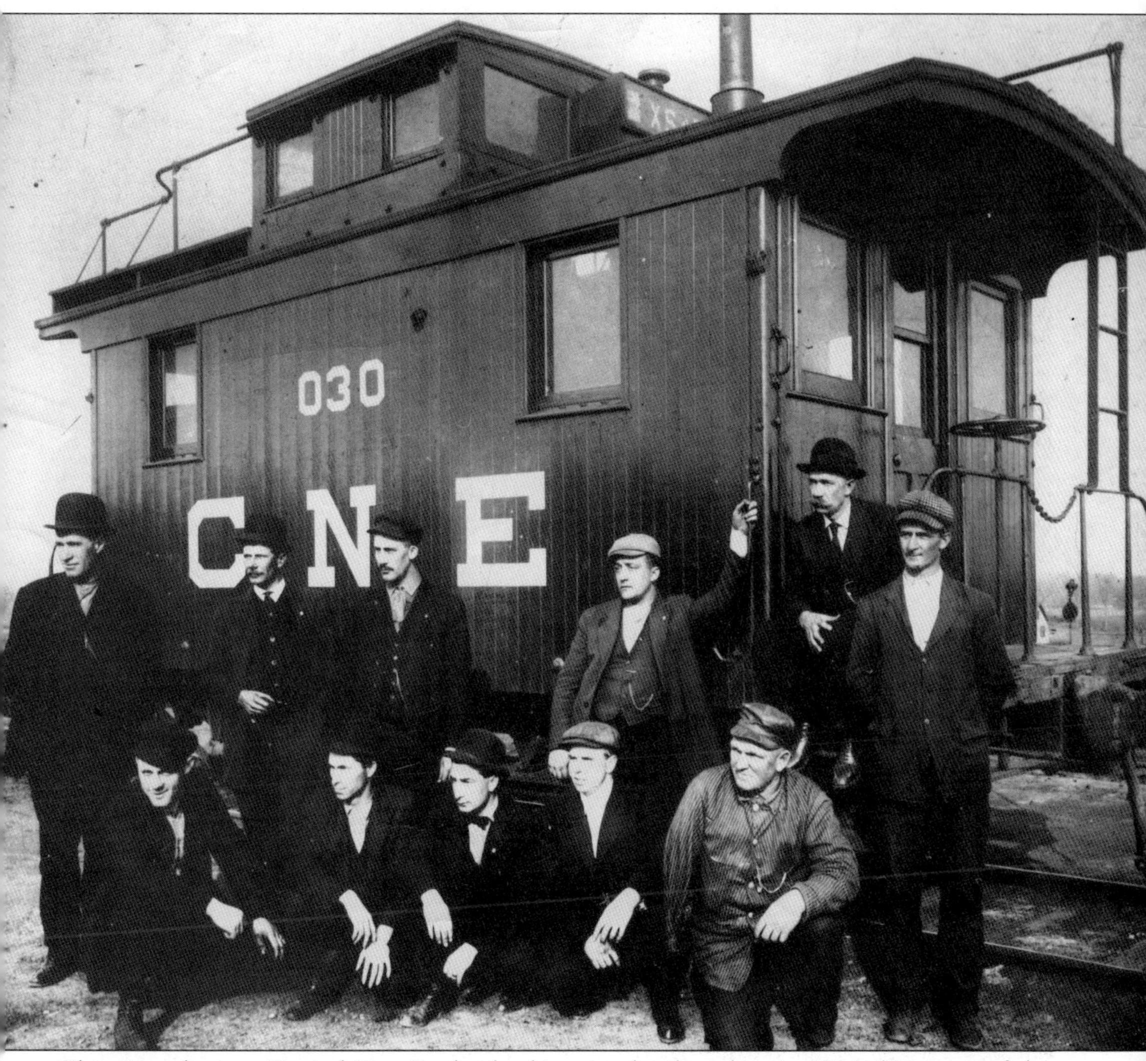

This view shows a Central New England caboose and rail workers in 1915. (Courtesy of the Maybrook Railroad Historical Society & Museum.)

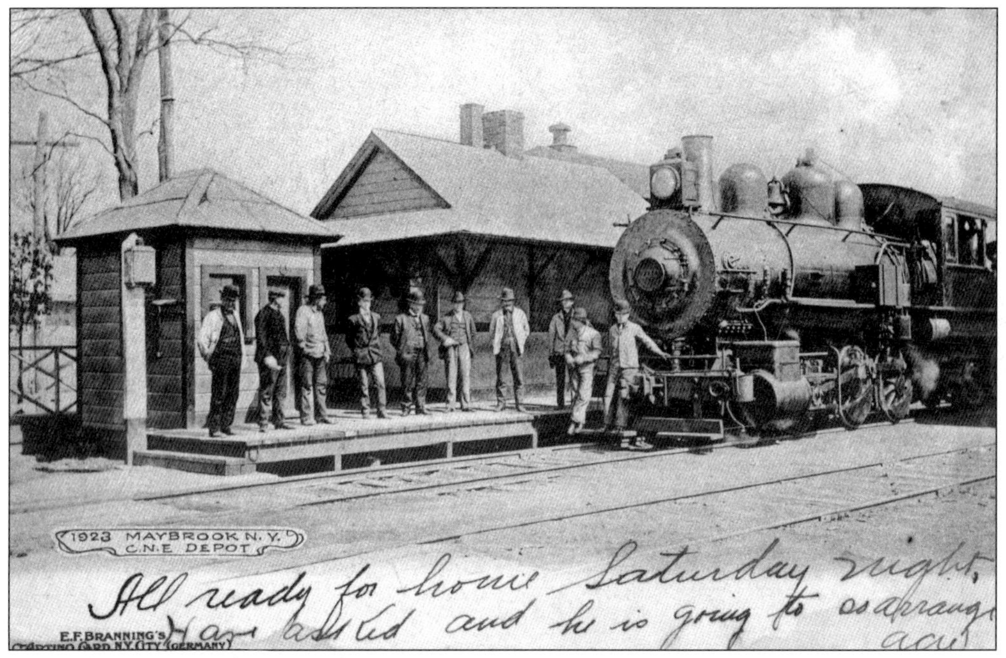

Pictured *c.* 1923 are the Central New England depot and ticket office in Maybrook. (Courtesy of Eric Kruger.)

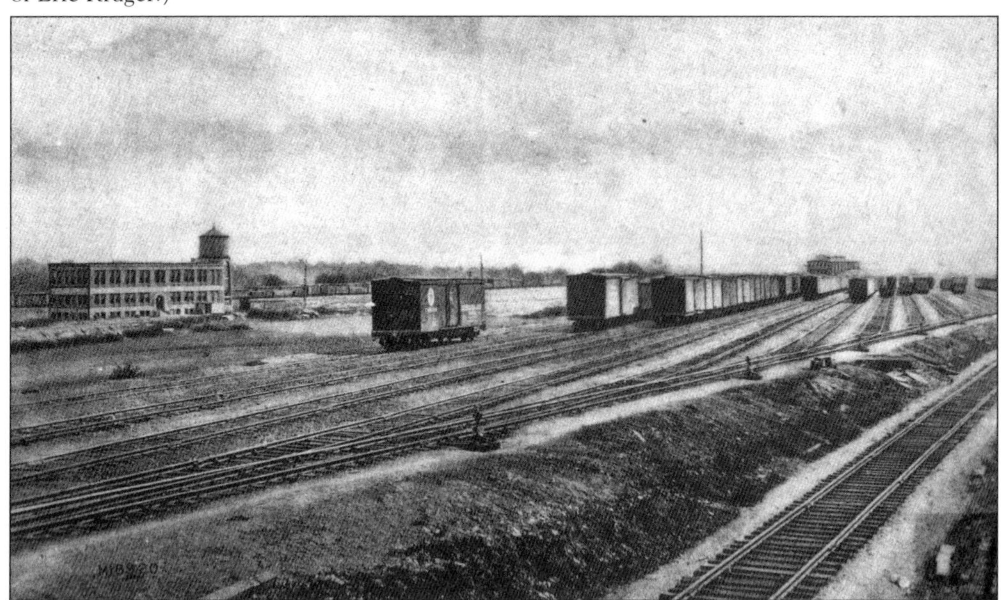

As the New York, New Haven, and Hartford Railroad began to transform its rail system into the largest switching terminal east of Chicago, Illinois, immigrants in large numbers migrated from New York City to the Hudson Valley. The national policy of the United States after World War I was to reduce the number of immigrants entering the county. Regardless of the limitations on this specific group, numbers of Italian immigrants came to Maybrook in search of jobs as laborers working on the rail line. With this additional labor, tracks were expanded and services were developed in the 1920s. Shown are the railroad offices and yards *c.* 1925. (Courtesy of Eric Kruger.)

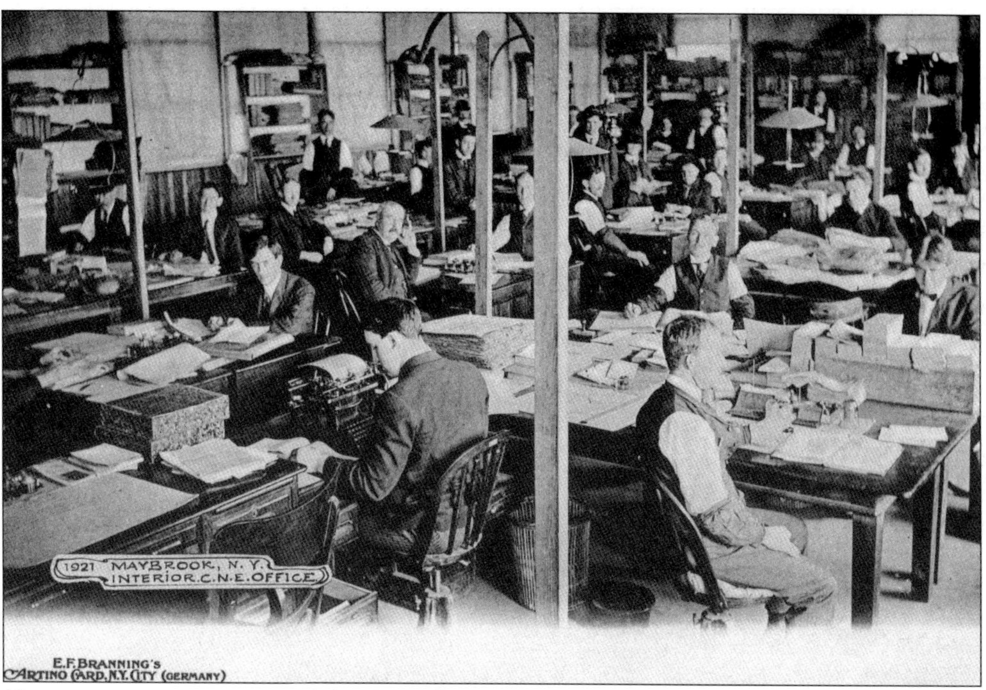

Shown are an interior view of the Central New England Railroad offices *c.* 1921 (above) and a *c.* 1922 view of the railroad's freight yard in Maybrook (below). (Courtesy of Eric Kruger.)

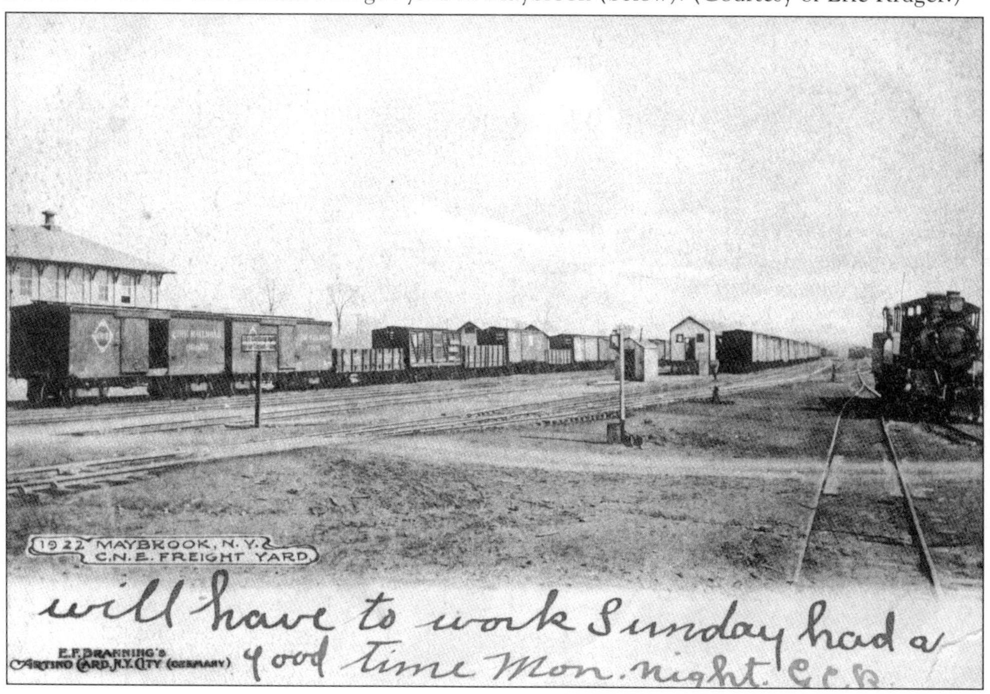

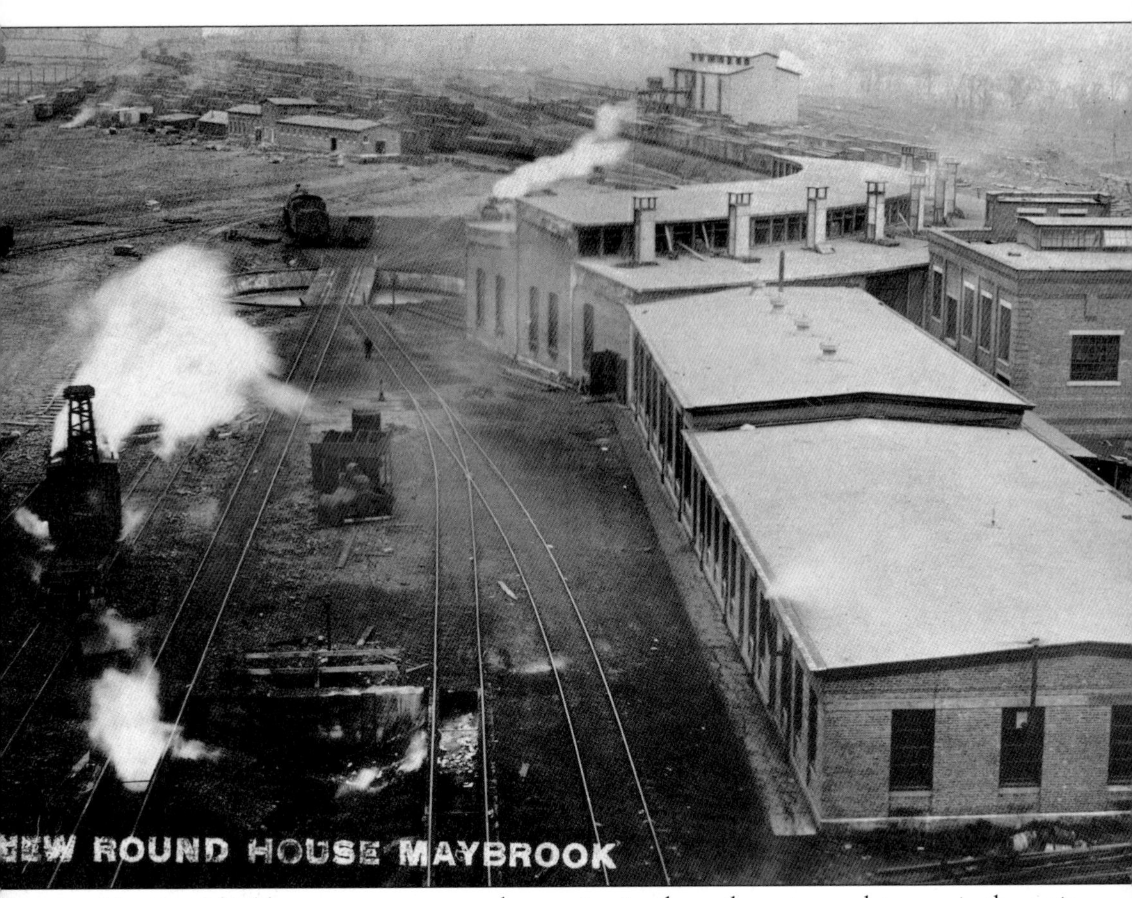

Numerous buildings were constructed to maintain the rail service and to repair the train engines and cars. There were boxcar shops, an engine house, machine shops, carpenter shops, rebuilding shops, boxcar repair shops, and a steam engine rebuilding shop. The most significant improvement under the management of the New York, New Haven, and Hartford Railroad was the new roundhouse and turntable, shown *c.* the 1920s. (Courtesy of Robert Kidd.)

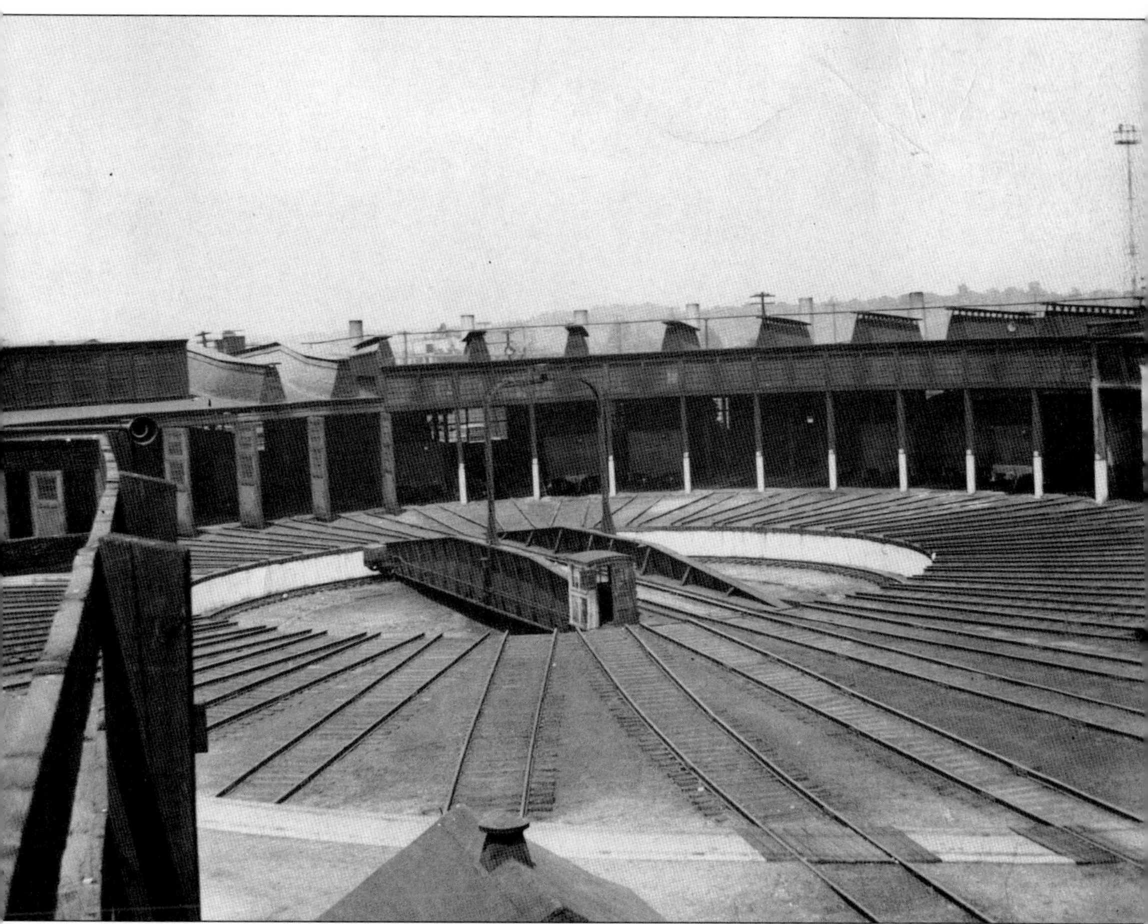

The Maybrook roundhouse increased from 9 stalls to 27 stalls. The turntable was enlarged to almost 100 feet in length. The Maybrook rail yard had 20 eastbound classification tracks and 20 westbound classification tracks. The switching terminal had a length of three miles and a width of one mile. It has been estimated that if the rails of eastbound and westbound tracks were laid in front of one another, the total track length of 75 miles could hold some 5,000 rail cars. Six major railroads brought their engines and cars into Maybrook for transfer and service in the period from the 1920s to the 1970s. This is a close-up view of the roundhouse, taken c. the 1920s. (Courtesy of The Maybrook Railroad Historical Society & Museum.)

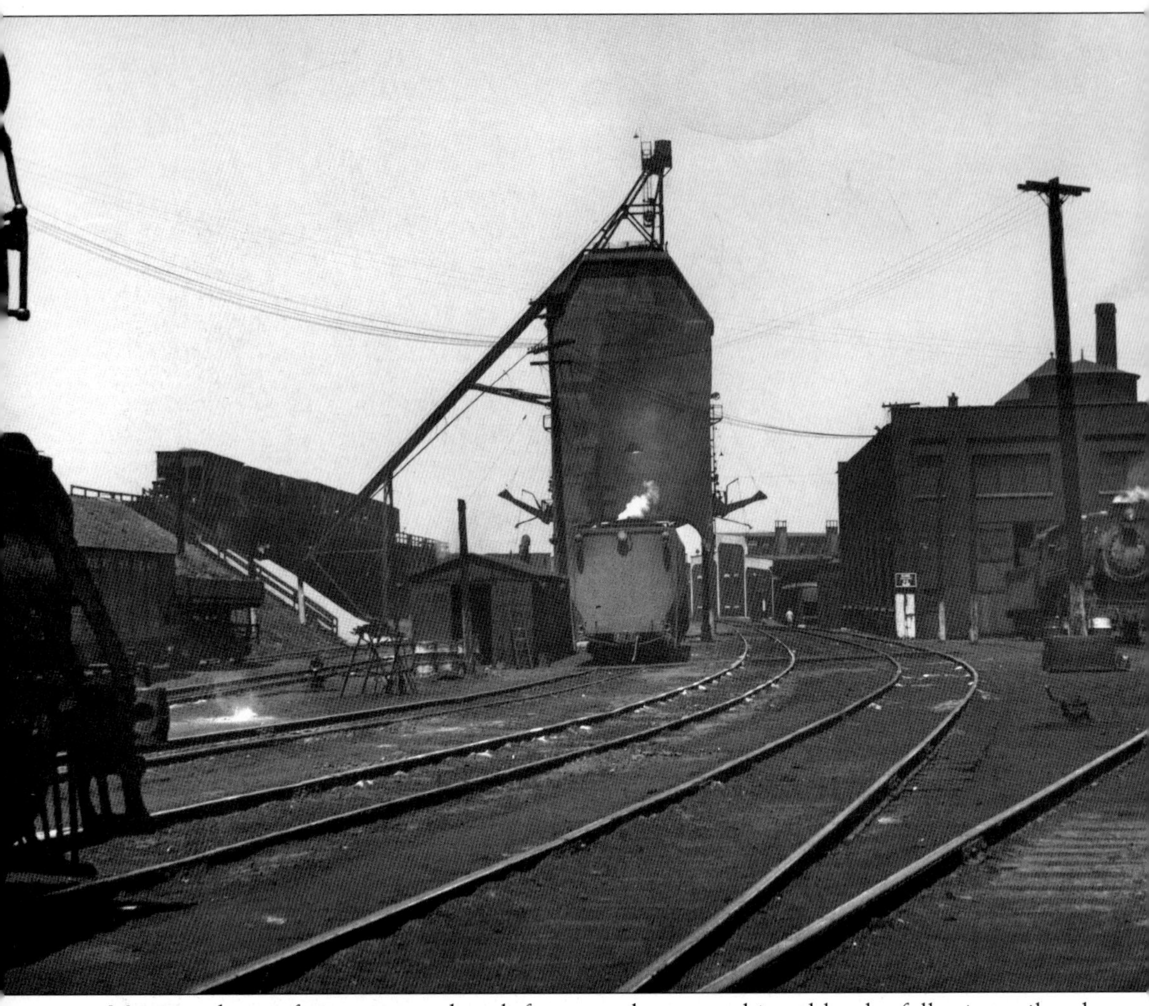

Many products—fruit, meat, and coal, for example—were shipped by the following railroads from as far west as California to Chicago and then routed across Pennsylvania to Maybrook and then on to Connecticut and Massachusetts: Erie-Lackawanna (E & L), Ontario and Western (O & W), Lehigh-New England (LNE), Central of New Jersey (CNJ), Lehigh and Hudson (L & H), and Pennsylvania. The photograph shows the coaling station and sandpit at the rail yard in Maybrook *c.* the 1940s. (Courtesy of the Maybrook Railroad Historical Society & Museum.)

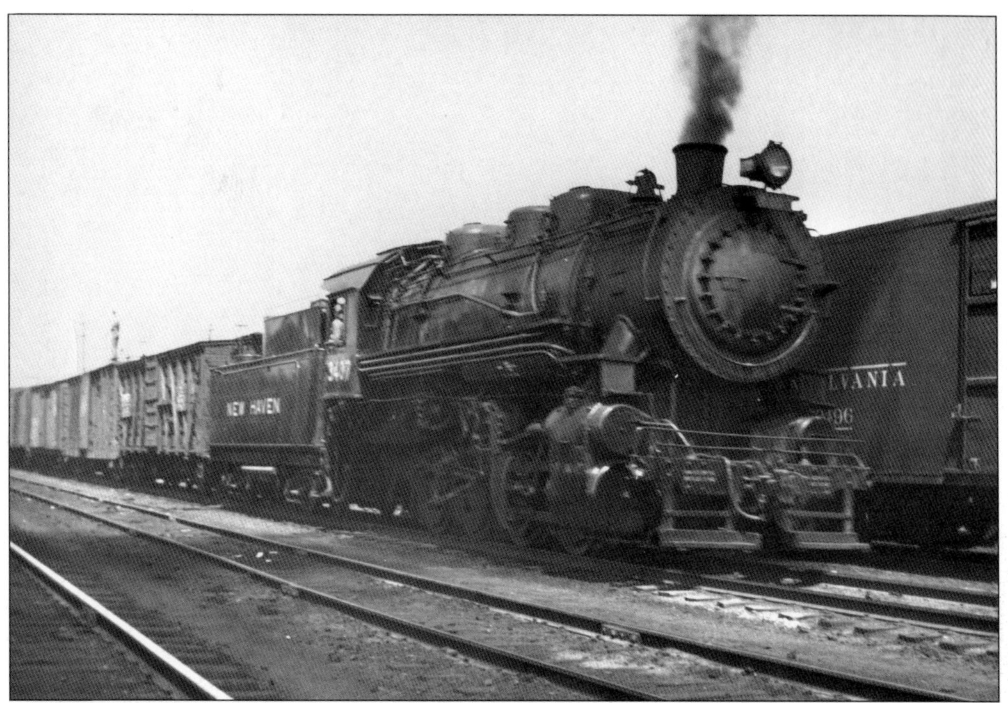

An engine with boxcars leaves the rail yard at Maybrook in the 1940s. (Courtesy of the Maybrook Railroad Historical Society & Museum.)

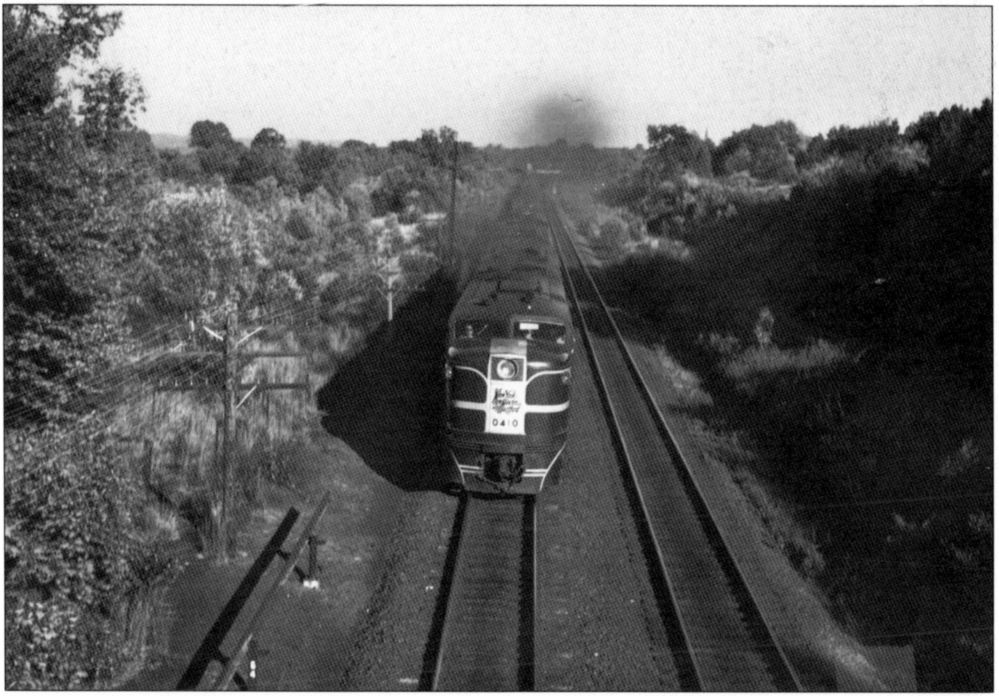

This is a view of the New York, New Haven, and Hartford Railroad in Maybrook *c.* 1954. (Photograph by Peter C. McLachlin, courtesy of the Maybrook Railroad Historical Society & Museum.)

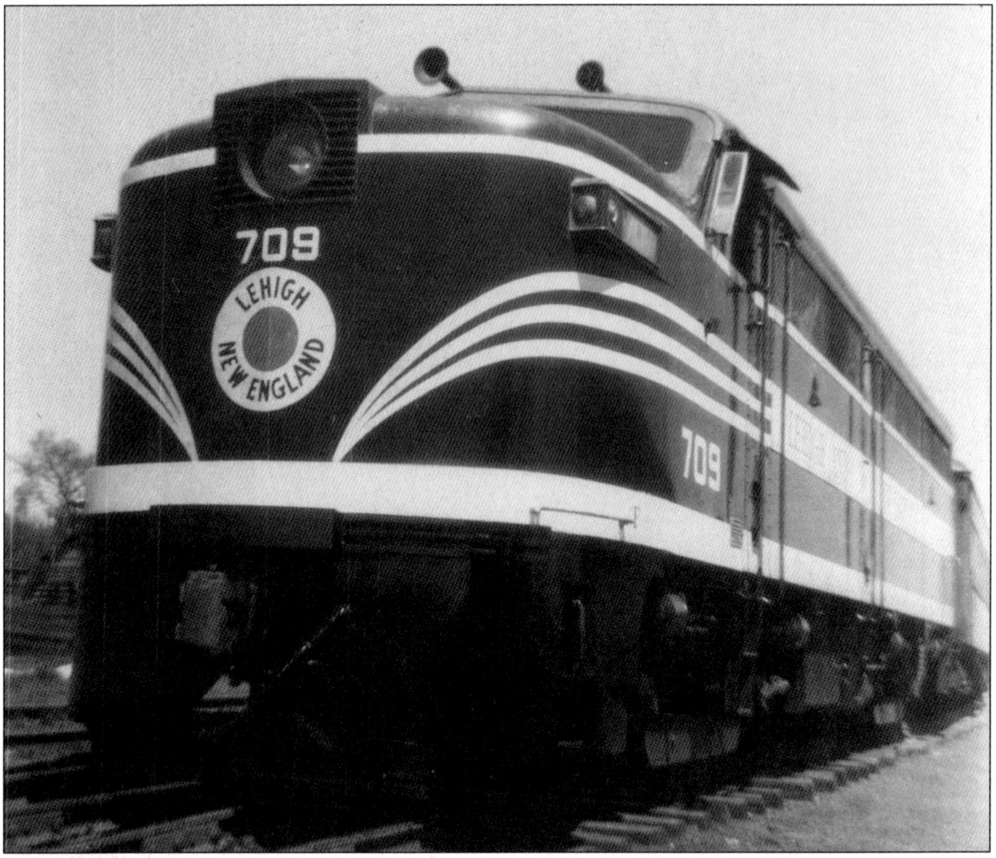

Shown in Maybrook are a Lehigh and New England Railroad train (above, *c.* 1957) and an Erie-Lackawanna Railroad train (below, *c.* the 1950s). (Courtesy of the Maybrook Railroad Historical Society & Museum.)

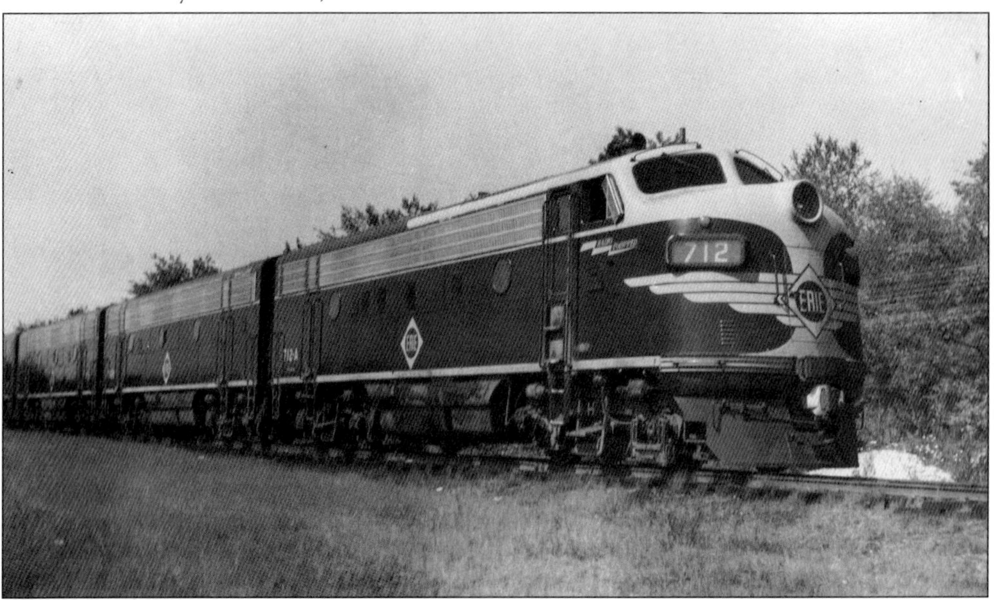

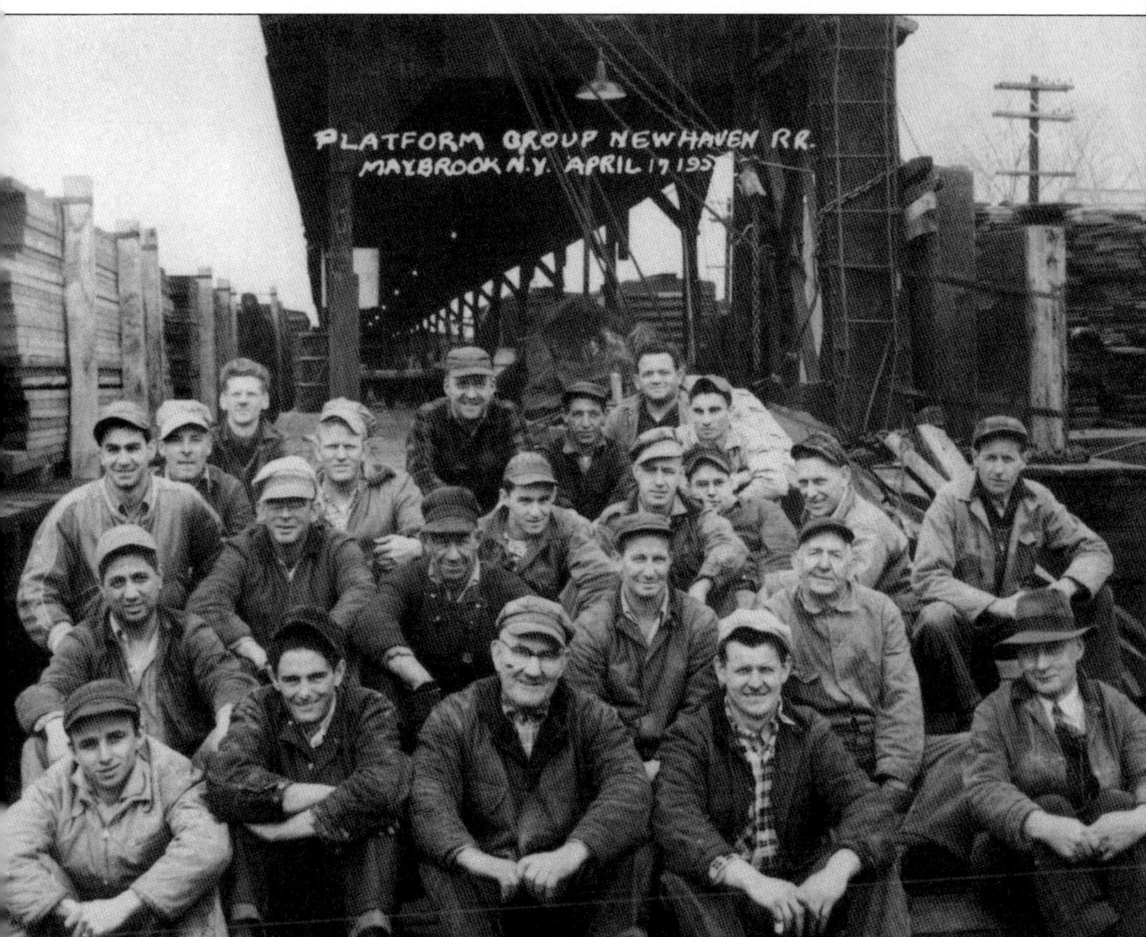

During the Great Depression, many of the workers were able to maintain their jobs because of the importance of the rail system. Maybrook became the "Gateway to the East." Trains from as far west as California, as well as the major rail terminal in Chicago, Illinois, were serviced and transferred in the Maybrook rail yard. During World War II, some 1,500 employees worked for the New York, New Haven, and Hartford Railroad. During the 1940s, the rail yard switched or transferred 54 trains in a period of 24 hours. Part of the success of the system was the effectiveness of the central office to coordinate the transfers, as well as the employees who through hard work accomplished such a monumental feat. Shown are platform workers of the New York, New Haven, and Hartford Railroad c. the 1950s. (Courtesy of the Maybrook Railroad Historical Society & Museum.)

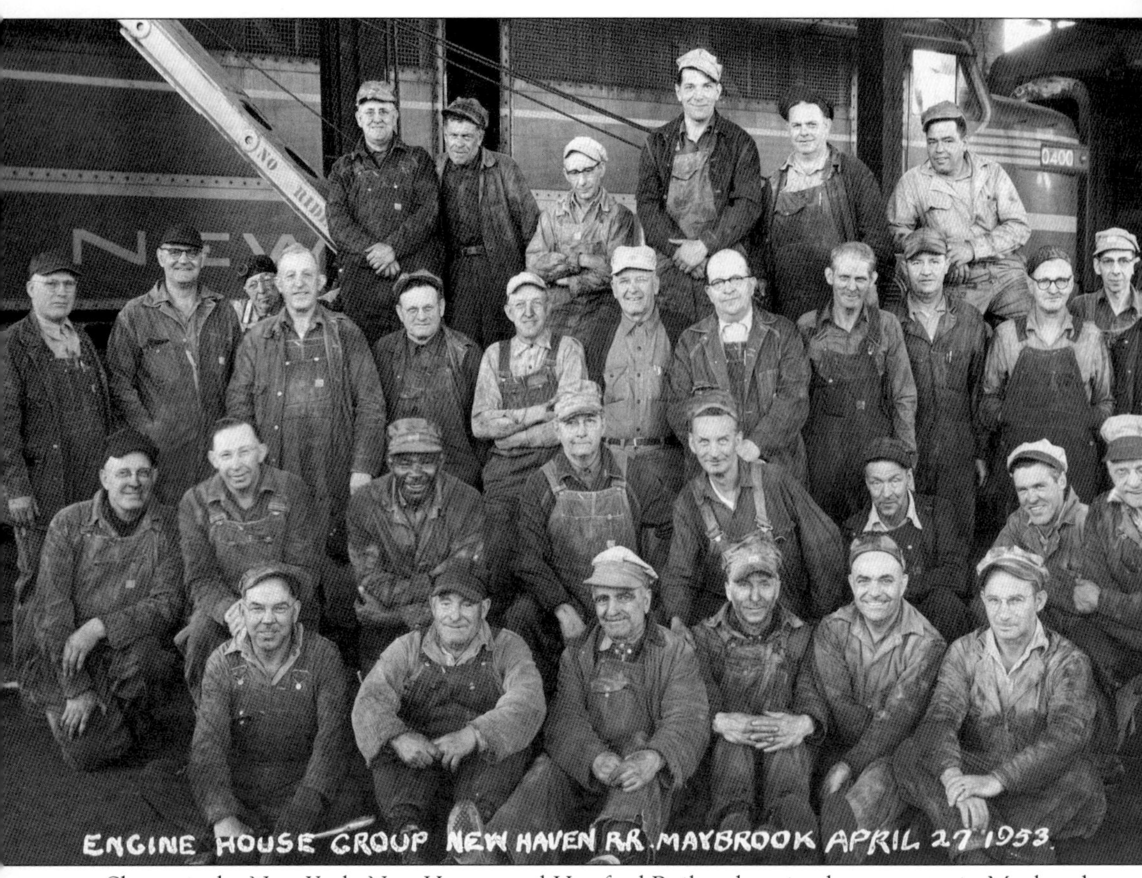

Shown is the New York, New Haven, and Hartford Railroad engine house group in Maybrook on April 27, 1953. On that day the group transferred and reassembled a total of 3,491 cars. (Courtesy of Cindy Yanello Badendyck.)

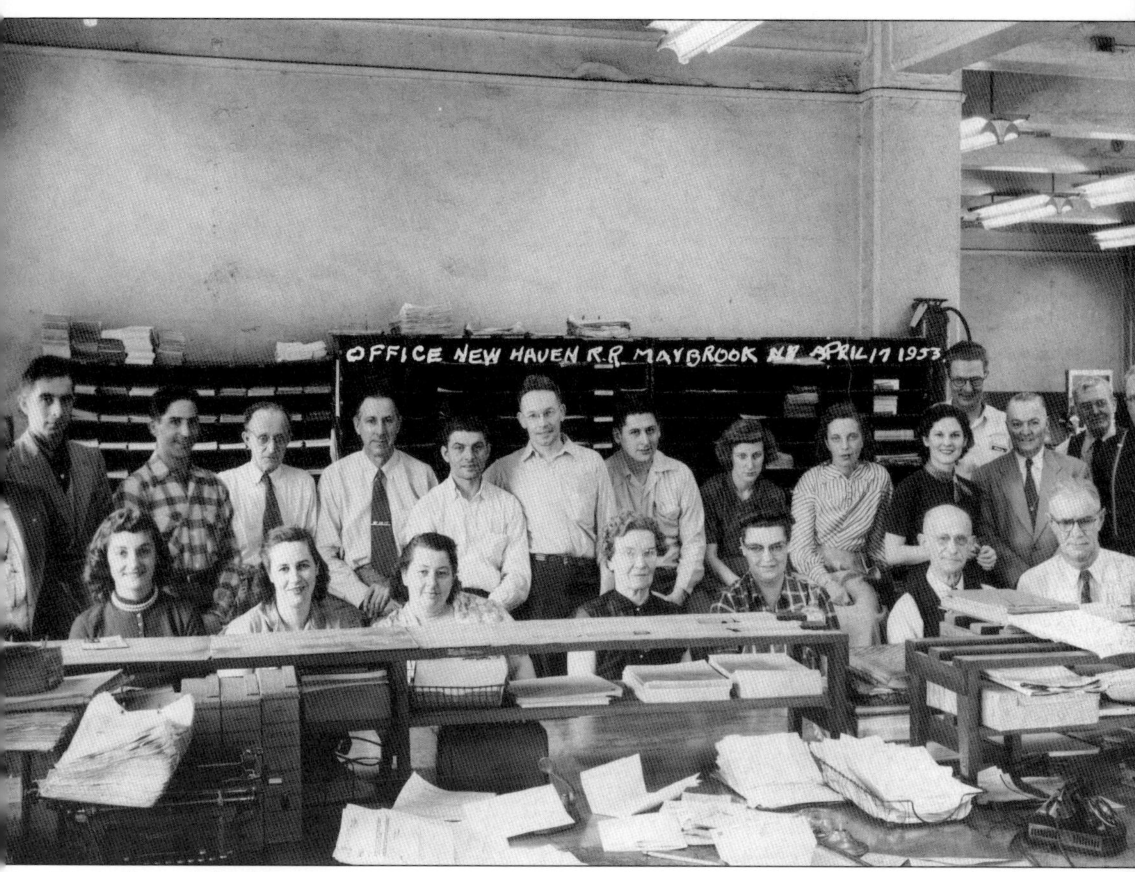

The office of the New York, New Haven, and Hartford Railroad in Maybrook is pictured c. 1953. The switching yards had one main purpose: "The switching yards were designed in such a way so as to keep the cars moving constantly in the same direction until their final arrival at the opposite end of the terminal where it would await movement to the final destination. Trains arriving at the terminal from the West would be left in the east bound receiving yard where they would be pushed over a gravity hump, and continue moving eastward into a Classification yard and then gathered together with other cars destined for New England destinations and placed in a train in the east bound departure yards. The administrative office, keeping records of the car movement, would be situated in the terminal . . ." —Albert Alexander, *The Birth and Death of the Maybrook Switching Terminal,* pages 3–4.

During World War II, troop trains passed through the Maybrook yards. Trains moving on the eastbound track brought young soldiers to the docks on New England ports to be embarked on U.S. naval transports to the Atlantic theater in North Africa, Sicily, Italy, and Europe. On some occasions, prisoner-of-war trains passed through the Maybrook yards, carrying men and young boys from the European theater in 1944 and 1945, destined for prisoner-of-war camps in the interior of the United States. Some of the boys were only 14 or 15 years old. From 1942 to 1945, mass production of war munitions, weapons, and food supplies was needed, and additional workers were hired from surrounding communities, including the village of Walden. (Courtesy of Jennie Gesso.)

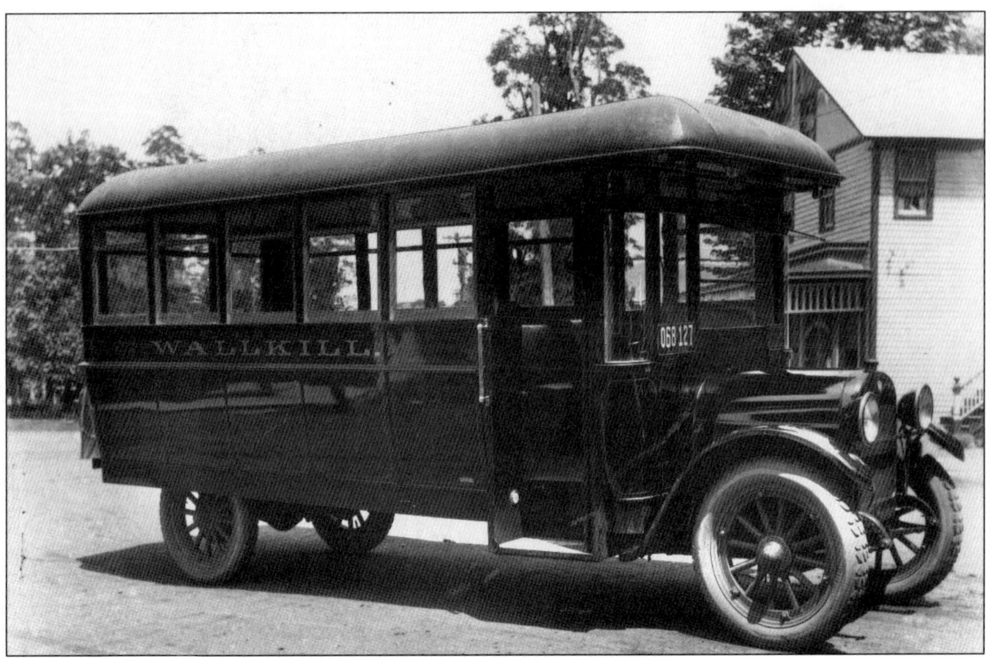

The Wallkill bus, which had existed since the 1920s and 1930s, was used to transport workers from Walden to Maybrook. (Courtesy of Marcus Millspaugh.)

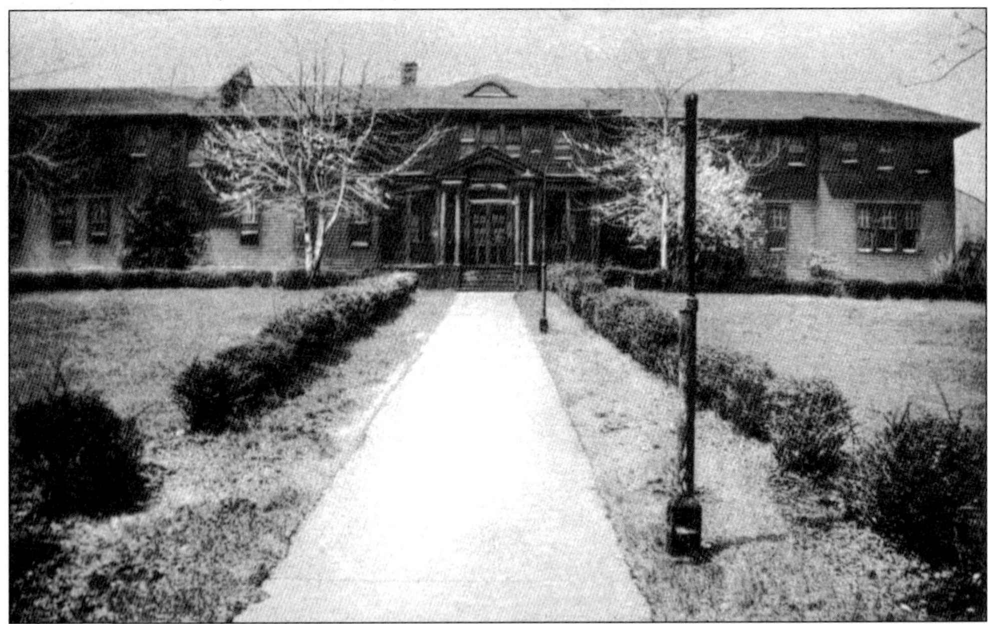

The New Haven Railroad built this YMCA, with bedding accommodations and a gymnasium, c. the 1930s. The YMCA accommodated the growing number of people in Maybrook, especially rail workers needing a place to stay overnight when transferring from one train to another, westbound to eastbound and eastbound to westbound. Employees lived in Orange County, Ulster County, Sullivan County, and Dutchess County. A passenger train from Poughkeepsie transferred workers from Dutchess County to Maybrook in Orange County. The train was referred to as the Scoot. (Courtesy of Roby Petzold.)

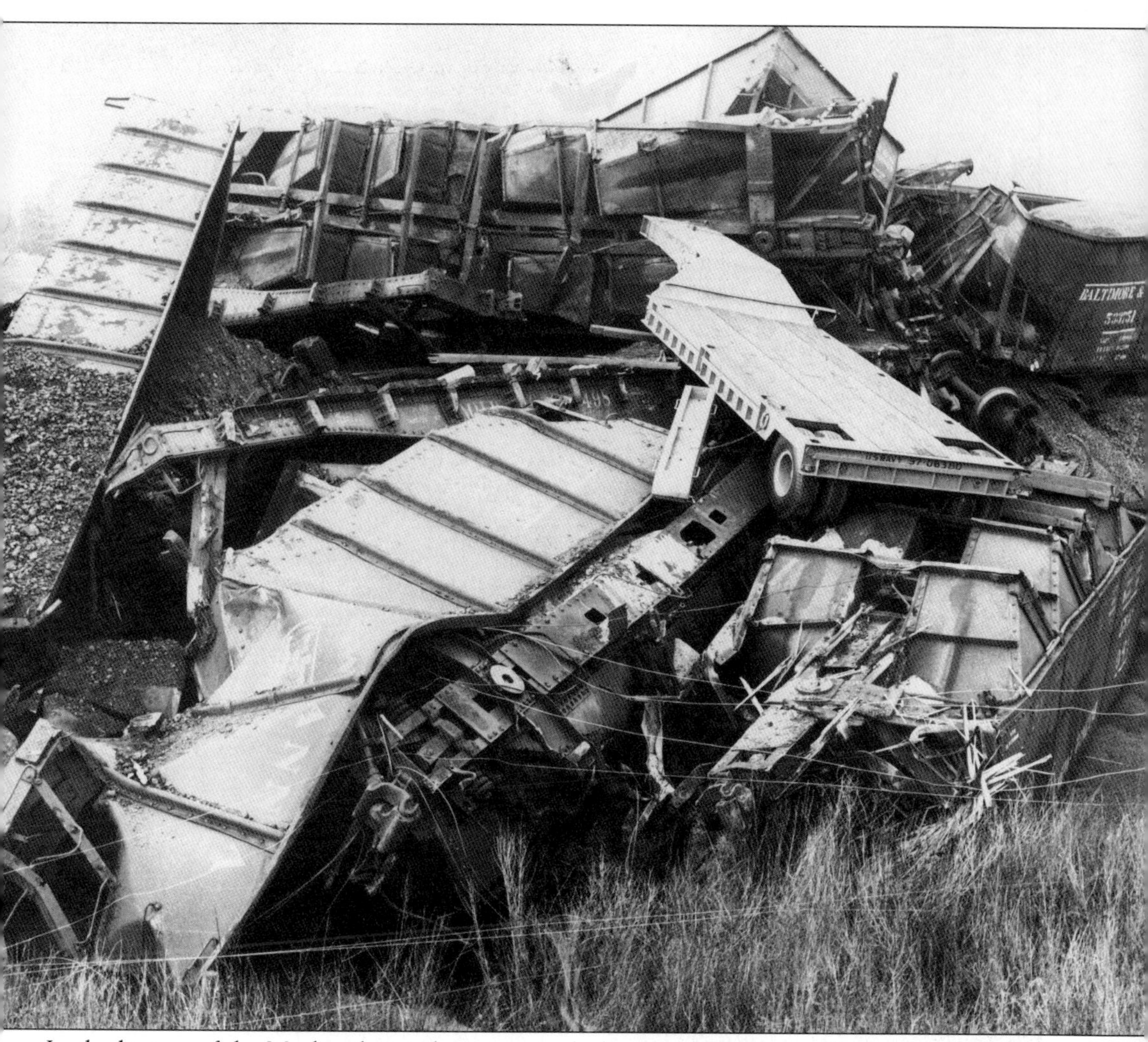

In the history of the Maybrook switching terminal, there were positive and negative moments that brought a great deal of laughter and a great deal of pain. There were episodes of danger and destruction. Numerous lives were lost or physically impaired in the course of the labors of the men of the Maybrook switching terminal. One such accident occurred in the 1950s, when an eastbound and a westbound train collided in Walden. (Courtesy of the Maybrook Railroad Historical Society & Museum.)

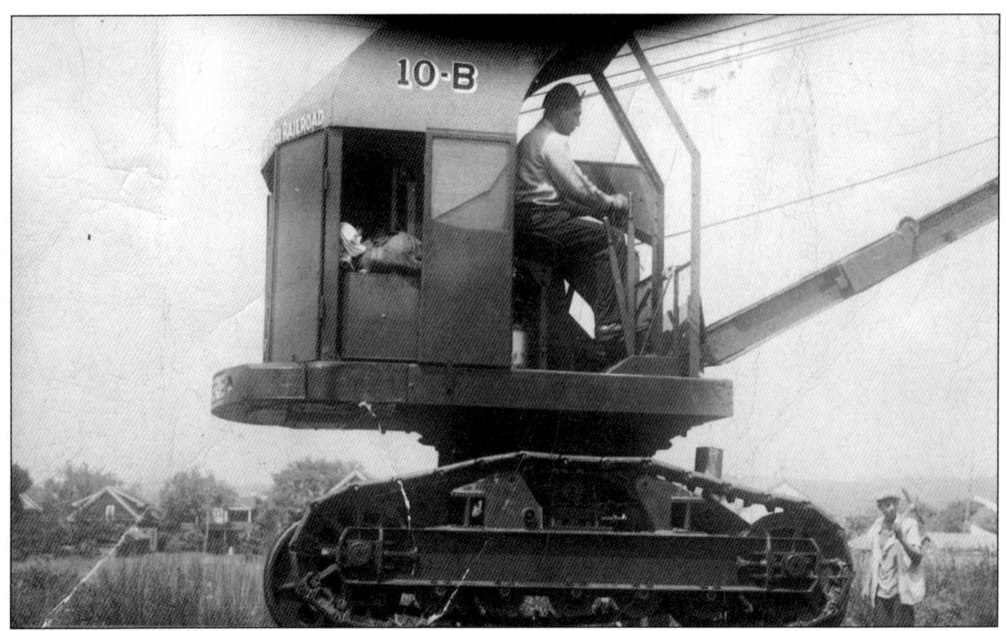

A special crane with a big hook was devised on a railroad car. The hook could lift a derailed car and take it completely off the track or place it back on the track. Joseph Yanello is shown working the railroad crane in Maybrook *c.* the 1940s. (Courtesy of Cindy Yanello Badendyck.)

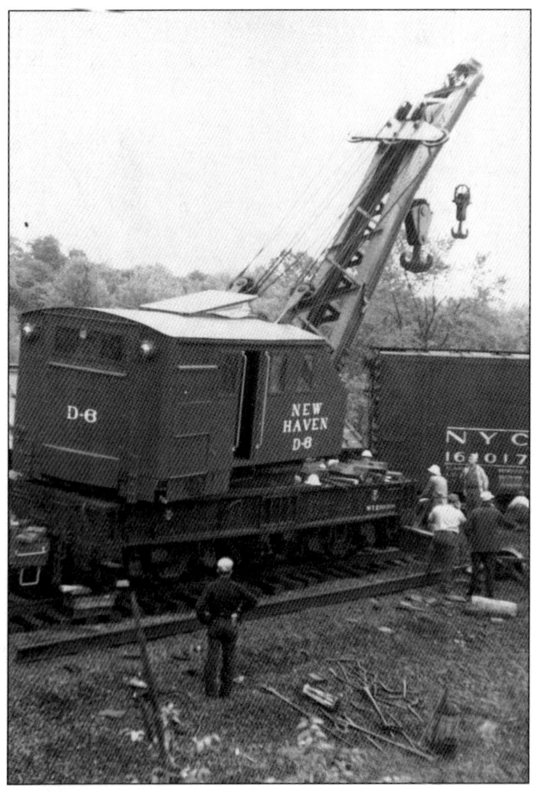

Repair crews were constantly at work, inspecting rails, switches, and ties as well as the amount of sand for traction that each train carried and the level of compressed air for the rail brakes, known as air brakes, originally developed by George Westinghouse in 1869. Some residents of the village of Maybrook were enrolled as support staff for maintenance of the terminal. After winter storms, Maybrook boys would be hired for excellent wages to shovel the snow and clear the switches in the rail yard. Pictured in the 1940s is the railroad crane with the big hook. (Courtesy of the Maybrook Railroad Historical Society & Museum.)

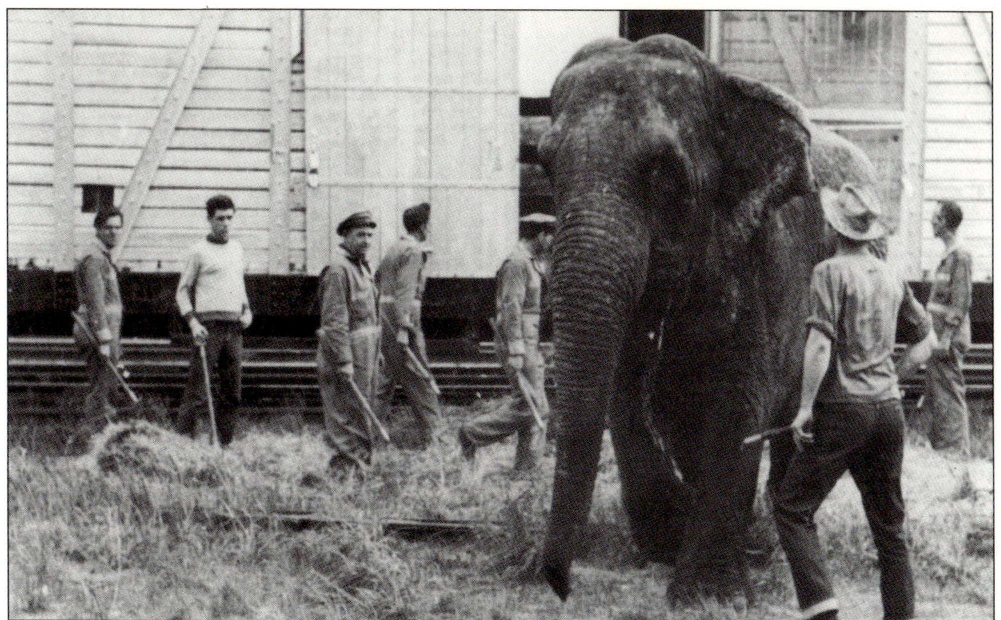

Residents of the village of Maybrook did not have to go to Madison Square Garden in New York City to see the circus. Ringling Brothers and Barnum & Bailey Circus came once a year to the village of Maybrook, specifically the Maybrook switching terminal. When the circus came to any city, town, or village, it was a unique occasion. While the circus boxcars were being removed and reassembled, the circus people spent the day enjoying the residents and sites of the village. One of the major attractions for young children was the unloading of the elephants from the boxcars, as seen here *c.* the 1950s. (Courtesy of the Maybrook Railroad Historical Society & Museum.)

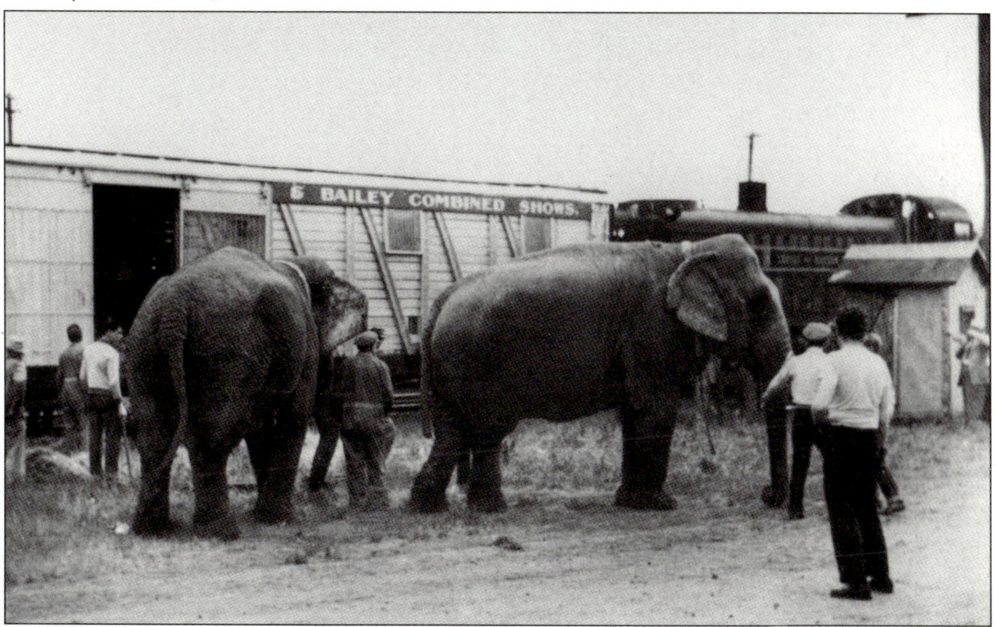

Several elephants are led away to a grazing area in Maybrook *c.* the 1950s. (Courtesy of the Maybrook Railroad Historical Society & Museum.)

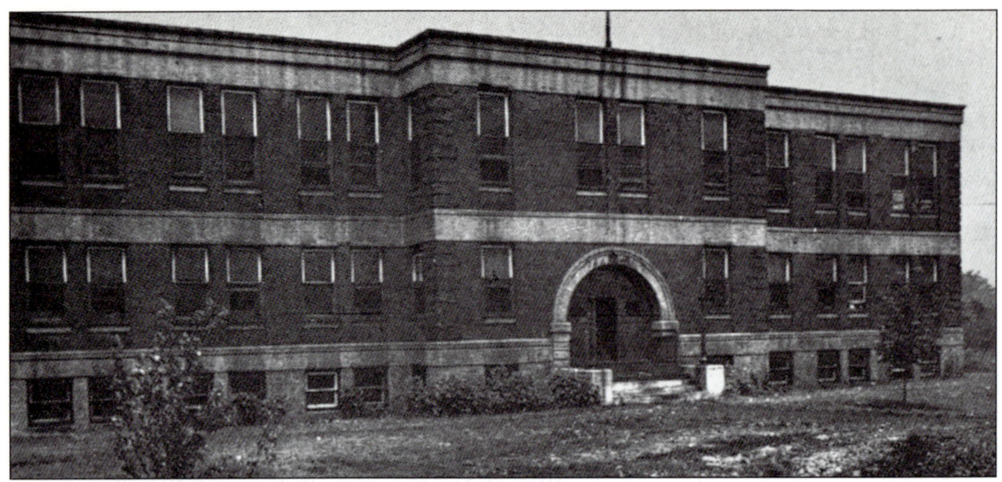

By the 1960s, the New York, New Haven, and Hartford Railroad had become part of the Pennsylvania Central Railroad, known as Penn Central. Most of the buildings that existed began to deteriorate by the early 1970s, and new facilities were expanded in the town of Selkirk. Shown is the administration building of the New York, New Haven, and Hartford Railroad *c.* the 1930s. (Courtesy of the Maybrook Chamber of Commerce.)

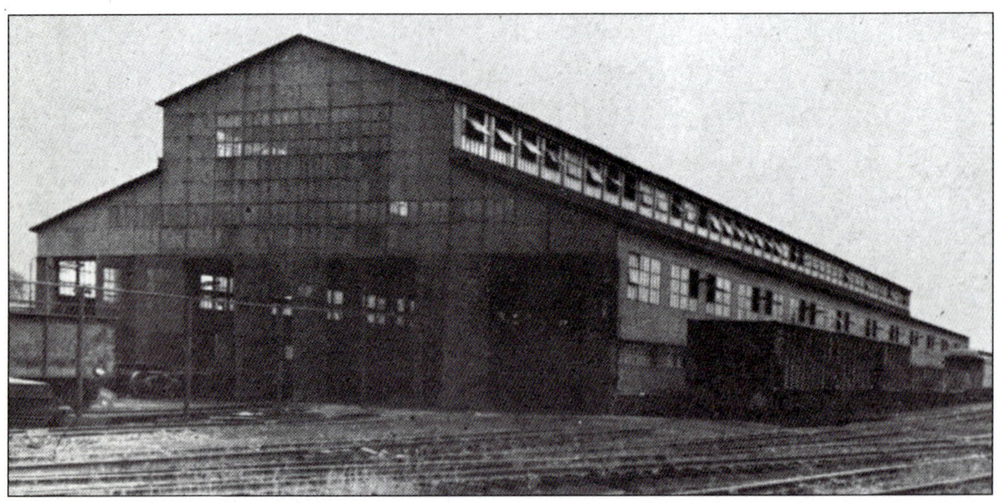

These were the car shops of the New York, New Haven, and Hartford Railroad *c.* the 1930s. (Courtesy of the Maybrook Chamber of Commerce.)

On May 8, 1974, a fire broke out on the Poughkeepsie Railroad Bridge. The bridge was more than 200 feet above the water and included parts of several Poughkeepsie streets. The bridge had a span of more than 6,500 feet in length. The fire consumed a 700-foot section of it. Fire departments were called to the scene but could do little because their ladders were not high enough to reach the tracks. Helicopters with water buckets and water cannons had not yet been invented. The amount of damage to the bridge was more than $200,000 (which today would be in excess of $1 million). The Poughkeepsie Railroad Bridge was sold for the nominal amount of $1 to Gordon Schreiber Miller. (Courtesy of the Maybrook Railroad Historical Society & Museum.)

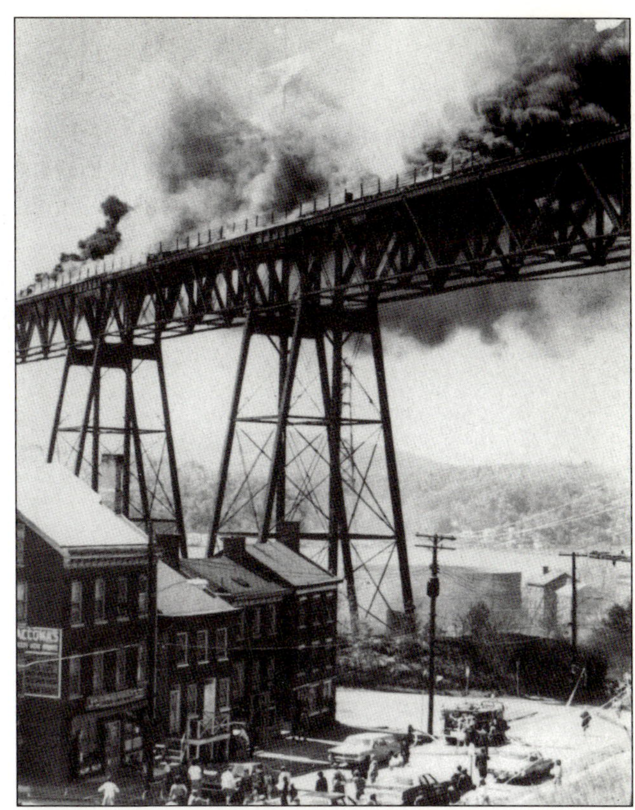

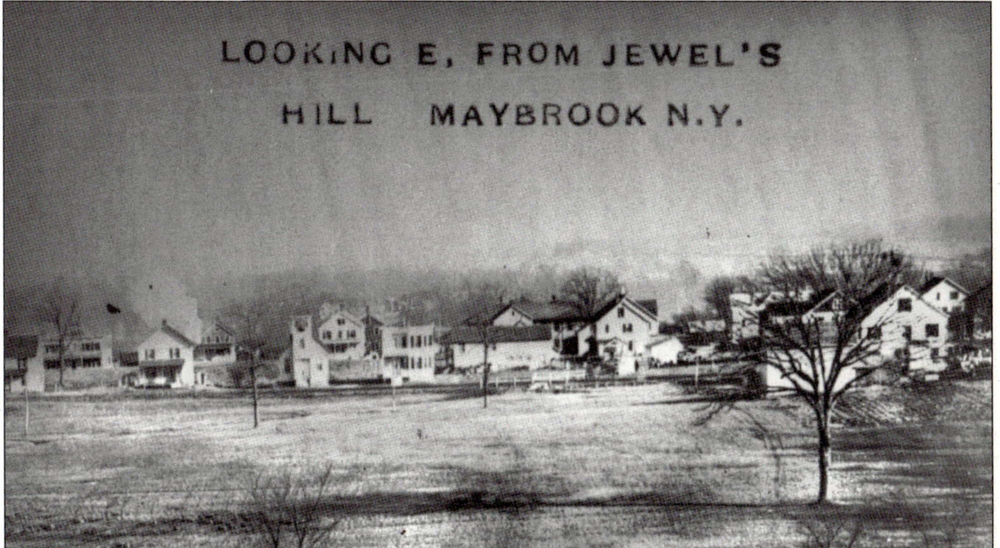

Life in a railroad town was filled with many hours of hard work but also many memories of the businesses and stores that served the needs of both the resident and the railroad worker. There were few buildings in Maybrook during the 1920s, but within several decades a commercial mercantile community developed that provided both the necessities and the comforts of the community. This view looks east from Jewell's Hill in Maybrook c. the 1920s. (Courtesy of Roby Petzold.)

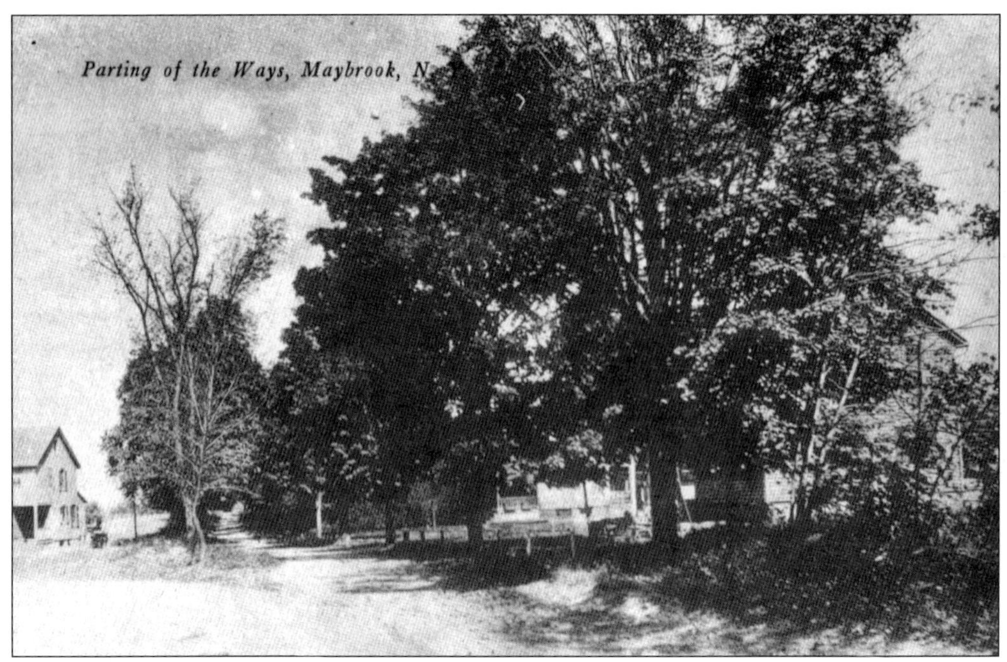

In the early years *c.* 1910, Maybrook was a farming community with more land and little housing. (Courtesy of Eric Kruger.)

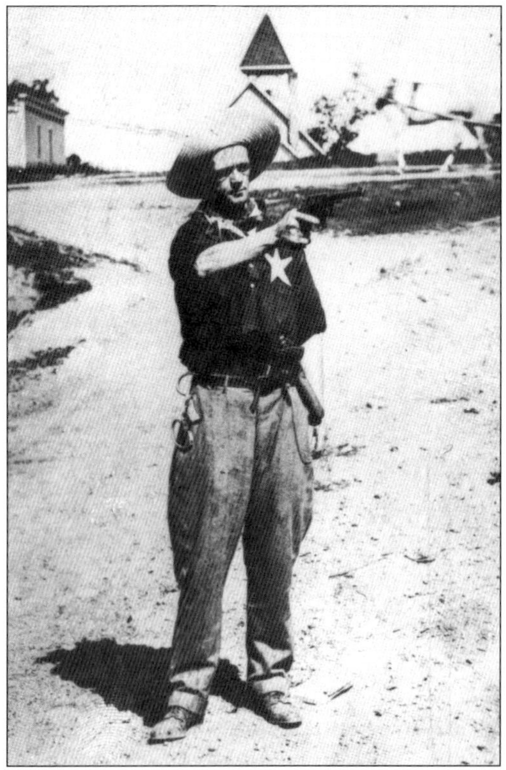

Life was very simple before Central New England's Harry Leonard, known as "Two Gun Harry," served as the Maybrook constable during the first decade of the 20th century. This picture was taken *c.* 1910. (Courtesy of Roby Petzold.)

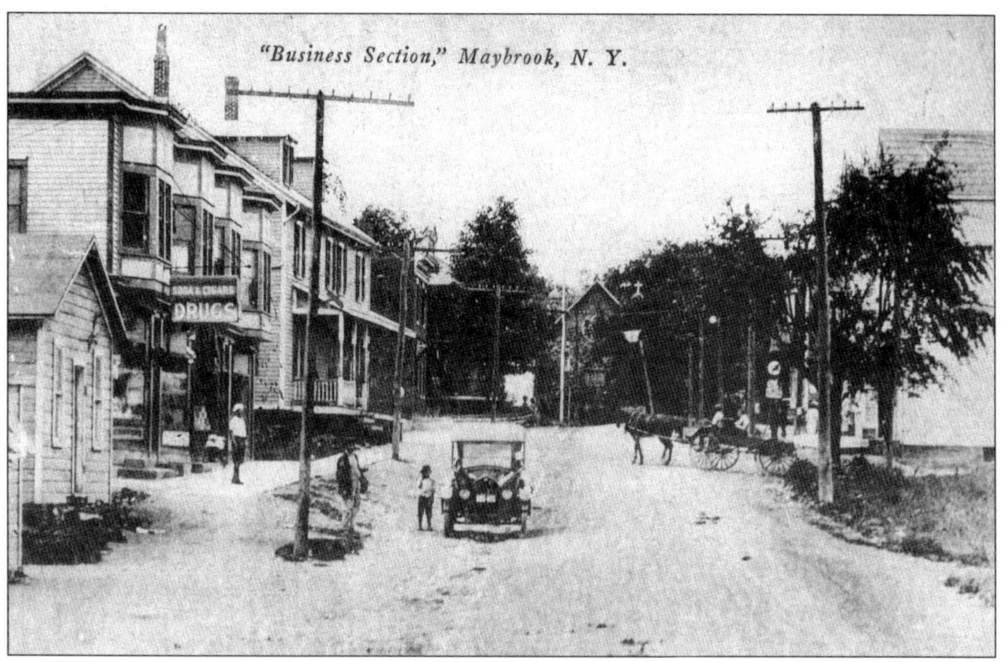

The business section of Maybrook, pictured *c.* 1924, was mostly on one side of the main street, Homestead Avenue, Route 208. There were only a few stores during the 1920s. (Courtesy of Eric Kruger.)

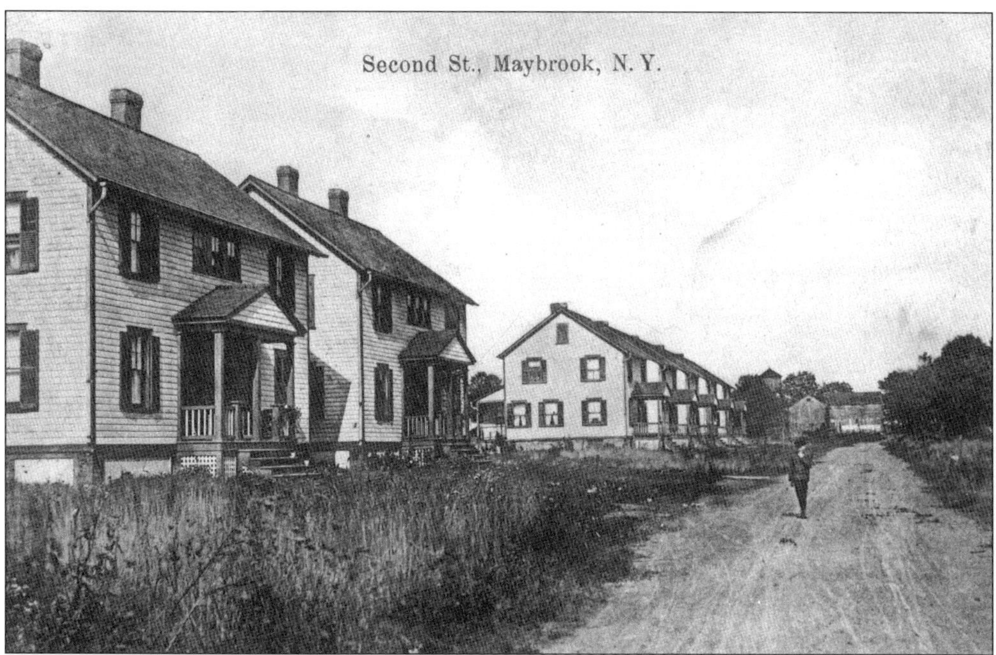

Housing for both the residents and the employees of Central New England Railroad was built along Second Street in the village of Maybrook. This photograph was taken *c.* 1909. (Courtesy of Eric Kruger.)

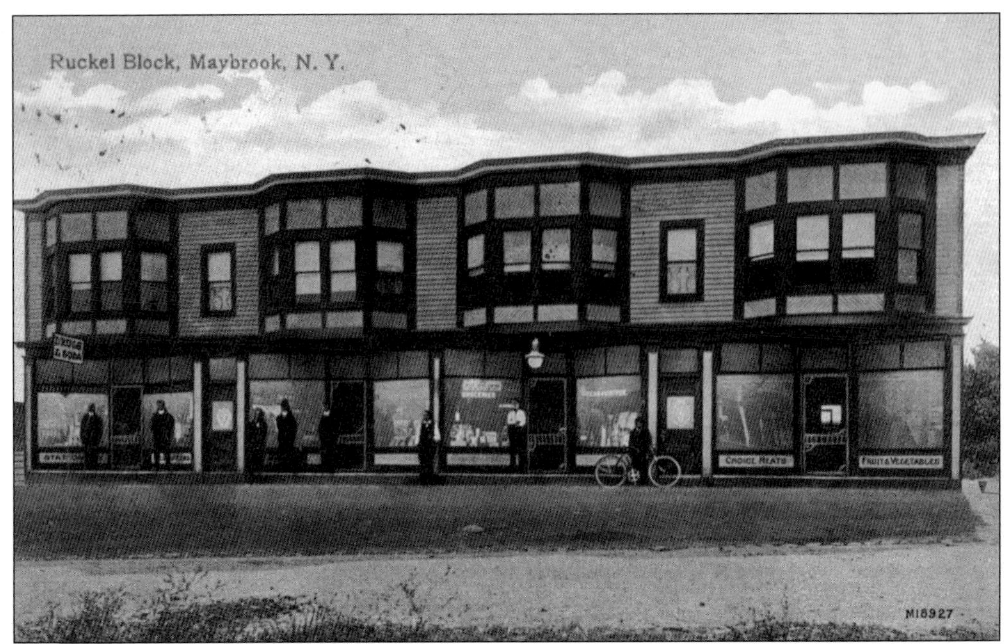

The Ruckel Block was the forerunner of the strip mall during the 1930s and 1940s. There were four businesses with apartments on the second floor. On the extreme left is the early home of Watts Drug Store, which was established by Glenn L. Watts in 1914. The photograph dates from the 1920s. (Courtesy of Eric Kruger.)

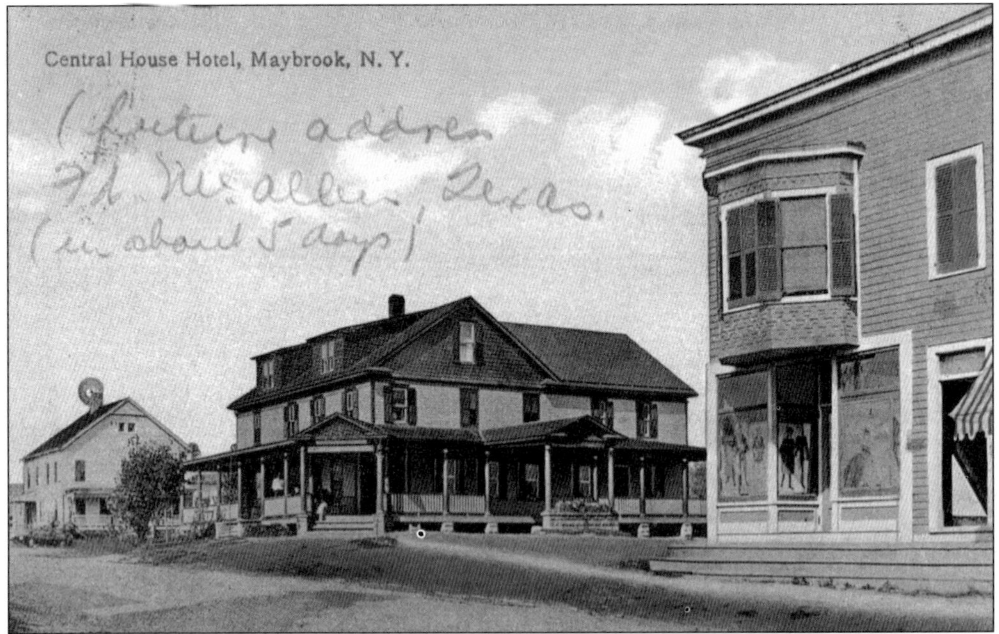

The village of Maybrook had more than a dozen bars, taverns, and restaurants, which catered to the resident, the visitor, and especially the hardworking railroad worker. The Central House Hotel, shown *c.* 1930, provided accommodations for visitors on their travels through the area, as well as for employees of the railroad who needed a place to stay overnight. (Courtesy of Eric Kruger.)

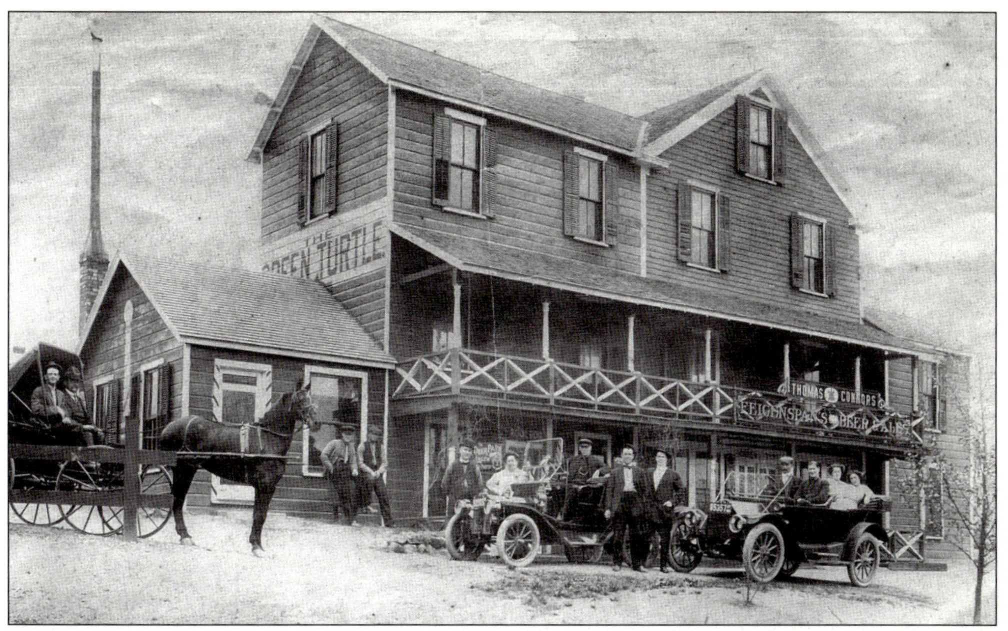

The Green Turtle Hotel, shown *c.* 1915, was another establishment that served visitors and others. Built in 1910 when the Central New England Railroad was established in Maybrook, it was owned by Thomas Conners. (Courtesy of Dan Saracino.)

MODERN MAYBROOK DINER

Highway 208 Maybrook, New York

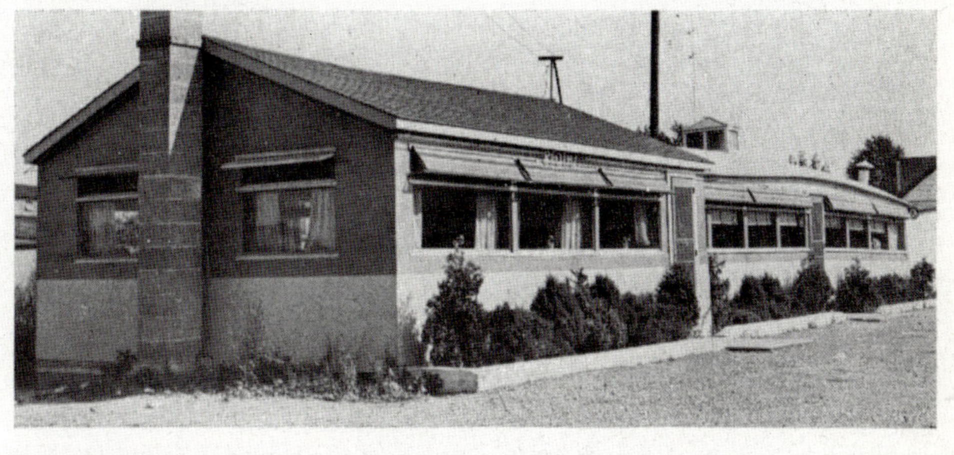

During the 1940s and 1950s, it was common to see some of the railroad employees at either the Modern Maybrook Diner, which was owned and operated by Frank "Pete" Bullis, or the Maybrook Inn, which was owned by Bob Sadler. Residents would go for pizza, sandwiches, or a full-course dinner at the Bastianos' Blue Mirror Restaurant. Walter Johnston's was another restaurant that was popular with workers who stopped in for a sandwich or a piece of pie with coffee. The photograph shows the Modern Maybrook Diner *c.* the 1950s. (Courtesy of the Maybrook Chamber of Commerce.)

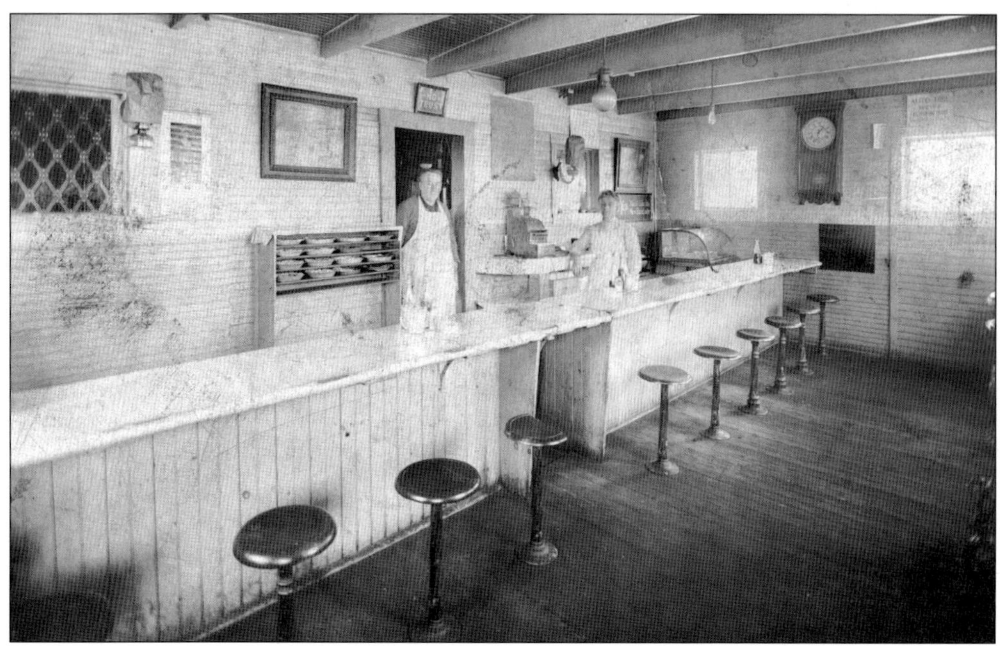

Martha Johnson's Beanery was another eating place *c.* the 1930s. (Courtesy of June Hess.)

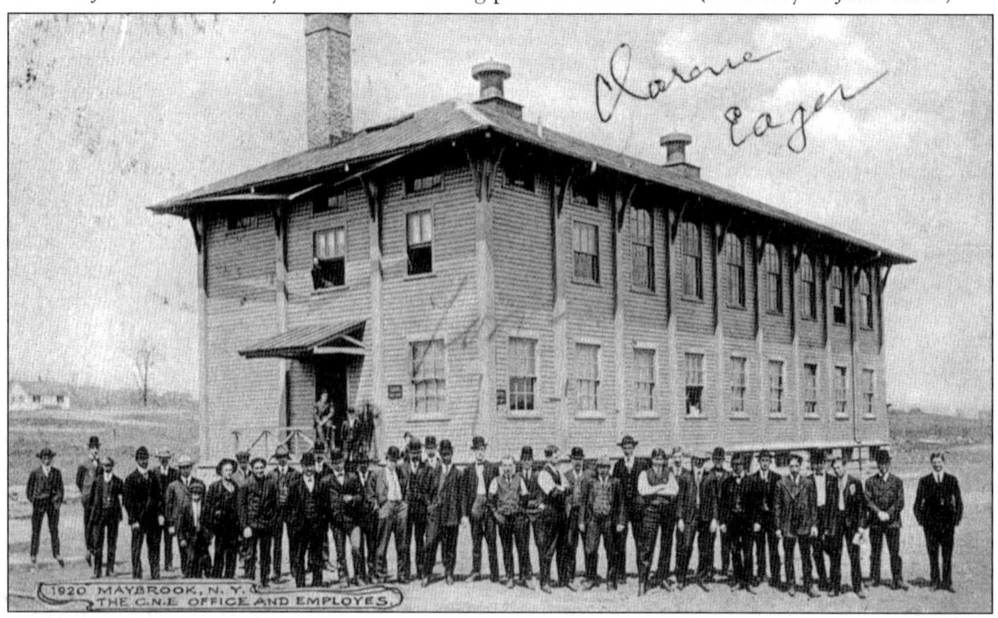

The growth of the railroad industry helped to establish numerous businesses within the community. Some of these were simple market stores while others were small industries that employed residents of the community. One of the larger businesses was a textile manufacturing company, Brook May, which was "Maybrook" in reverse. The top floor of the old Central New England office building was converted into a textile garment company. Clothes made here were sold in fashionable stores in New York City. The company had a reputation for high quality. Many of the garments were made by the working women of Maybrook. This is a *c.* 1920s close-up view of the Central New England office building, which later became Brook May. (Courtesy of Roby Petzold.)

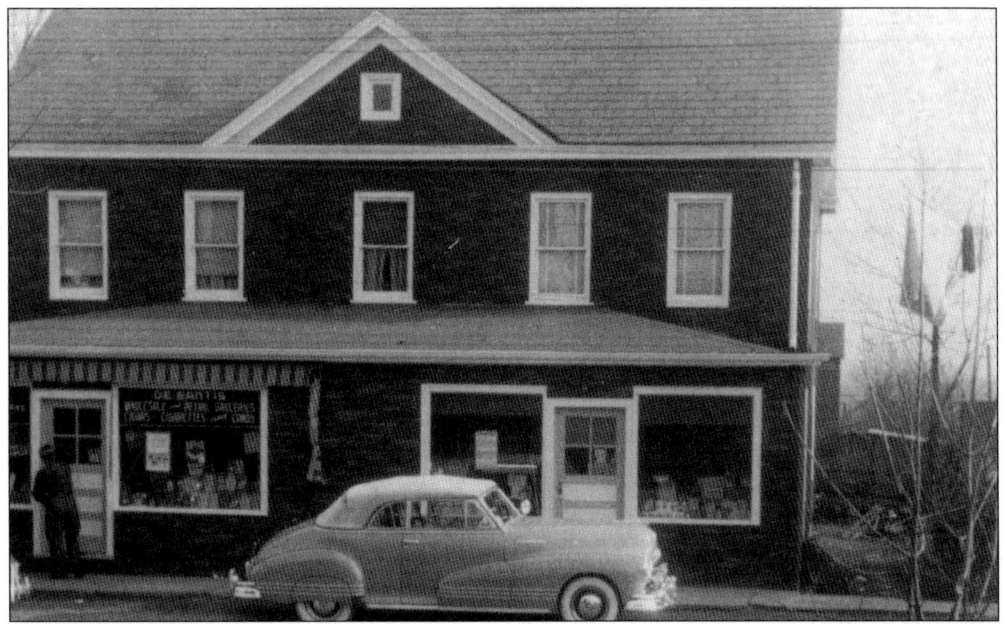

There were numerous bars and grills such as the Yellow Dog, the Red Onion, the House of Blazes, the Blue Goose, the Wallace House, and the Blue Mirror. Aside from them there were grocery stores and meat markets, such as De Santis Grocery Store, pictured *c.* the 1950s. (Courtesy of Cindy Yanello Badendyck.)

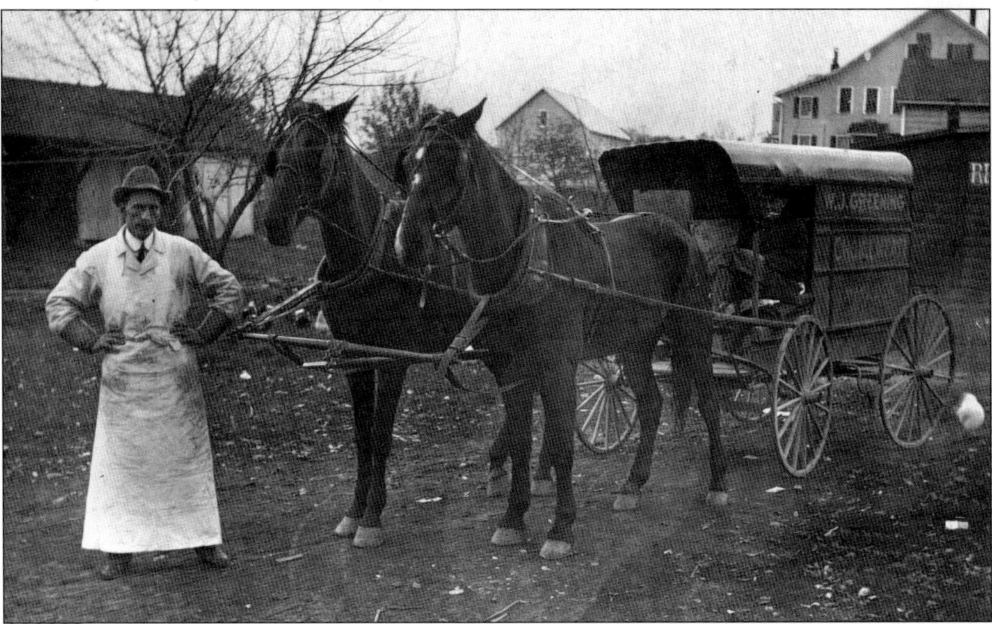

The community had grown from the horse-and-wagon days of Walter Greening, traveling within the community and neighboring communities selling grocery and food items, to the storefront businesses that were popularized by the period of the 1920s. Greening's Grocery Store and Meat Market, as well as other businesses on Main Street, provided important services for the community. Residents did not have to leave the community to purchase these essentials. Greening is shown with his grocery wagon *c.* 1911. (Courtesy of Nancy Mitchell.)

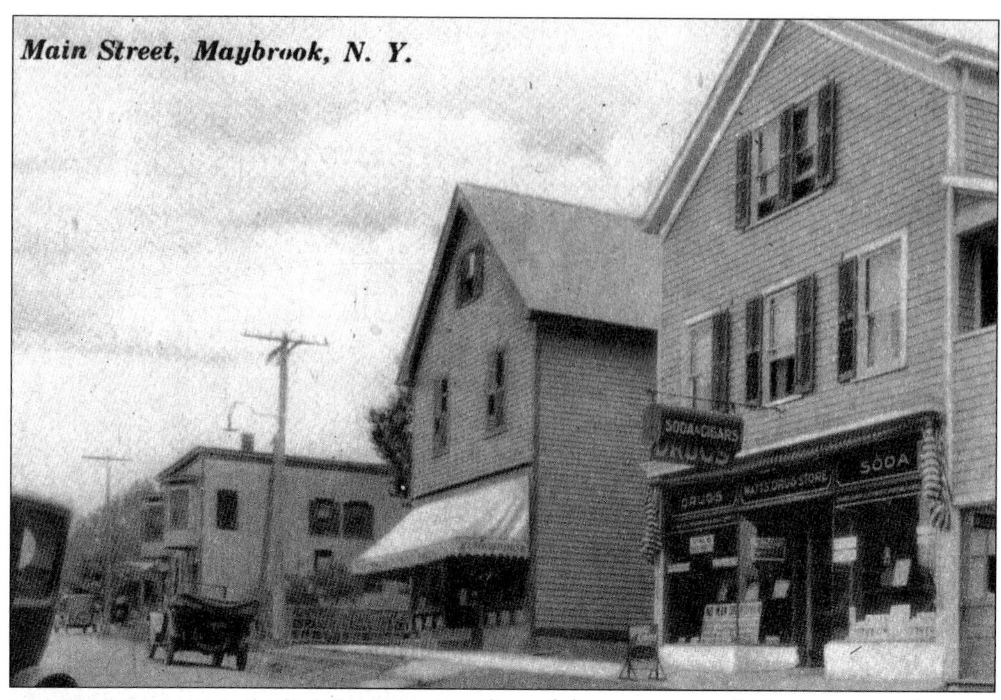

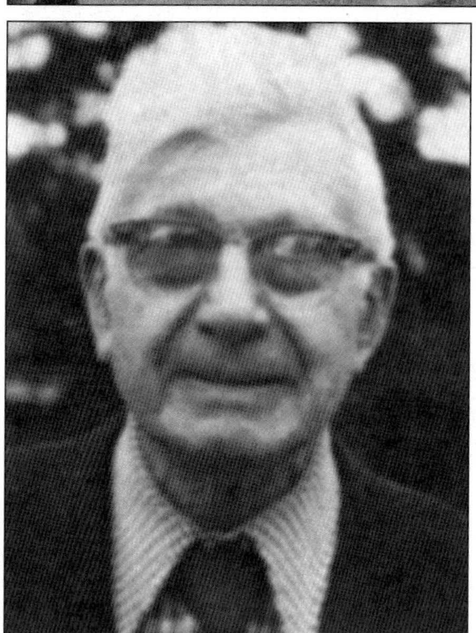

One of the very successful businesses in the village was Watts Drug Store. Pictured above *c.* the 1930s, it was located on the corner of Main Street. It not only provided the community with medicines but also served as a meeting place for young people. Customers were greeted and served at the soda fountain by assistant John M. Bodle (left). Many of the children in the community came in after school, sat on the floor, and read comic books that were on the newsstand—Superman, Batman, Archie, Lulu, and western heroes Gene Autry and Roy Rogers. Eventually, Bodle would ask a child either to pay for the comic book or to place it back on the rack—but well after enough time had elapsed to read all or most of the story. (Courtesy of Eric Kruger.)

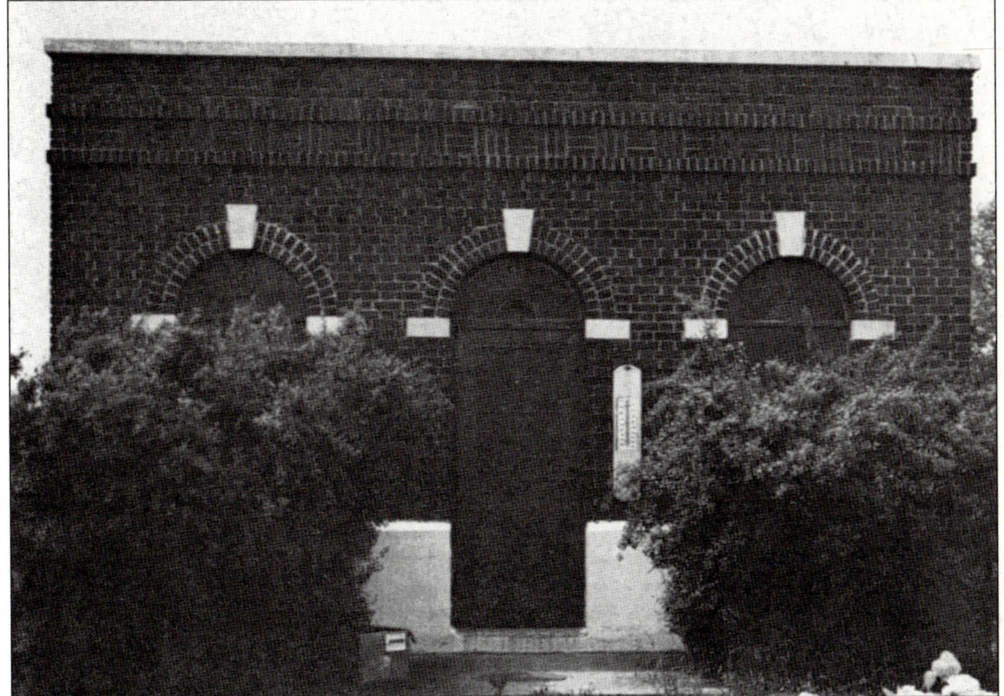

The Maybrook switching terminal had to lay off some of the workers during the Great Depression. Unemployed railroad workers were able to find some relief during those years through municipal construction projects. MayΩor George Bullis was able to obtain government funding through the New Deal agencies of Pres. Franklin D. Roosevelt. At the beginning of the 1930s, the village constructed a pump house (above, *c.* 1931) for its water supply. In the mid-1930s, it built a sewage disposal plant (below, *c.* 1936). (Courtesy of the Maybrook Chamber of Commerce.)

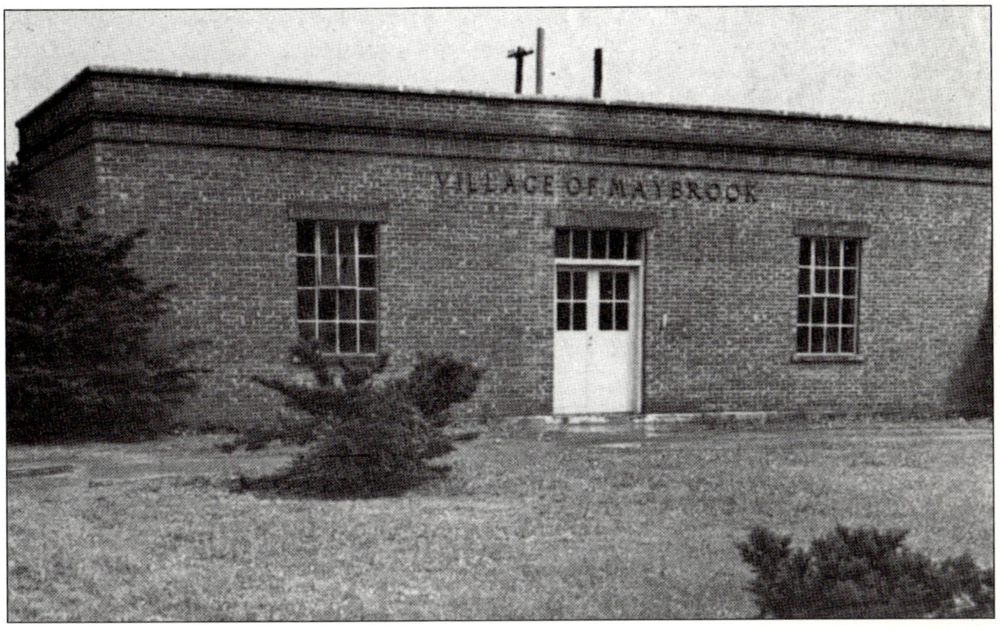

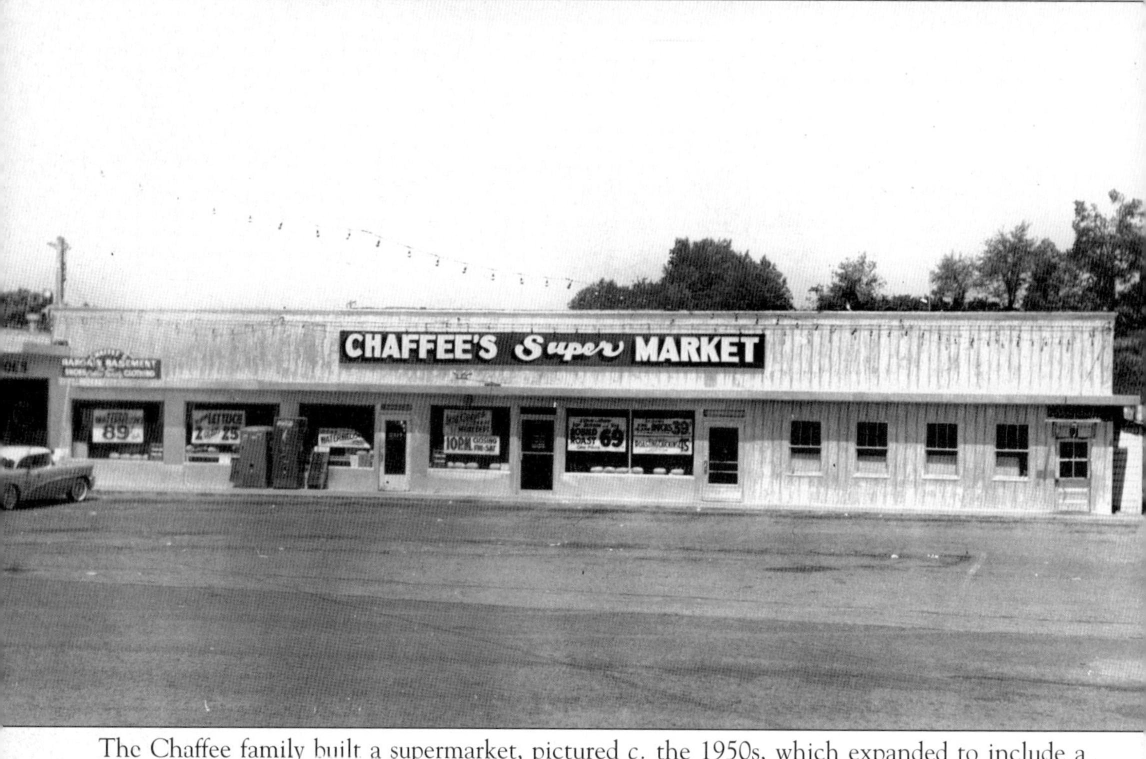

The Chaffee family built a supermarket, pictured *c.* the 1950s, which expanded to include a drugstore and a 5-and-10 cent store. Many of the young people growing up in Maybrook worked at one time or another at Chaffee's Super Market. The shopping mall, later called the strip mall, continued to develop, and a drive-in movie theater was built. (Courtesy of Pat Bullis Feldman.)

By the 1950s, the Maybrook switching terminal employed some 1,500 workers and had tracks and buildings that dominated the area for miles. A host of businesses thrived. Johnstons Garage expanded to include a Toyota dealership managed by John Jardine. The Sandbothe Service Station was always busy. The Panaro family, including daughter Emanuela Panaro, opened a custard stand in the south end. Village fathers, including George C. Bullis, A.J. Di Benio, and Walter Greening, upgraded municipal services. Along with the business expansion came new housing, constructed in the mid-1960s.

Then, toward the mid-1970s, the economy and prosperity of Maybrook began to decline. The Poughkeepsie Bridge Fire of 1974 led to layoffs. Workers who were not laid off were sent to Selkirk to work at the rail terminal. The railroad industry and the traditions that developed around this railroad community became part of the past.

After the railroad closed its doors to local residents, Yellow Freight Transit opened its facility in Maybrook. With assets in the billions of dollars, Yellow Freight purchased a large section of land, the westbound classification yards, from the Penn Central Railroad. Many of the railroad buildings that belonged to the New York, New Haven, and Hartford Railroad were demolished, with the exception of part of the roundhouse. Track was ripped up and a truck bay was created.

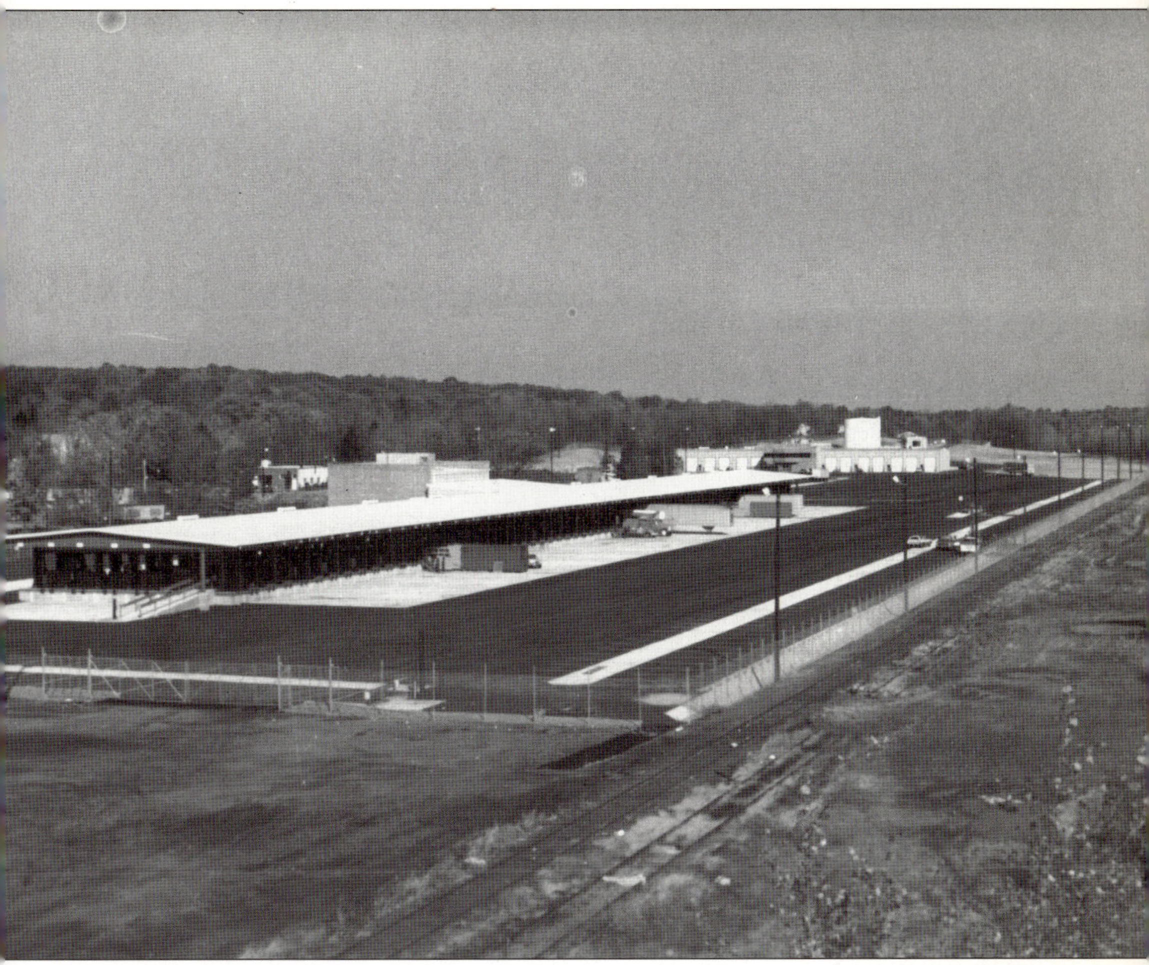

Shown is the Yellow Freight Company, Maybrook, c. the 1980s. (Courtesy of Yellow Freight Systems and Tom Kirby.)

Maybrook was an ideal location for the freight carrier. The construction of Interstate 84 from New York east to Connecticut and west to Pennsylvania opened the way to greater service and business for the company. The trucking terminal in Maybrook replaced the railroad terminal, brought business to the community, and provided jobs for men and women.

Yellow Freight was the outgrowth of various transportation services provided by brothers Cleve and A.J. Harrell in Oklahoma City, Oklahoma. There was Yellow Cab—originally a Model T Ford painted bright yellow—Yellow Transit, and then Yellow Freight after it was sold to Arlington W. Porter.

In 1981, Yellow Freight Systems earned revenue of over $1 billion. Less than 10 years later, the company had more than doubled that amount of revenue, making it one of the largest trucking corporations in the country. In the late 1990s, under Maurice Myers as chairman and Thomas L. Smith as president, revenues rose to $2.5 billion.

By 2001, Yellow Freight Systems had not only established freighting services across the United States but as far north as Canada and as far south as Mexico. The corporation also had added freighting services in Europe. Bill Zollars was named the new chairman and Yellow Freight, as part of the Yellow Systems Corporations, celebrated more than 85 years of service since its launching by the Harrell brothers in 1916.

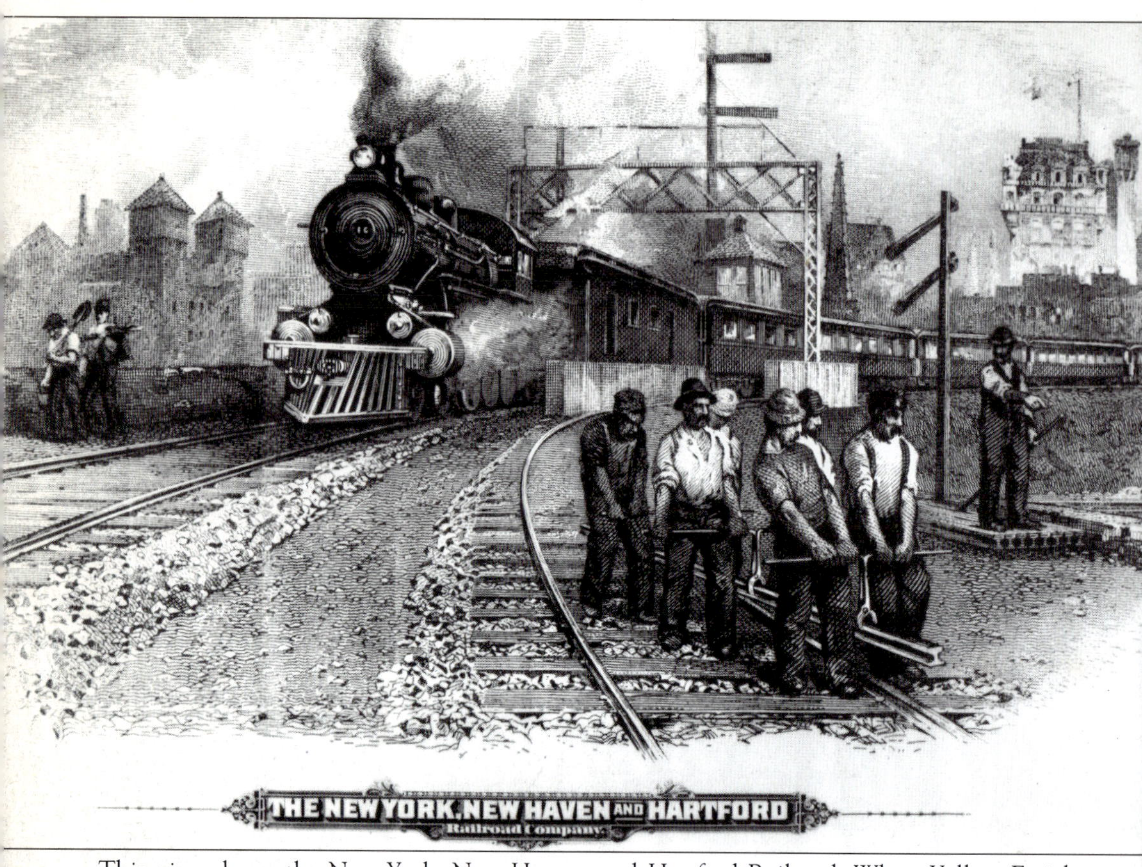

This view shows the New York, New Haven, and Hartford Railroad. When Yellow Freight Transit arrived in Maybrook, many of the remaining railroad buildings were demolished and track was ripped up. (Courtesy of the Maybrook Railroad Historical Society & Museum.)

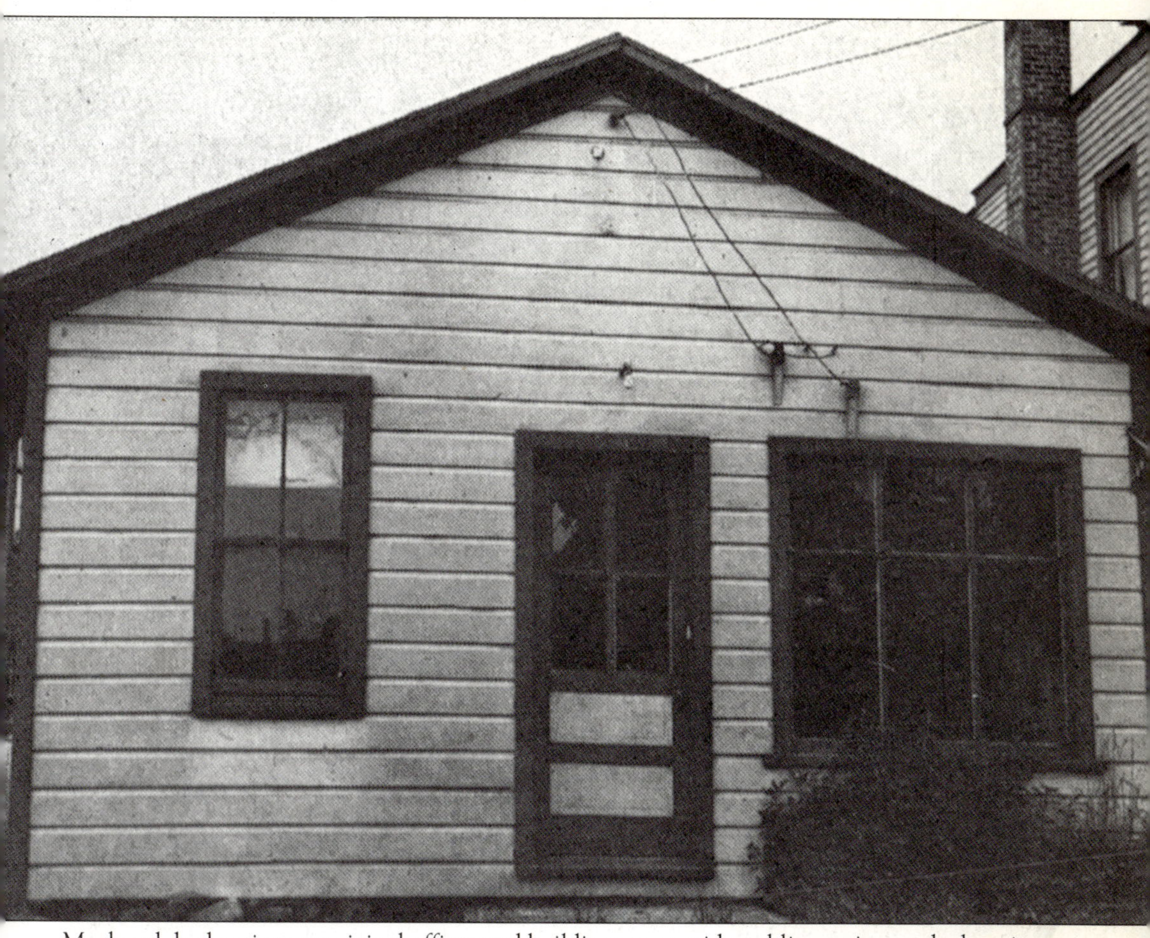

Maybrook had various municipal offices and buildings to provide public services and education. This is the Maybrook village office *c.* the 1930s. (Courtesy of the Maybrook Chamber of Commerce.)

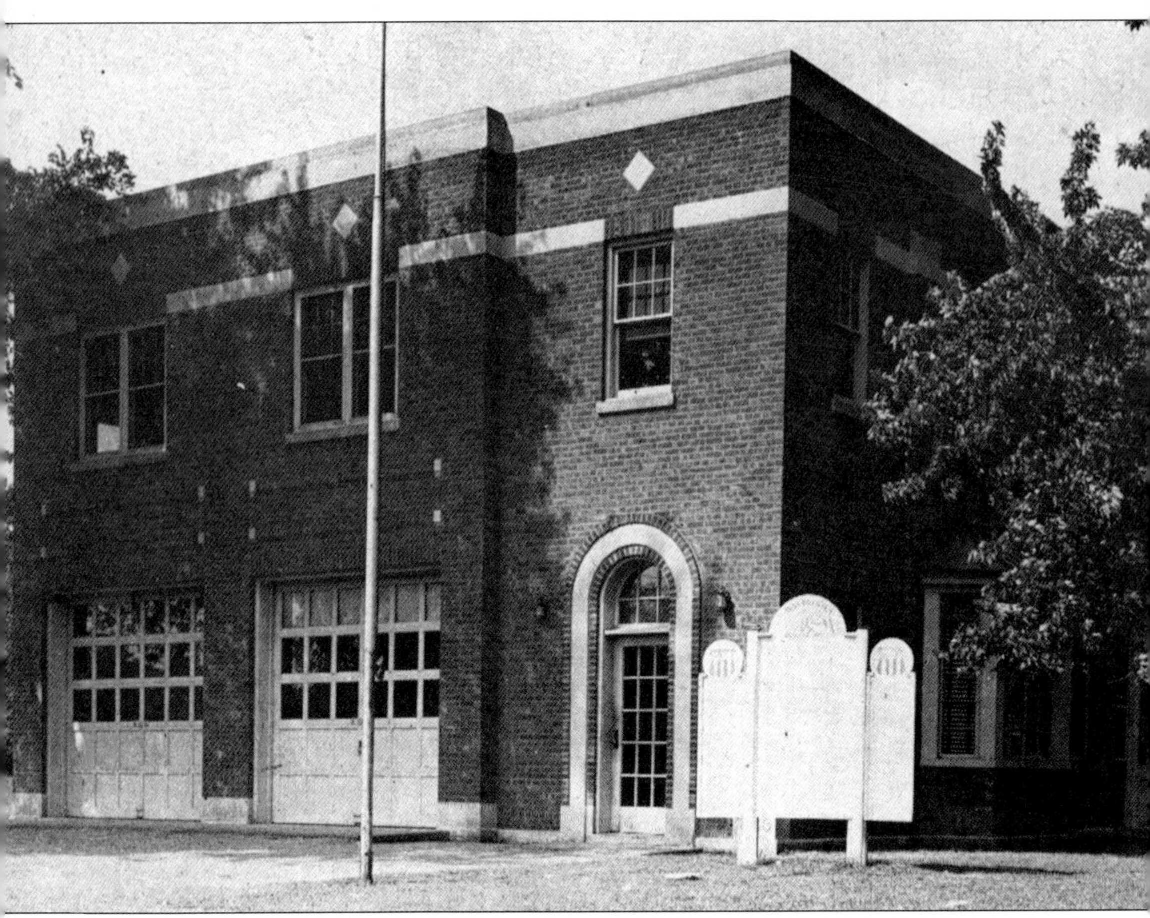

This is a c. 1940 view of the Maybrook Municipal Building. (Courtesy of the Maybrook Chamber of Commerce.)

Eight
Social and Recreational Life

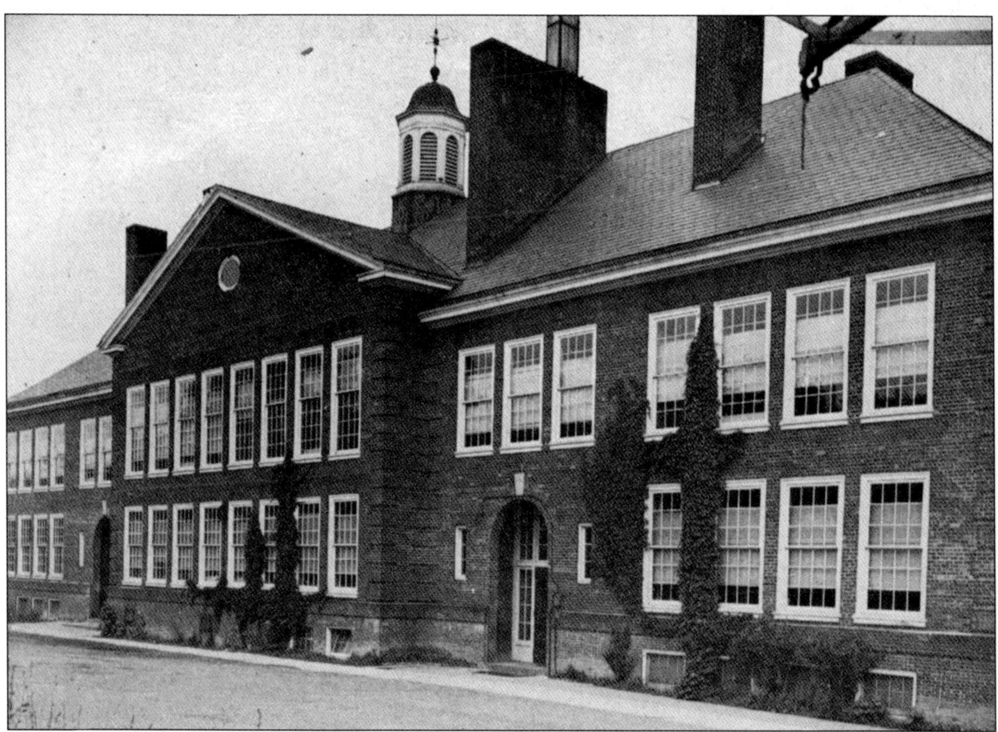

There were three centers of social and recreational life in the village of Maybrook. One was the Maybrook High School, pictured just after it was built in 1923. The school provided activities through clubs, organizations, and athletics, which dominated many of the hours that young people enjoyed after school. (Courtesy of the Maybrook Chamber of Commerce.)

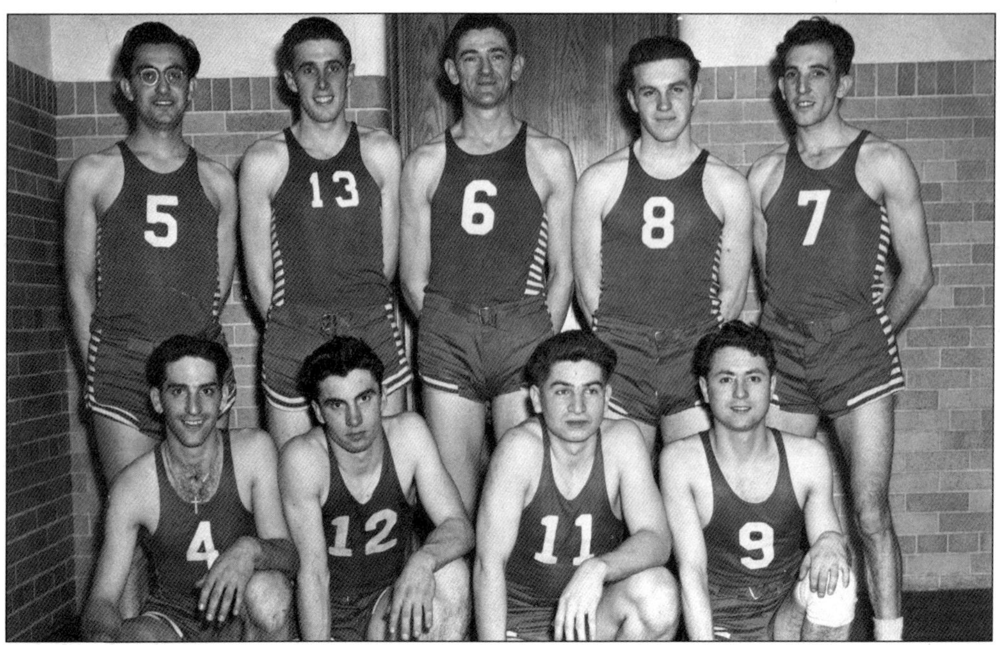

Some of the basketball teams that were developed in the 1930s and 1940s were considered the very best within the town and county. Maybrook High School's 1947–1948 team played in the finals but was beaten by Warwick. Pictured, from left to right, are the following: (front row) Danny Saracino, "Corky" Shields, Angie Iorlano, and Nunzy Mondello; (back row) Joe Iorlano, Brad Conklin, Si Thorpe, and Everett McCormick. (Courtesy of Dan Saracino.)

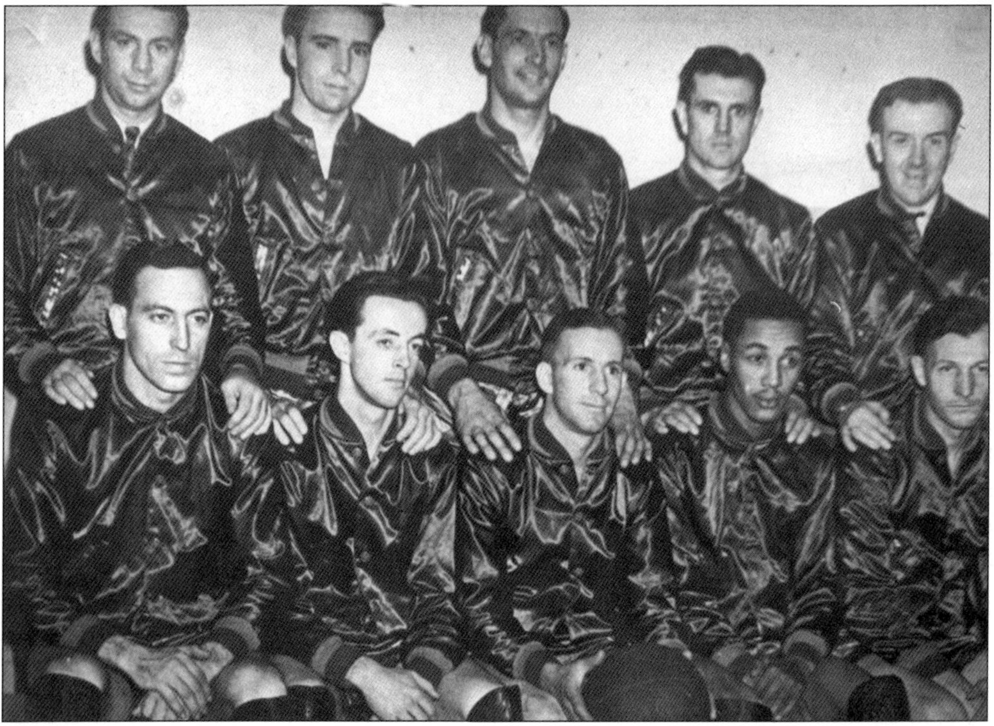

Shown is the Maybrook High School basketball team *c.* the 1950s. (Courtesy of Eric Kruger.)

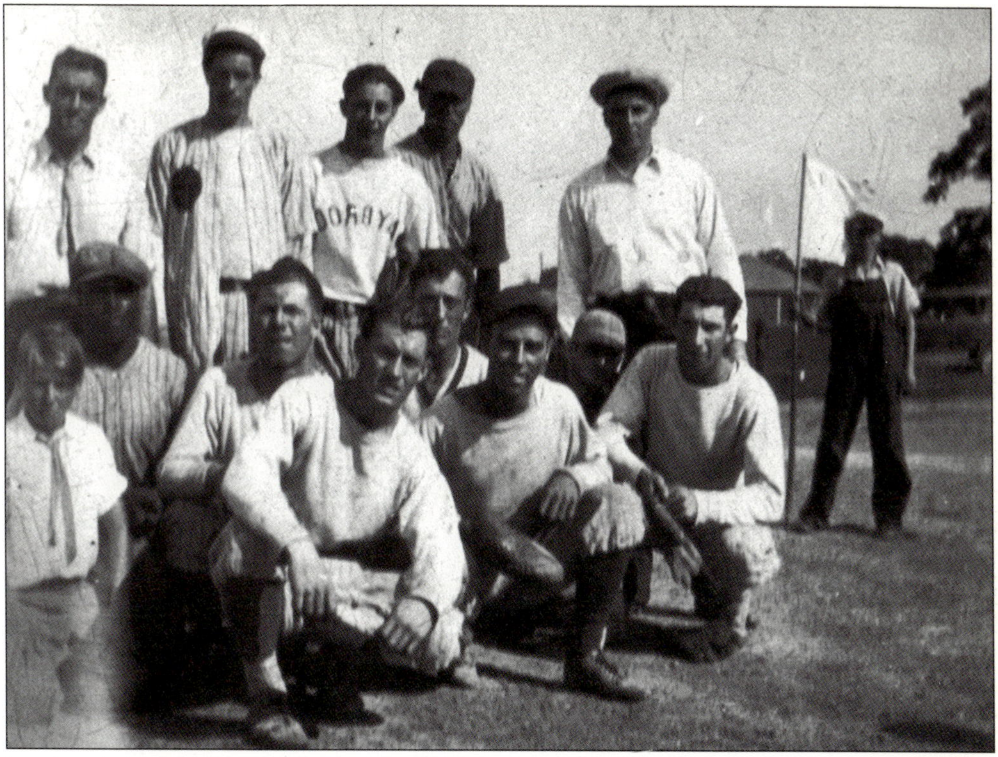

Maybrook had some semipro baseball players who had the chance to try out for the New York Yankees. Robert Brown Sr. was one of them. This pictured was taken c. the 1940s. (Courtesy of Carole Brown Jennings and Robert Brown Jr.)

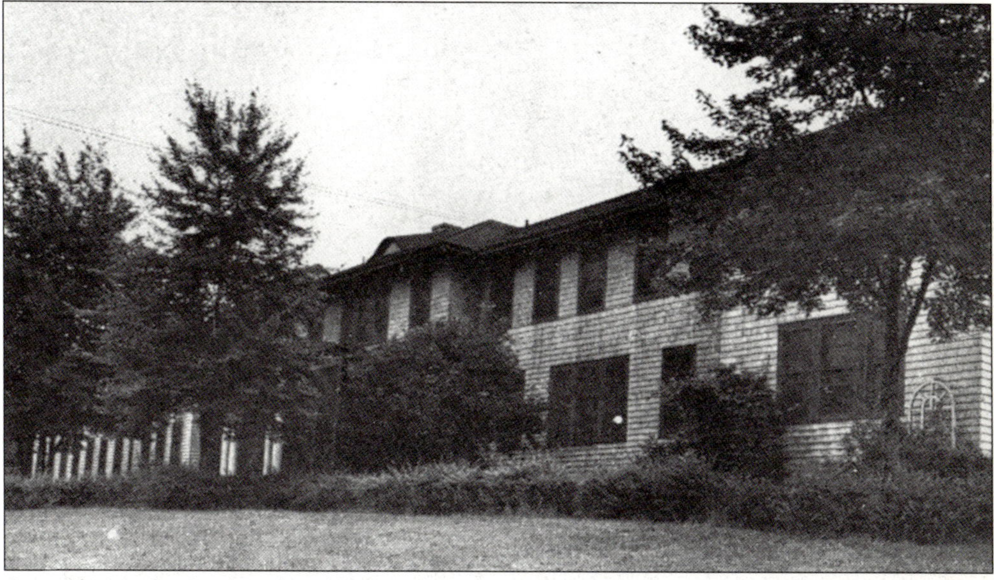

Central New England Railroad built a YMCA, offering recreation to workers who stayed over to board a train the next day. The building included rooms for guests, but the major section was an indoor gymnasium, used for dances as well as basketball games. This view of the YMCA was taken in the 1940s. (Courtesy of the Maybrook Chamber of Commerce.)

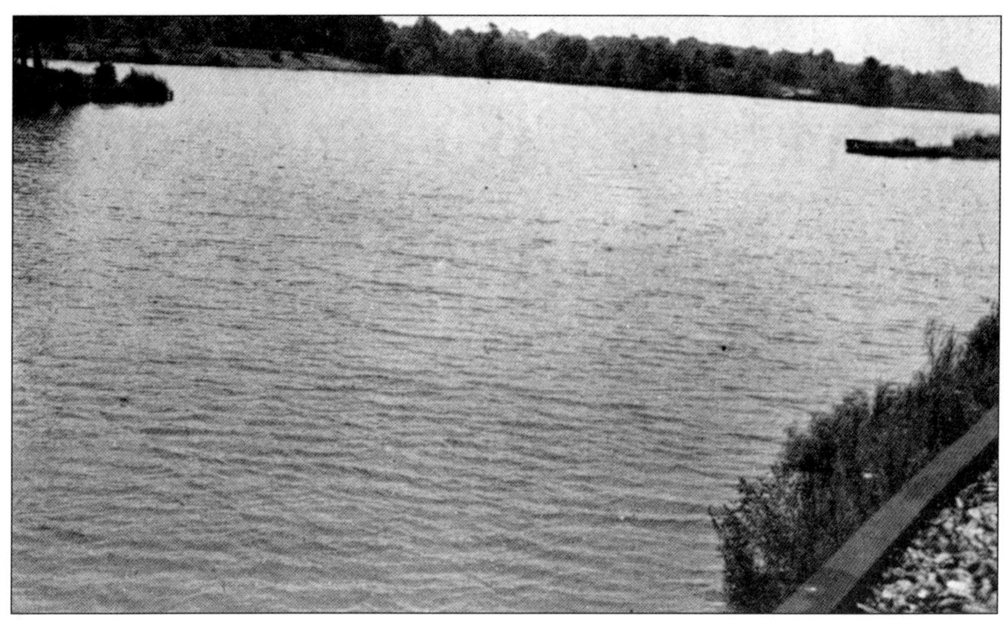

When the Central New England Railroad established its terminal in Maybrook, a reservoir was created for a water supply for the trains. Not long after that, an icehouse was constructed at the Maybrook switching terminal to provide ice for those rail cars used to transport meat and fruit west to Chicago and beyond. The reservoir, shown *c.* the 1940s, was named Indian Lake; it served as a recreational area for the community. Young boys often dove off the ledge into the water or sat on the ledge and fished. (Courtesy of the Maybrook Chamber of Commerce.)

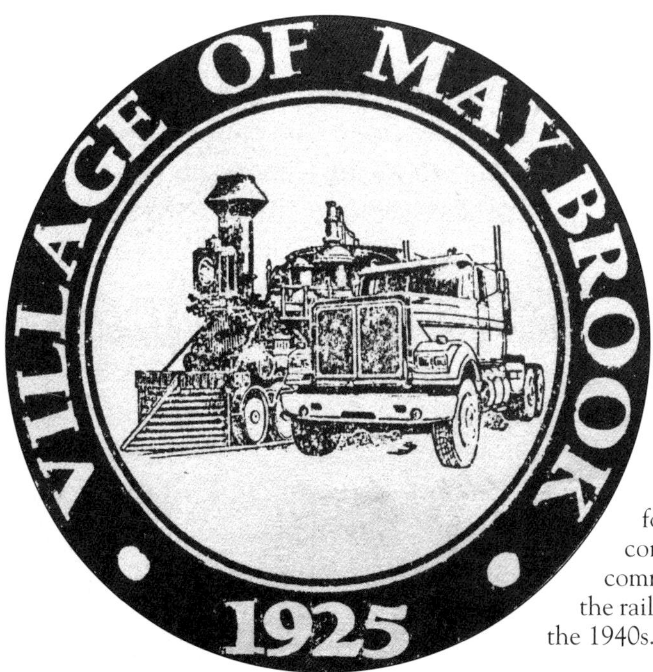

The largest gathering of the community was for the Feast of the Assumption. Members of all faiths attended the annual feast. Delicacies were laid out on table after table. For Roman Catholics, the feast was part of their religious observance, as well as a day of celebration. The event became a tradition in Maybrook for decades. It reinforced the common bond of many in the community who were employed by the railroad. Shown is the village seal *c.* the 1940s. (Courtesy of Roby Petzold.)

Nine

MEMORIES

When the Ringling Brothers and Barnum & Bailey Circus came to town, schoolchildren were given a half day off from school to go down to the railroad tracks to see the elephants and other animals being unloaded from the boxcars.

Everyone growing up in a small village knew everyone else. During Halloween, festivities lasted from Monday through Friday. Every night, the children and their parents went to a different section of the village. The costumed children entered a home and paraded around until the host family guessed each one's identity. Often that took 15 minutes.

Youngsters played games in the streets around the post office—Ringaleveo or Johnny on the Pony, in the 1950s. The Midway Diner had pinball machines and jukeboxes, but the best place to go was Watts Drug Store. Doc Watts called all the children either "Sonny" or "Girlie," even though he knew all their names. A trusting person, he devised a charge card plan that allowed the youngsters to buy sodas and comic books, and then pay for them after they earned some money mowing lawns or shoveling snow. During the winter months, boys of 16 or older prayed for a large storms so that the railroad would need help shoveling snow off the switches on the tracks. In the mid-1950s, the minimum wage was 60 cents an hour; depending on the number of hours worked, that wage could double or triple.

When the school system was centralized in 1959, Maybrook students entered Valley Central High School, on Route 17K in Montgomery. Seniors spent the year making pies and cakes to raise money for their senior trip to Washington, D.C. Discontinued for a while, the trip was later reinstated and continues to this day. The school prom was prepared and hosted by the students and their parents and supported by the entire village. Movie night was Tuesday, in the gymnasium. Square dancing, called by the Kentucky Moonshines, was held on a Friday night. Maybrook was a community within a community.

—Bonnie Greening Van Wagenen and Neil Van Wagenen

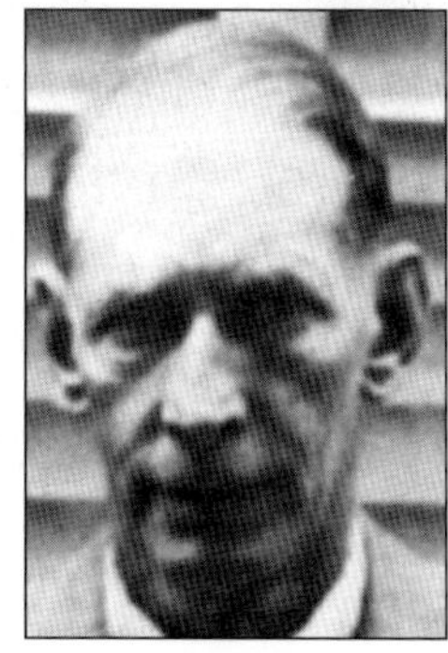

Early settlers of Sullivan County who relocated to Orange County included the Greenings, the Van Wagenens, and the Van Leuvens. The Greenings came originally from England and Germany; they were butchers and ran Greening's Meat Market, on Main Street. The Van Wagenens and Van Leuvens were Dutch. Mr. Van Wagenen worked for the railroad maintenance shop in the roundhouse. Walter Greening (right, *c.* 1925–1927) was the first mayor of Maybrook, incorporated as a village in 1925. (Courtesy of the Maybrook Golden Jubilee Committee.)

The Panaros came from Italy and Sicily and arrived as immigrants in New York City. Mr. Panaro worked on the railroad and later had a bar and grill, landscaping service, and nursery. Dan Green's family came from Rhode Island and intermarried with the Jewell family in Maybrook. The original tract of land of the Jewell House and Estate was part of the Kirkland Tract, which dated back to King George III. The Panaro family bought the Jewell Estate years later. Green started as a fireman and became an engineer for the New York, New Haven, and Hartford Railroad.

Residents walking down the streets of Maybrook knew every family and every house, having been inside each year during Halloween week. The Duffy and McVey families came from Ireland, according to Caren Duffy Aiello. Maybrook was a melting pot of different ethnic groups, with Italian Americans dominating the eastern section of the village. The school system became the equalizer. Students in the lowest grades had classes in the basement. The seniors had the top floor. All of them mingled with others of all ages.

Maybrook's homeless people were referred to as gandy dancers. Some made money shoveling snow off the switches in the railroad yard. The community gave them food other items, and over the years more and more homeless people came to Maybrook as hobos or on foot, having heard of the community's hospitality toward strangers.

Some 500 families became the core of the village of Maybrook. Often, they intermarried and within several decades could trace their roots to numerous other families within the community. In Maybrook, residents were introduced to many different aspects of life and ethnic traditions that helped make people hardworking and well-rounded.

—Dan and Emanuela Green
—Michael and Caren Aiello
—Norman and Kathy McVey

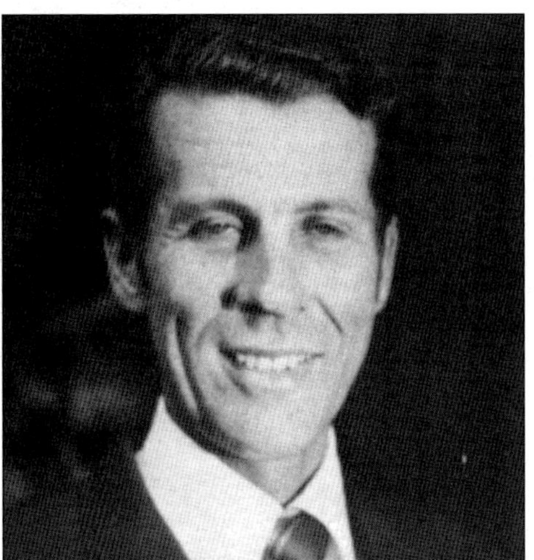

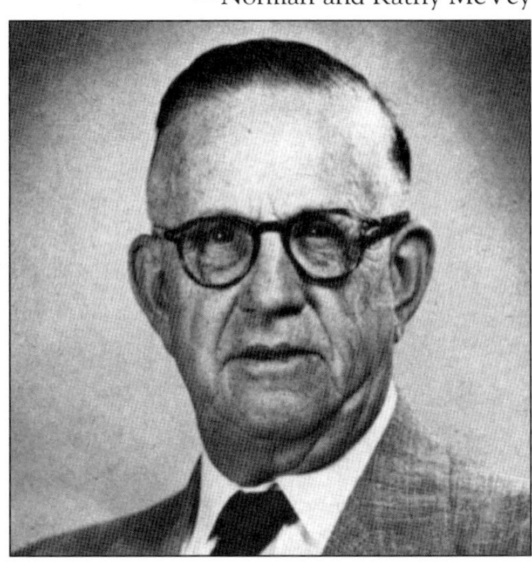

The Browns of Maybrook came from England, where they were descended from the Oglethorpe family, including James Oglethorpe, who helped settle the province of Georgia in the 1730s. The family name Oglethorpe was shortened to the family name of Thorpe. The Thorpes were early settlers in New York, dating back to the early 1730s. The Browns were from the Republic of Ireland and were employees of the railroad. Before Robert Brown Jr. (left, *c.* the 1970s) was elected mayor of Maybrook, he worked for the railroad, as members of his family had before him. Under the leadership of Mayor George Bullis (right, *c.* the 1940s), the village grew and survived the Great Depression. Most of the early modernization of the village is credited to Bullis, whose insight and business ability was able to keep many of the men in the village employed. (Left, courtesy of the Maybrook Golden Jubilee Committee; right, courtesy of the Maybrook Chamber of Commerce.)

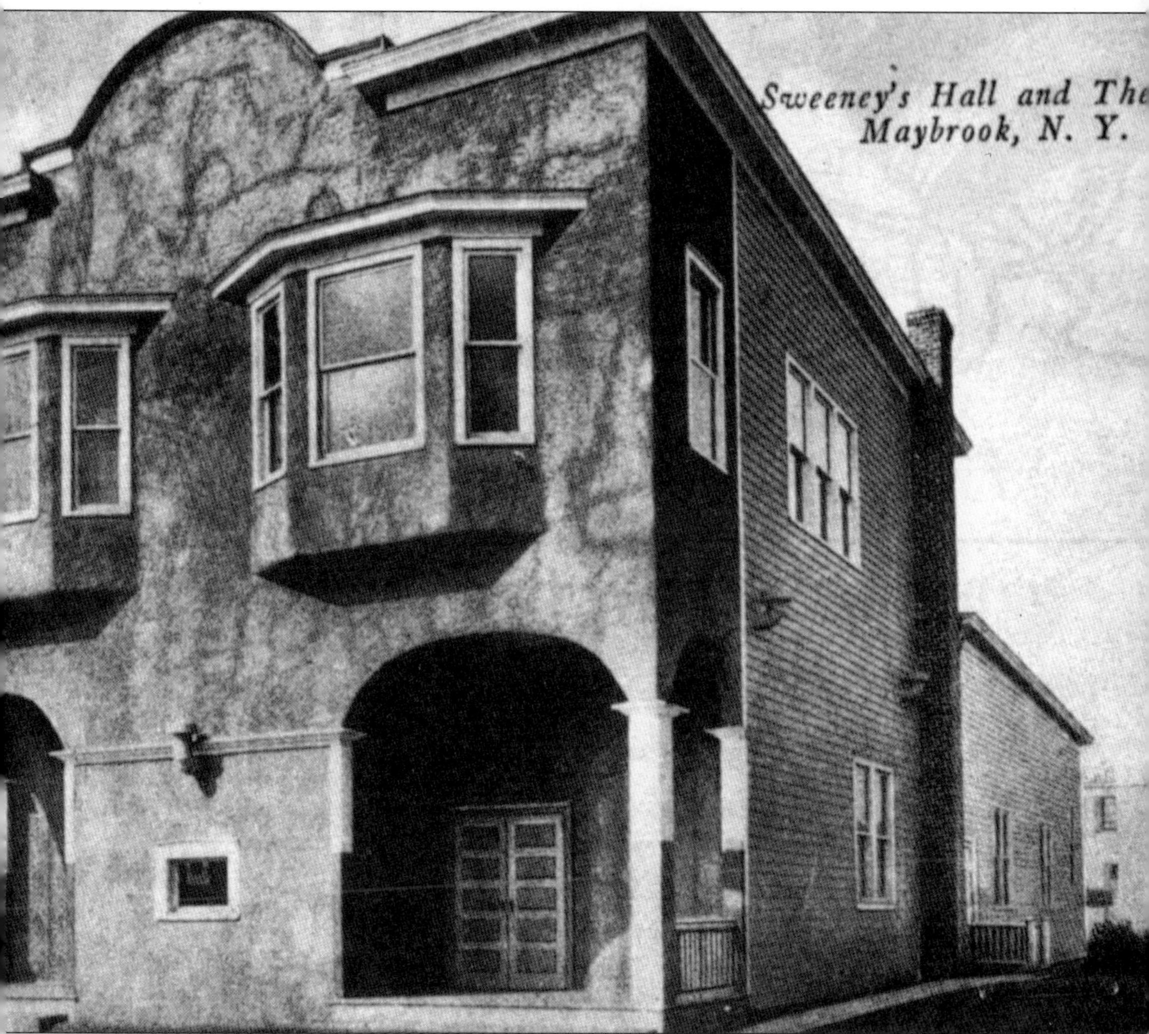

Maybrook had its own movie and stage theater, Sweeney's Hall and Theater, picture *c.* the 1920s. Here, residents saw vaudeville shows and movies—first, silent films and, later, talkies. (Courtesy of the Maybrook Golden Jubilee Committee.)

Children in the community used imagination and innovation to occupy their time. Very little money was in circulation. Young people could not afford many of the luxuries of life, but they certainly enjoyed the pleasures of the day. Many people observed the weekend ritual of having their extended families come for Sunday dinner. Visitors at any time were always invited in for a cup of coffee, and it was considered an insult to refuse the hospitality. People enjoyed spending time together, talking about current issues and past memories.

The most successful business in Maybrook, aside from the railroad and the trucking industry, was Brook May, a coat factory owned by Bill Consorti. The factory, which made cloth winter coats, was in the former Central New England Railroad office building. When Interstate 84 was constructed, the building was torn down and the company relocated to Newburgh.

—Doris Brown Christian
—Carol Brown Jennings
—Robert Brown Jr.

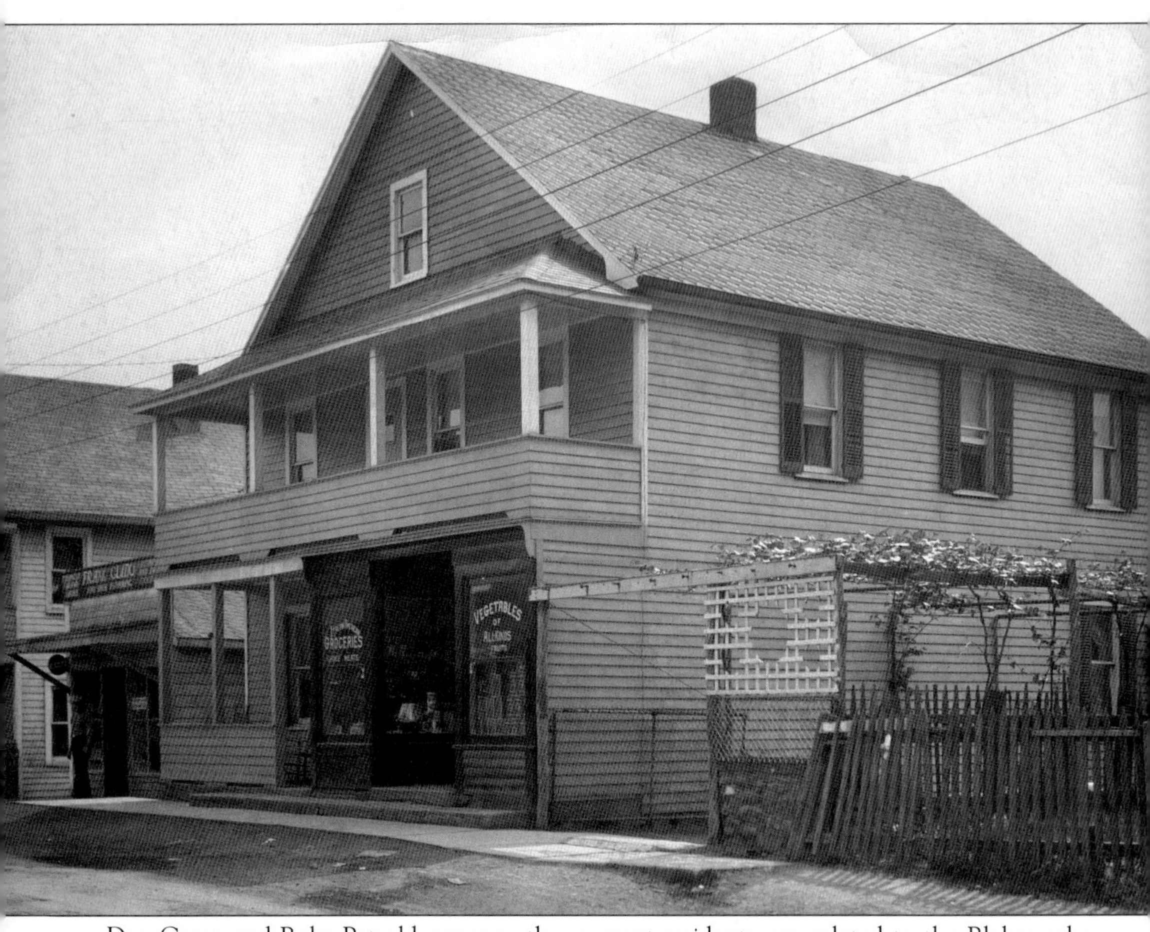

Dan Green and Roby Petzold, among other current residents, are related to the Blakes, who were involved in railroads. Maybrook children liked Guido's Shoe Repair, on Main Street. Guido always greeted them with a smile, as they examined the penny candy in the glass container while shoes were being repaired. Shown above are Saracino's grocery store and Guido's Shoe Repair shop c. the 1930s. (Courtesy of Dan Saracino.)

There were no shopping centers in the village at the time. Sweeney's Hall was used for dances and movies and sometimes for classes—for instance, when the school roof leaked. The largest room at Sweeney's Hall was partitioned to accommodate different classes. Maybrook had the distinction of having the smallest number of pupils within the town of Montgomery. Education was highly individualized because there were so few students in each class and each family was known on a personal level. Hastings, an English teacher, accompanied the students on their annual trip to Washington, D.C. Pepe, the gym teacher, made the activities fun. As one former student put it, "They were not just teachers . . . they were our friends."

—Roby Petzold

Pasquale "Patsy" Iorlano's parents were immigrants from Leone and San Marco, Italy. They lived near the railroad tracks by Tower Avenue. Matthew Iorlano, who began as a track worker, worked for the railroad for 30 years and never missed a day. Youngsters had a variety of activities from which to choose. They could go down to Johnson Toyota to see a car that had been wrecked on the road. They could or play ball in the sandlots or go swimming and fishing at Indian Lake. One of the best sports teams was the Montgomery Farmers, which was made up of some of the best athletes from the village of Maybrook.

—Pasquale Iorlano

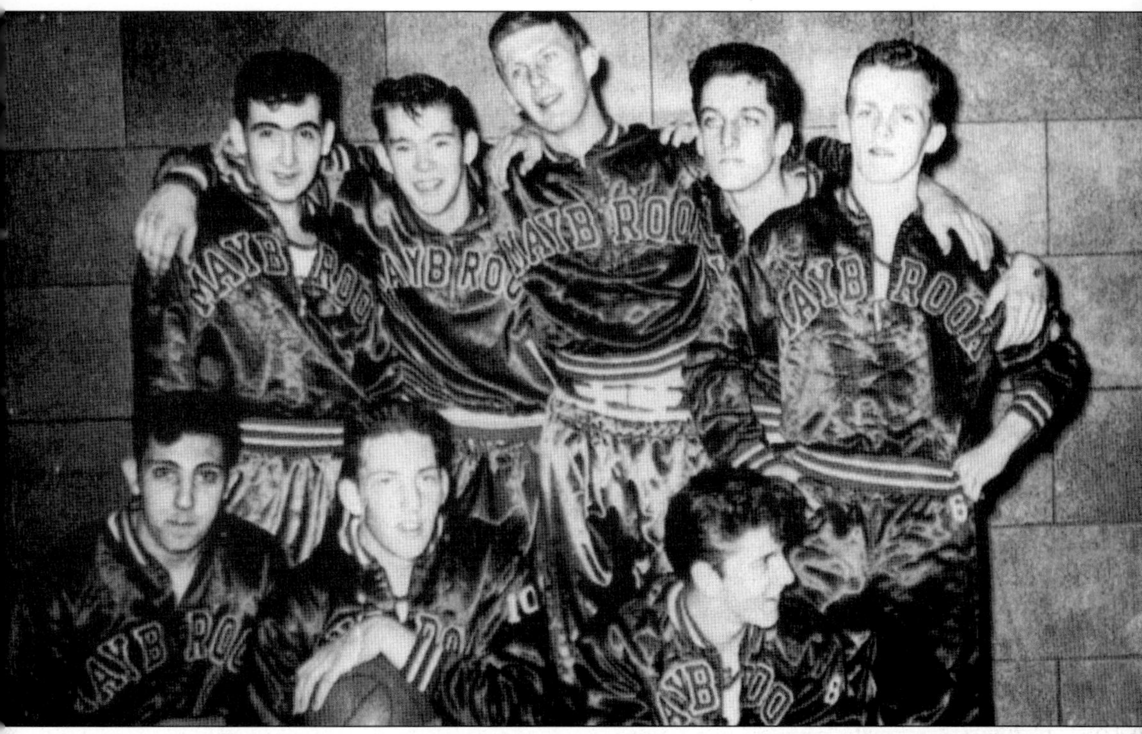

Shown in this 1958 photograph are the following members of the Maybrook High basketball team coached by Tony Gesso, from left to right:(front row) Patsy Iorlano, Lou Capazzoli, and John Jardine; (back row) Neil Van Wagenen, Billy Green, Buddy Blake, Bill Gill, and Pete Calley. This was the last team at Maybrook High School before centralization. (Courtesy of Pat Bullis Feldman.)

The Yanello family lived on Abbey Avenue in Maybrook. The grandparents were immigrants from Italy, some from Calabria. Joseph Yanello ran the crane with the big hook to take cars off the rails that were derailed. Aunt Tess De Santis had a grocery store known as Pepe's, or De Santis Grocery Store. For entertainment, Aunt Tess would read tea leaves to some of the patrons who entered the store. On Sundays, the De Santis family had gravy (sauce) and pasta. Aunt Tess invited any customer who came into the store early in the morning to return for dinner at noon. Tables were set with plates and napkins—one never knew how many people would come for dinner. While Uncle Pepe was waiting on a customer, Aunt Tess would throw some spices into the sauce, and while she waited on a customer, Uncle Pepe would throw a handful of spices into the pot, not realizing that she had already done so. The sauce, or gravy, would continue to grow and grow and never lost its taste.

—Cindy Yanello Badendyck
—Doug Badendyck

The Bastianos were immigrants from Tuscany, Italy. Arriving in New York City in 1915, Antonio Bastiano started as a taxicab driver with a horse and buggy and Amelia Bastiano modeled for the garment industry. In the 1920s, the Bastianos started the Maybrook Inn, referred to as Lola's, offering homemade wine free with a full-course meal. Once, investigators came to the restaurant after hearing reports that wine, was being served—in violation of the Prohibition amendment. After the men ate their meal, with several servings of wine, they proceeded to arrest Bastiano for violating the Volstead Act. Bastiano pleaded innocent to the charges, stating that since he not charged for the wine, he was not guilty. Later, Lola's was sold and the Bastianos opened the famous Blue Mirror restaurant.

—Gene Bastiano

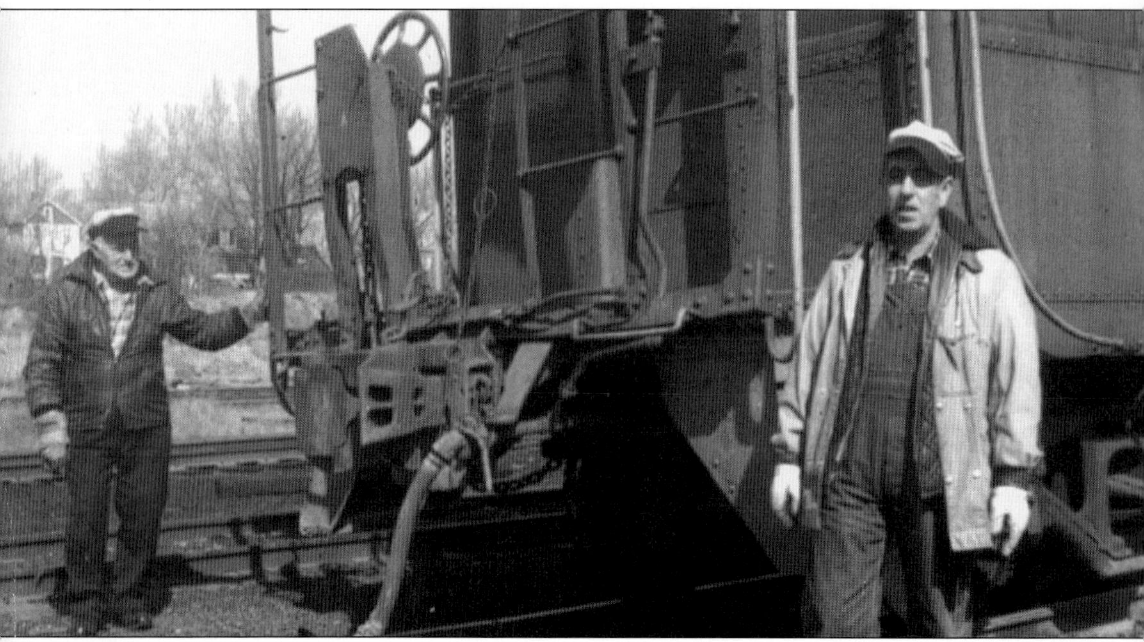

The Christiano family came from Calabria, Italy. Sam Christiano worked for the railroad from 1937 to 1940, first as a welder and then as a yard brakeman. His father was a blacksmith employed by the New Haven Railroad and the Lehigh and Hudson Railroad. Christiano and Jim Marano are shown on the last train to cross the Poughkeepsie Bridge before it burned in 1974. (Courtesy of the Maybrook Railroad Historical Society & Museum.)

A.J. Harrell and his brother started Yellow Freight, which dates back to the formation of the Yellow Cab Company in 1916. Today, the company is known as Yellow Freight Corporation and distributes products worldwide. Maybrook became a distribution center in 1980. The company chose Maybrook as a center because of its availability and the location of Interstate 84, the New York State Thruway, and other interchanges, plus the proximity to New York City and the metropolitan area. The company is located on the westbound classification yard that dates back to the New York, New Haven, and Hartford Railroad. Today there are 312 doors on the loading dock, with an enrollment of 650 employees.

—Tom Kirby, Yellow Freight Corporation

The Marano family came to the United States in 1906 from Calabria, Italy. Antonio Marano began working for the New Haven Railroad in the mid-1940s and worked his way up to the position of conductor. Conductors instructed the engineers and made sure that all the bills were in order. The railroad hump was in a receiving yard with receiving tracks. Its purpose of the hump was to have a brakeman sit on top of a car and ride the car over the hump, where it would be switched to the proper rail. The brakeman would slowly tighten the brake on the rail car, as gravity brought the car into that specific rail. Later, it would be reassembled as part of a full train with engine, which would be routed to its destination.

Many hobos would ride the train toward Maybrook and get off the train before it reached the rail yard. Outside of Maybrook, these unemployed workers created a hobo camp. At times, they visited some of the homes in Maybrook, asking for food. Many of the residents of the community opened their doors to these people to help them. This proud community not only took care of its own but also helped strangers as they traveled through the "Gateway to the East."

—Sam Christiano
—Tony Marano
—Albert Alexander

Ten

Historical Sites and Monuments

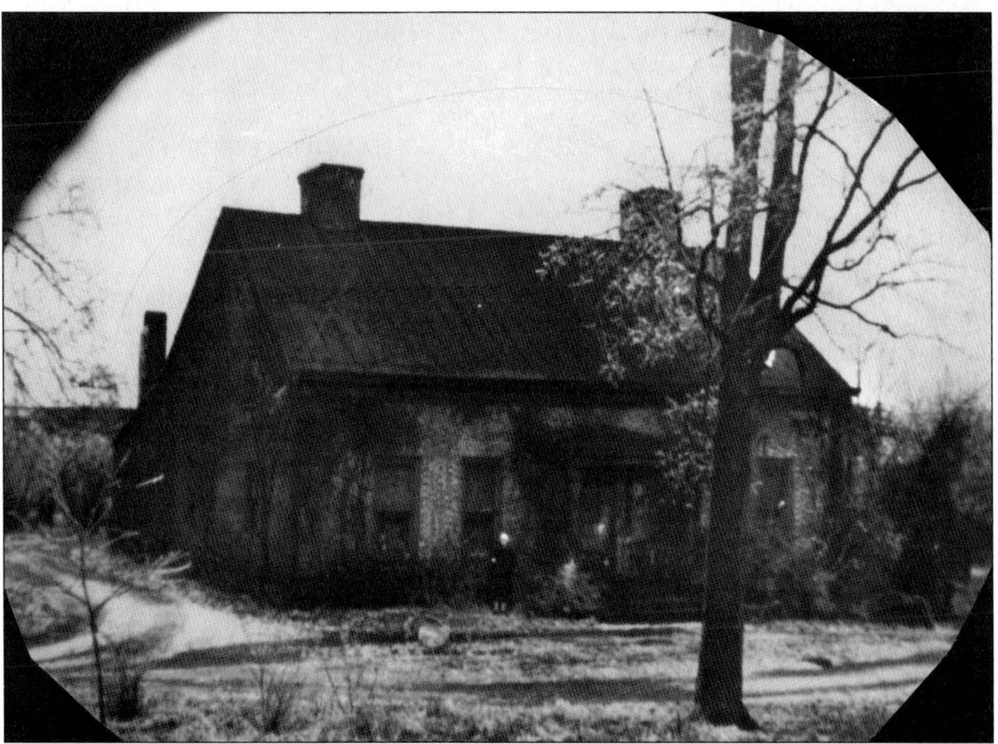

This is the John Blake House, which dates from c. 1770s to the 1820s. The estate was deeded in 1764 to John Blake Jr. The 220 acres of land cost 224 pounds and 10 shillings at the time. A great deal of the original house deteriorated and has since been rebuilt in New England Saltbox style. Although privately owned, it is a historic site and the oldest dwelling of the community. (Courtesy of Nancy Mitchell.)

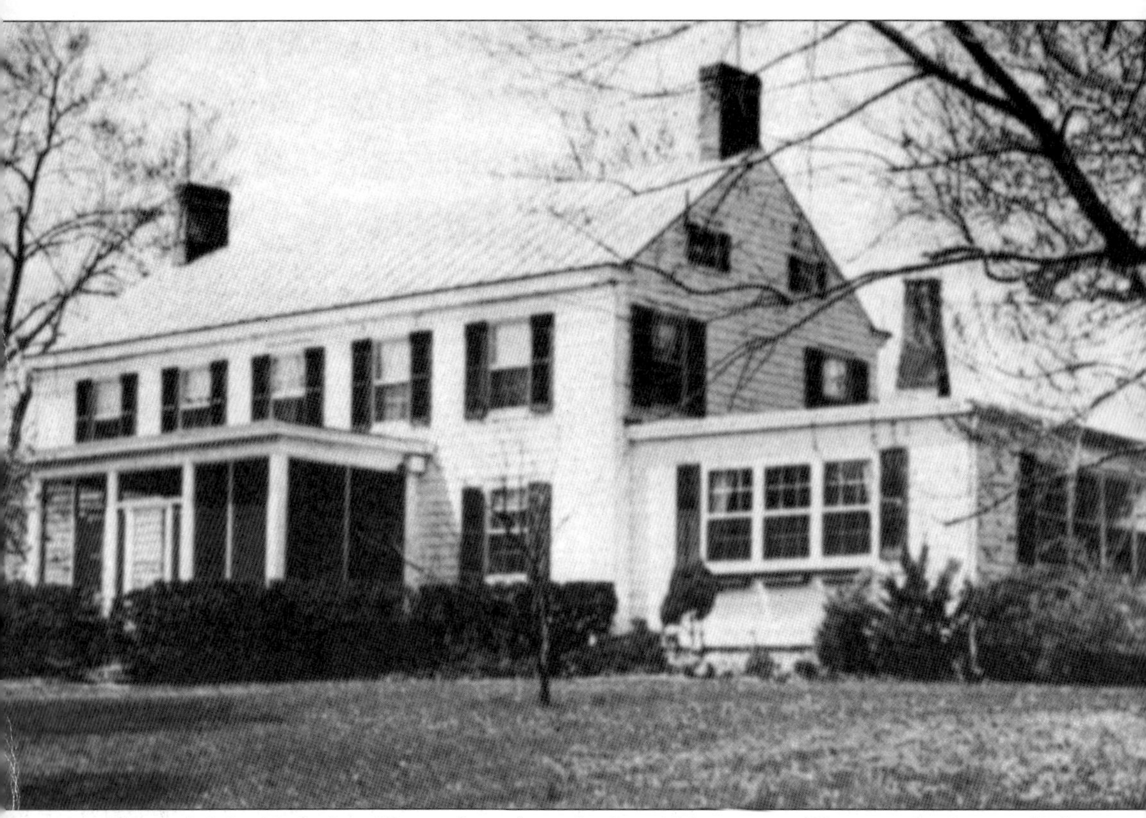

The Col. John Nicholson House dates from the late 18th century. This was the home of John Nicholson, a Revolutionary War hero. Today, it is a private residence. The roofline is in the Georgian style and there is a New York State Historical Marker denoting its historical significance. (Courtesy of the Maybrook Golden Jubilee Committee.)

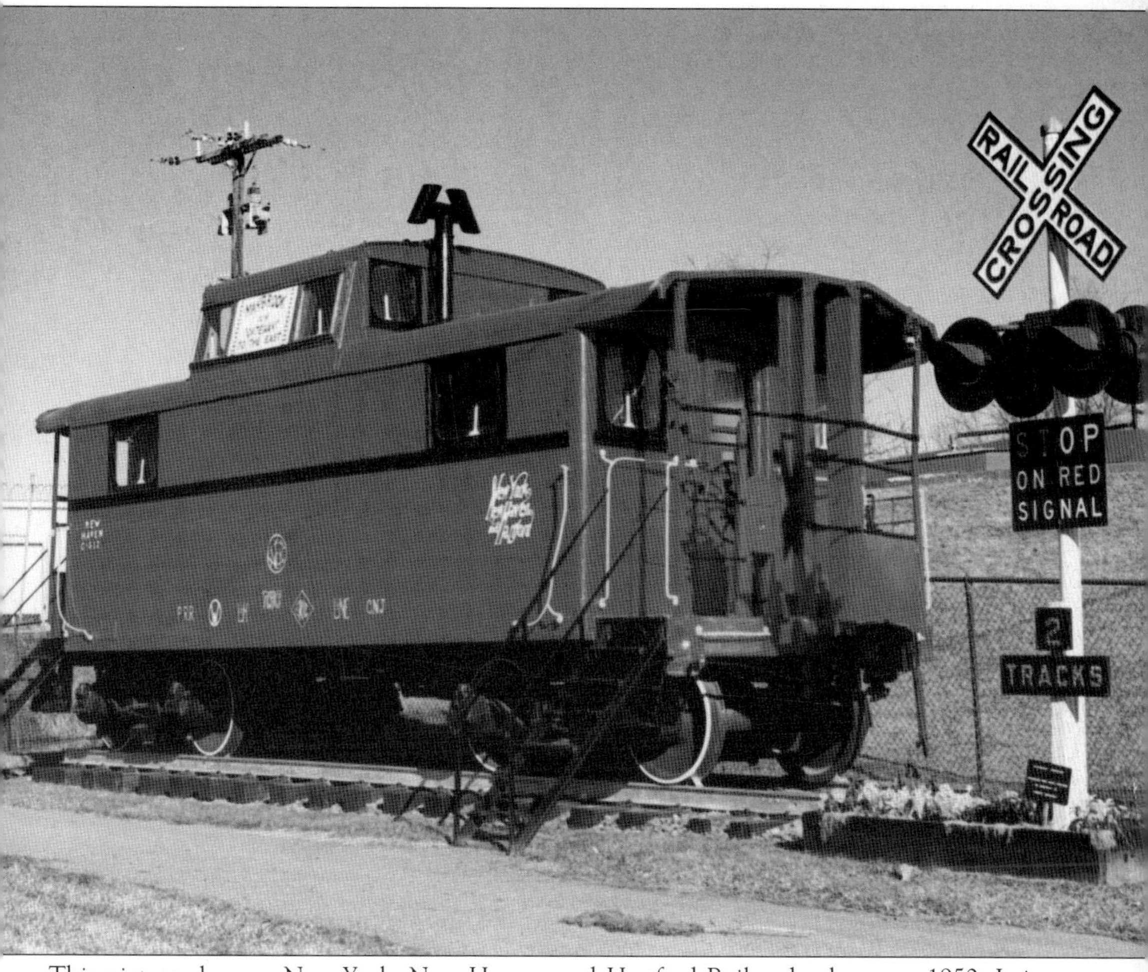

This picture shows a New York, New Haven, and Hartford Railroad caboose *c.* 1950. It is located in the Maybrook Railroad Caboose & Museum, a small museum on the north side of Maybrook. It has numerous photographs of the railroad era, with some of the artifacts from the 1940s and 1950s. It is maintained for the community, the public, and those interested in railroad history. (Courtesy of Roby Petzold.)

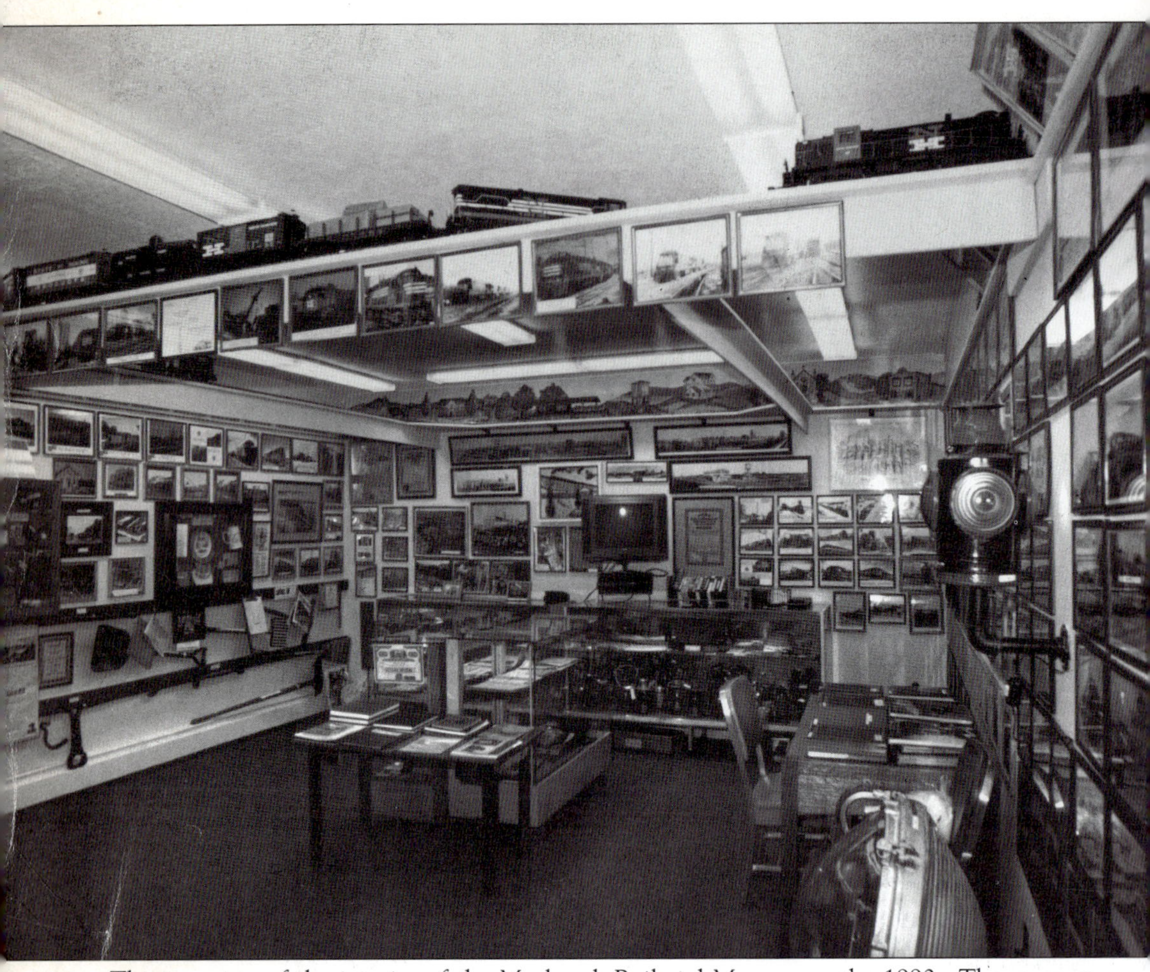

This is a view of the interior of the Maybrook Railroad Museum *c.* the 1990s. The museum houses a railroad train set of the New York, New Haven, and Hartford Railroad, as well as original artifacts that relate to that railroad and the New York, New Haven, and Hartford Railroad. Many photographs line the walls of the museum, and a dozen scrapbooks with photographs trace railroading from the 1880s to the 1970s, especially in the village of Maybrook. (Courtesy of Roby Petzold.)

INDEX